Canada, the Spell

Lilian Whiting

Alpha Editions

This edition published in 2024

ISBN : 9789364737203

Design and Setting By
Alpha Editions
www.alphaedis.com
Email - info@alphaedis.com

As per information held with us this book is in Public Domain.
This book is a reproduction of an important historical work. Alpha Editions uses the best technology to reproduce historical work in the same manner it was first published to preserve its original nature. Any marks or number seen are left intentionally to preserve its true form.

Contents

CHAPTER I   THE CREATIVE FORCES OF CANADA ....- 1 -
CHAPTER II   QUEBEC AND THE PICTURESQUE MARITIME REGION ....- 26 -
CHAPTER III   MONTREAL AND OTTAWA ....- 37 -
CHAPTER IV   TORONTO THE BEAUTIFUL ....- 49 -
CHAPTER V   THE CANADIAN SUMMER RESORTS ....- 58 -
CHAPTER VI   COBALT AND THE SILVER MINES ....- 74 -
CHAPTER VII   WINNIPEG AND EDMONTON ....- 81 -
CHAPTER VIII   ON THE GRAND TRUNK PACIFIC..........- 91 -
CHAPTER IX   PRINCE RUPERT AND ALASKA..............- 110 -
CHAPTER X   PRINCE RUPERT TO VANCOUVER, VICTORIA, SEATTLE, AND THE GOLDEN GATE...........- 127 -
CHAPTER XI   CANADA IN THE PANAMA-PACIFIC EXPOSITION ....- 133 -
CHAPTER XII   CANADIAN POETS AND POETRY ....- 144 -
CHAPTER XIII   THE CALL OF THE CANADIAN WEST .- 183 -

CHAPTER I

THE CREATIVE FORCES OF CANADA

"All parts away for the progress of souls,
All religion, all solid things, arts, governments—all that was or
    is apparent upon this globe or any globe, falls into niches
    and corners before the procession of souls along the grand
    roads of the universe.
Of the progress of the souls of men and women along the grand
    roads of the universe, all other progress is the needed
    emblem and sustenance."
                  WALT WHITMAN (*Song of the Open Road*).

"The flowering of civilisation is the finished man, the man of sense, of grace, of accomplishment, of social power—the gentleman. What hinders that he be born here? The new times need a new man, the complemental man, whom plainly this country must furnish.... Of no use are the men who study to do exactly as was done before, who can never understand that to-day is a new day."—EMERSON.

Against a background of bewilderingly varied activities which projects from the earliest years of the sixteenth well into the twentieth century and reveals itself as a moving panorama of explorers, pioneers, adventurers, traders, and missionaries, there stands out a line of remarkable personalities whose latter-day leadership has largely initiated as well as dominated the conditions of their time and the bequest of century to century. Among these were men, lofty of soul and tenacious of high purpose, who saw the potential Empire in a vast and infinitely varied region which seemed compact of unrelated resources. They were kindled by the growing achievements of the constructive genius that had already projected the wonderful steel highways carrying civilisation into the trackless wilderness. This constructive genius bridged the mighty rivers; created extensive waterways by means of canals connecting lakes and flowing streams; in still later years this genius commanded the cataracts and rapids to transform their ceaseless motion into motor power for traction, and lighting, and other service of industrial and economic value.

Each successive civilisation of the world, indeed, has shown an unbroken line of exceptional personalities in whom has been focussed the power of their epoch. They are the centres through which this power becomes manifest in applied purposes and special achievements. Civilisation itself is but the evolutionary representation of successive conditions of increasing enlightenment. With each succeeding age does man recognise more and more clearly his relation to the moral order of the universe. The guidance of unseen destiny leads him on, and in the records of no country is this working out of the invisible design more unmistakably shown than in those of the Dominion of Canada. This golden thread discloses itself to retrospective scrutiny through a period of three centuries of time. "Man imagines and arranges his plans," says Leblond de Brumath in his biography of Bishop Laval; "but above these arrangements hovers Providence whose foreseeing sets all in order for the accomplishment of His impenetrable design.... Nor must man banish God from history, for then would everything become incomprehensible and inexplicable."

The creative forces of an Empire include various and varying agencies. If to the courage and heroism of the original discoverers of the land too great recognition can hardly be given, yet to those who have made these discoveries of value by bringing the resources of a continent into useful relations with humanity recognition is not less due. John and Sebastian Cabot, Jacques Cartier, Champlain, Mackenzie, Fraser, and La Salle, were great pathfinders. But the very greatness of their achievements required such men as James McGill, Donald Smith (Lord Strathcona and Mount Royal), Sir George Etienne Cartier, the Right Honourable Sir John Alexander Macdonald, Sir Charles Tupper, and others, to stamp the early life of the pioneer with the seal of statesmanship and education. Here were vast areas of land; enchanting rivers, noble lakes, majestic mountains; untold wealth in minerals and in the boundless potentialities of agriculture; a marvellous country that is not only a land of promise, but a veritable Promised Land. Yet are its possibilities like those of the ether of space, until it is rendered accessible to restless, struggling humanity by the indomitable power of great spirits, of wise and forcible leaders of progress who are perhaps the pioneers of the physical world in a degree similar to that of lofty beings in the realms unseen. It is such as they who create the conditions which render all these immeasurable resources of practical value to humanity. Such men as Sir William Cornelius Van Horne and Charles Melville Hays; men who have courage as well as vision; who see beyond all barriers; men who dare do that which weaker souls fear to attempt—such men are as truly among the creative forces of their country as are its original discoverers.

FALLS ON GRAND FORKS RIVER

Falls of the Grand Forks River

Little reference to these earliest years of Canadian history could be made, even in the mere outline which alone is possible in these pages, without a vivid recognition of episode and adventure so startling, so often brilliant and romantic, so often tragic in its heroic endurance and ultimate fatality as to illuminate the horizon of history with a flame not unlike the dazzling lights in Polar skies. There were miracle hours that condensed experiences as significant as those often diffused throughout an entire cycle of time. Mingled with these were the long, slow periods of patient labour. It is not with sudden leaps and bounds alone that life progresses, but by the steady, normal advance of persistent endeavour. Nor can demands for improved conditions be always unmingled with some measure of judicious compromise. James Mill, referring to his experiences while in the London office, engaged with the affairs of India, says: "I learnt how to obtain the best I could when I could not obtain everything. Instead of being indignant or dispirited because I could not entirely have my own way, to be pleased and encouraged when I could have the smallest part of it; and when that could not be, to bear with complete equanimity the being over-ruled altogether." Something of this philosophy the makers of Canada were compelled to accept. The incomers from France, the incomers from Great Britain, represented two distinct, even if not unfriendly nations. There were differences of race, of language, of creed. There were differing convictions as to institutions and laws. Until the Confederation the interests of the people were largely local rather than united. The unifying of a country of such enormous geographical extent and including such vital differences among its widely scattered inhabitants, must always prefigure itself as one of the signal feats in the statesmanship of the world.

The very magnitude of the resources and the infinite riches of Canada presented themselves in the guise of difficulties and obstacles to be conquered. Nature provided the vast systems of lakes and rivers; but these required vast schemes of engineering construction to render them of fullest service as continuous waterways. The broad rivers must be bridged. Triumphs of construction have arisen, such as the Victoria Jubilee Bridge across the St. Lawrence at Montreal, a marvellous feat of engineering, and the splendid steel arch bridge over the Gorge of Niagara. Again, in the interests of transcontinental transit, the mountain ranges, whose peaks seem to pierce the sky, must be overcome. Unmapped tracts of almost impenetrable forests; wastes of rocks, and swamps, and the treacherous muskeg; or immense plains, still inhospitable to the destined tide of settlers, must all be subdued in the interests of the advancing civilisation and the development of a country bordering upon three oceans with an extent of coast-line exceeding that of any other country in the world. Then there were incalculable mining possibilities, precious metals, copper, iron, coal; there were unlimited resources of lumber, but the trees must be felled, and there must be railways or waterways to transport the timber. Canada offered water-power enough to turn the wheels of all the manufactories of Europe, but this power was useless until harnessed by the constructive genius of man. Another valuable asset was the pulpwood, the vastness of which suggested this country as the very centre of the pulp and paper manufacturing industry; but between the thousands of acres covered with white spruce trees, and the lakes and rivers contiguous ready to furnish the power, what marvels of mechanism must be duly constructed to bring the pulpwood and the water-power into service of man. As an indication of the proportions to which this industry has already grown it may be cited that for the fiscal year ending on June 30, 1916, the Canadian pulp print papermakers shipped to the United States alone seven hundred and ninety-four and a half millions of pounds, an increase of one hundred and eighty millions over the amount shipped to the States in the preceding year.

Here, indeed, was a country rivalling any other in the world in the largess of nature, but whose every aspect was a challenge to the constructive enterprise of man. Nature, with unsurpassed lavishness, presented the raw material; it rested with man to stamp it with value. Thus the stimulus to industrial and commercial activities was second to none other in the history of nations.

These were the conditions that confronted, as well as rewarded, the early discoverers and pioneers. Did some prescience of all this potential wealth awaiting the centuries to come drift across the ocean spaces and touch minds sensitive to its impress?

"The Future works out great men's purposes."

John and Sebastian Cabot were impelled by a destiny as unrevealed to them as was that of Columbus. Each bore a magic mirror turned forward to reflect the promise of the future. In the hand of each was carried the lighted torch. It was passed from each explorer to his successor. Cartier, who navigated the St. Lawrence to Quebec and then on to Hochelaga (the name given to the primitive Indian village on the site of which now stands the stately and splendid city of Montreal), carried the lighted torch still farther, and passed it on to Champlain who, three-quarters of a century later, came to found a trading-post on the island of Montreal—"La Place Royale" it was then called, the picturesque mountain that rises in the midst of the modern city of to-day having been named by Cartier "Mont Royale," from which is derived the present Montreal. There followed La Salle, Marquette, Joliet, and others. Sieur de Maisonneuve consecrated the site of Montreal as the first act of his landing. It is little wonder that the visitor to this entrancing city to-day feels some unanalysed and mystic touch pervading the air, something that must forever haunt and pervade his memories of stately, magnificent Montreal. No other city on the continent has this indefinable element of magic and of charm.

The seventeenth century was an almost unbroken period of bold and daring adventure and of missionary activities. All over the world, at this time, was there manifested the passion for exploration. It prevailed over the entire continent of Europe. It recorded its progress on the new continent of North America.

The discovery of Hudson Bay has been placed by some statisticians as early as 1498, when it is surmised that Cabot may have reached it; but the absolute and authentic date still lingers somewhat in the region of conjecture and mystery. It was in 1607 that Henry Hudson is known to have first seen it as he sailed in search of the North Pole. Intrepid adventurer! He found, not the goal of his quest, but, instead, that "undiscovered country" we shall all one day see. "Hudson's shallop went down in as utter silence and mystery as that which surrounds the watery graves of those old sea Vikings who rode out to meet death on the billow," says a Canadian historian. Hudson Bay became a centre of intense interest to all the exploring navigators. Admiral Sir Thomas Button sailed in search of Hudson, or of some tidings of his fate. He returned without the knowledge he sought for, but with much information regarding all the western coast. Still later came Foxe and James. In 1631 Foxe discovered a fallen cross which he judged had been erected by his predecessor, the English Admiral, and he raised it and affixed an inscription and the date.

An organisation that was pre-eminently one of the creative forces of Canada was that of the Hudson's Bay Company, which traces its origin to a voyage of adventure made by two Frenchmen, Pierre Esprit de Radisson and Menart Chouart sieur Degroseillers, who were allured by rumours of the "inexhaustible harvest of furs" that awaited enterprising traders. Baffled for the time by obstacles that seemed insurmountable, they returned to England to ask the assistance of King Charles II., and in 1666 was formed a company that included Prince Rupert (a cousin of the king), the Duke of Albemarle, the Earl of Craven, Sir George Carteret, and other noblemen and merchants, as the incorporators, to whom, in 1670, the king granted a charter to comprise "the whole trade of all the seas, bays, rivers, and sounds, in whatever latitude, ... and territories of the coasts which are not now actually possessed by any of our subjects, or by the subjects of any other Christian prince or state." In the following year two vessels were sent out within a short period and there sprang up a group of trading posts. Radisson remained for life in the service of the Company.

Against the living background of Canadian history in all its varied activities, no one contributing factor stands out with such prominence as that of this Hudson's Bay Company which, for two and a half centuries, dominated the country and whose commercial importance played so large a part in her development. Let no one mistake the purpose of the Company, however, as one inspired by purely philanthropic or patriotic ardour. The dominant aim was by no means primarily that of the development of the new and almost unknown country. The servants of the Company were not braving the terrors and hardships of the wilderness on exclusively altruistic inspirations. On the contrary, it was their policy to conceal the existence of the vast riches of the land and to represent it as inaccessible to any one beyond Indians and hunters. Even as late as the comparatively recent date of the decade of 1860-70, the pupils in Canadian schools were taught that all the Hudson Bay region was uninhabitable; that it was a desolate "No Man's Land," so to speak, covered with ice and snow. No effort to change this impression was made by those concerned with the administration of the Company, but, rather, they were more or less untiring in assisting to confirm it. They had their occult reasons for not being averse to the representation of the entire North-West as being quite valueless for the purposes of civilisation. The impression, if not the conviction, was well authorised that the climate rendered the region quite impossible for habitation; and the region in which now lies the most wonderful wheat-growing belt of the world, and whose fertility under cultivation renders it capable of supporting a population as large as that of the entire United States at the present time (estimated at one hundred millions), was assumed to be a region only capable of sustaining wild animals, Indians, and the most hardy hunters and traders. Now it is traversed by three transcontinental railways which have opened an immense business of travel and traffic; and beside dozens of prosperous young towns and villages it contains Winnipeg with its quarter of a million people; Edmonton, Calgary, Saskatoon, Regina; the important new terminal seaport of Prince Rupert, and the still older and more developed port of Vancouver; to say nothing of the scenic grandeur through all the Mount Robson locale, that has captured the enthusiasm of the world. The tradition of the rigours of climate has become so popularised that even as late as the summer of 1915 a New England tourist faring forth for a trip through the great North-West of Canada was urged to provide himself with furs and rugs enough to fit out an expedition to the Polar regions. As a matter of fact the only embarrassment encountered as to temperature was that of trying to discover sufficiently thin clothing for Winnipeg in the opening September days, where the sunshine poured down just then with a flood of radiance that fairly rivalled that of a summer in the Capital city of the United States. Yet, even in all this splendour of sunshine and discomfort of heat, that wonderful quality of the Canadian air was not wanting—a peculiar invigoration which one who has visited the Dominion misses for a long time after leaving the country. Edmonton repeated the same wonderful luxuriance with the same delicious coolness at night; and the journey on through the magnificent mountain scenery to Prince Rupert had the exquisite temperature of an Italian spring.

The Hudson's Bay Company, however, was not organised on the basis of a bureau of publicity for the general benefit of the country and of posterity. Their aim was the gaining of wealth and it was one signally successful. Immense quantities of valuable furs were shipped homeward every year; the shares in the Company became more and more valuable as magnificent dividends were continually declared. They controlled a territory exceeding an area of two million square miles. It was peopled only by the Indians. Yet all through the seventeenth century run the records of that self-sacrificing and heroic band, the Jesuit missionaries, whose devotion to the Christian ideal led them on with a faith and fervour that consecrates their memory.

CAPE SANTÉ (QUEBEC), ST. LAWRENCE RIVER

Cape Santé (Quebec), St. Lawrence River

The ambition of the Company to extend their trading posts still farther and farther inland incited still more explorations into the unknown North-West. They built better than they knew, for while their aim hardly went beyond that of increasing their own revenues, the results were inevitable factors in the development of the country. That this is true is not in any wise, as has already been said, to be regarded as in the nature of philanthropic or patriotic zeal. They regarded the country and its wealth in the light of a personal perquisite for their exploiting and financial benefit. They circulated the information that this was a "Great Lone Land," as undesirable as it was inaccessible. From motives of self-interest, if not entirely those of humanity, the Company had treated the Indians with kindness and justice and had thus made the British flag something to be held in respect by the tribes. Thus they had built up a strong reliance for themselves of friendliness on the part of the dusky natives. One of the eminent historians, George Bancroft, of Boston, U.S.A., calls attention to this attitude of the Hudson's Bay Company, saying that both the officers and the servants of the corporation "were as much gentlemen by instinct in their treatment of the Indians as in their treatment of civilised men and women." Thus, whenever they should wish to exclude, as enemies, those who came among them representing any other enterprise, they had strong supporters and coadjutors among the tribes. "No trespassers allowed" was practically their motto. Explorations, or the extension of trade, were alike vigilantly discouraged. "Notwithstanding the efforts put forth by the Company," says one chronicle, "it was realised that unless the active co-operation of the Indians could be secured, white trespassers would inevitably make inroads into the trade of the Territory. Steps were therefore taken to unite the tribes against all whites not officially connected with the Company. The means adopted were worthy of the object desired, but could only have been the outcome of an extraordinary disregard of the ordinary amenities of life. The Indians were told that these outsiders would rob and cheat them in the barter of their furs." Still, the very prominence of the Company was its own enormous and inevitable advertisement, so to speak, of untold resources connected with the mysterious regions, and both trade and further exploration were stimulated.

The first quarter of the eighteenth century had but just passed when (in 1727) Pierre Gaultier de Varennes (Sieur de la Verendrye), who was stationed on Lake Nipigon, became imbued with ardour regarding the great question of the day, the North-West Passage; and in 1731 he, with his three sons and an armed force of about fifty men, left Montreal for the West, reaching the shores of Lake Superior within two months, and pushing on—trading and exploring meanwhile—through the all but impenetrable wilderness until he sailed up the Red River, and in the autumn of 1738 established a fort near the site now occupied by the city of Winnipeg.

The great profits accruing to the Hudson's Bay Company inspired rivalry, and in 1795 its keen competitor, the North-West Company, was formed under the leadership of Simon M'Tavish, a Scottish Highlander, of "enormous energy and decision of character." Still another company came into being, organised by two merchants of Montreal, John Gregory and Alexander Norman McLeod, which during its brief life was known as the X Y Company, to whose purposes was attracted a young Scotsman who was destined to be immortalised by his remarkable explorations and his discovery of the great river which perpetuates his name. This young man was Alexander Mackenzie, who came to Canada in 1779, and immediately entered the fur trade. He became connected with the North-West Company and the X Y Company and left for the west to take charge of the Churchill River district. Later, owing to personal dissensions and conflicts of the Company with another of its agents, Mackenzie was commissioned to the Athabasca district, and it was there, apparently, that his project of exploration to the Arctic Ocean took possession of him. From the Indians he heard traditions of a mighty river like that of the Saskatchewan, and in June 1789 he had crossed Athabasca Lake and reached the Peace River which "displayed a succession of the most beautiful scenery," as he recorded. He journeyed to Great Slave Lake after encountering immense difficulties—rapids, long portages, boiling caldrons, and treacherous eddies that threatened to engulf his barque; but at the end of the month he found himself on the river that now bears his name, and on the 12th of July he first sighted the Arctic Ocean. Then there intervened a visit to England before his second expedition in 1792. His memorable inscription on a rock, on the coast near Vancouver: "Alexander Mackenzie from Canada by land, 22 July, 1793," tells its own story. It is not, however, with the long-familiar details of his expeditions that we are here concerned, but with the recognition of their result as one of the constructive factors of the Dominion. The story of these undertakings, of the adventurous journeys of the many explorers, inclusive of Hudson, La Verendrye, Mackenzie, Henry, Thompson, Fraser, Franklin, is a part of the story of Canada. To trace out the contributing causes and the influences investing each of these would be to throw a new illumination on the inter-relations of the factors that have sprung into activity over a long series of years as involved in the evolution of a wonderful country whose great destiny impresses the civilised world.

Sunset on Canyon Lake

The opening years of the nineteenth century were marked by a noble project that apparently ended in failure at the time and yet whose significance is not lost. In every worthy purpose, cosmopolitan, national, or individual in its scope, there is the germ of vitality, and dying in one form it is resurrected in another. Truly of such purposes may be said, in the sublime words of the apostle, that they are "sown in weakness, but raised in power."

"The good, though only thought, has life and breath."

Such a project was that of the Earl of Selkirk to assist numbers of his poorer countrymen by founding a colony for them in the Hudson Bay Territory, where they should find homes and engage in pleasant and profitable agricultural work. With Lord Selkirk it was not the dazzling opportunities of the fur trade that impelled his journey, when, in 1815, he with Lady Selkirk and their son and two daughters landed in Montreal, having already sent out three parties of his country people to the tract of land whose area was that of a hundred and ten thousand square miles which he had purchased in the Red River Valley. His scheme for the betterment of these people included free transportation and temporary support for the settler until he could begin to make his own way, together with a free gift of the land. It was in 1810 that Lord Selkirk had matured his scheme and purchased the land; but on arriving with his family he found himself assailed with charges of conspiracy, condemned to the payment of fines that he contended were totally unjust, and confronted with a strange network of alleged misrepresentation and accusation. It would seem that his chief desire was that of generous and noble aid to his countrymen. His experience is not without its parallel pervading all history in the lives of men whose single-hearted aim has been to make the world a better place. Who shall penetrate the spiritual mystery in that he whose efforts are noble and unselfish not infrequently confronts the same results as might properly belong to him whose objects were quite the reverse of these? "And that all this should have come to you who had meant to lead a higher life than the common, and to find out better ways," exclaims George Eliot's Dorothea to Lydgate, in the great novel of *Middlemarch*; and the heroine adds: "There is no sorrow I have thought more about than that—to love what is great and try to reach it and then fail."

Lord Selkirk took this experience greatly to heart. However much to be regretted is the failure of sufficient courage and faith to enable one to stand strong, "and having done all, still to stand," before a flagrant injustice or the pain of misconception, it is yet hardly to be wondered at that a sensitive spirit, conscious of its own integrity and unmeasured good-will, falters and faints before so unfortunate an experience. To the Scottish Earl it seems to have been more than he could endure. In 1818 he returned to Scotland, and soon after died, at the early age of forty-nine, in Pau, having gone to southern France in search of renewed health. The Red River settlement that he founded was in the neighbourhood of the present city of Winnipeg.

Historians differ, however, as to the motives of Lord Selkirk, some authorities taking a view quite opposite to the one cited here, and gathered, too, from trustworthy sources. The truth may lie somewhere between the two extremes. It is as unnecessary as it would be futile to endeavour to invest every leader of a movement with a golden halo like that of the mediæval saints of the Quattrocentisti. The world's progress has always been carried forward by mixed forces and both ideas and institutions owe their vitality to complex aims and to a variety of conditions.

In the spring of 1821 the Hudson's Bay Company and the North-West Companies united. This marked an epoch in Canadian progress; and in 1838 occurred another event, unnoted as of any significance at the time, yet which proved to be the advent of one of the greatest of the creative forces of Canada. "Any one watching keenly the stealthy convergence of human lots," says George Eliot, "sees a slow preparation of effects from one life on another, which tells like a calculated irony on the indifference or the frozen stare with which we look at our unintroduced neighbour. Destiny stands by sarcastic with our *dramatis personæ* folded in her hand." Surely the arrival at Montreal of a Scottish lad of seventeen years of age could hardly be held as bearing any direct relation to the future development and the cosmopolitan importance of Canada. Yet what a romance of history lies between the unnoticed landing of Donald A. Smith, in 1838, and the solemn grandeur of the scene in Westminster Abbey, in January of 1914, when representatives of the Crown, with the peers, the statesmen, the scholars, the social leaders of London; with a great concourse drawn from all ranks, met for the memorial service for Donald Alexander Smith, first Baron Strathcona and Mount Royal. "The memory of ten centuries of England's illustrious dead haunted the scene."

Donald Smith crossed the Atlantic in a small supply craft belonging to the Hudson's Bay Company and took up his duties as a clerk in one of the most unimportant branches of the service. He made the 1200 miles' journey from Montreal to Labrador. He was stationed in a place where only once a year could any tidings reach him from the outside world. Was he lonely in this exile? He himself said that he never knew what the feeling of loneliness was. He had books; he had thoughts. Such a psychologist as the late William James, who to his profound grasp of psychology and philosophy added the unmapped power of spiritual divination, would have found, in these long, solitary years of meditation and thought, the key and clue to the lad's future greatness. In the infinite and unmeasured force generated by thought-vibrations lies power that may transcend a universe. "Mind with will is intelligent energy," declares a recent scientific writer, who adds: "intelligent energy is enough to supply a cause for every known effect within the limits of the universe."

Sir Oliver Lodge has recently said that life is simply "utilised and guided energy to produce results which otherwise would not have happened." If the distinguished British scientist had been seeking a phrase to define the life of

Donald Alexander Smith he could hardly have created one more felicitous. That the results that were called into activity for a period of over fifty years, of momentous importance to Canada, by the causes set up by the young Scotsman, matters that would never have happened but for him, is evident to all who study closely the modern history of the Dominion. Lord Strathcona's biographer, Mr. Beckles Willson, introduces the reader to a long record of interesting details of the early years of Donald Smith, all of which contributed to the development and the nurture of the marvellous qualities which rendered him one of the most determining of the forces that shaped the destiny of Canada. The brilliant John Jay Chapman, writing of the remarkable man who may be said to have initiated the abolition of slavery in the United States, remarks of his subject: "Garrison plunged through the icy atmosphere like a burning meteorite from another planet." Not thus, however, did Donald Smith enter on his great career. Exiled in a far and frozen region, his service in Labrador lasted for thirteen years "with no companionship save a few employees and his own thoughts, learning the secrets of the Company, how to manage the Indians, and how to produce the best returns."[1] Thirty years had passed since his landing in Canada when, in 1868, on the death of Governor Simpson, of the Hudson's Bay Company, whose office was in Montreal, Mr. Smith was appointed by the London office to succeed him. He was then in his forty-ninth year. Born on August 6, 1820, he died on January 21, 1914, in his ninety-fourth year. The forty-five years which preceded his passing from the physical realm were the years in which Canada entered on her great destiny, and of this momentous period Lord Strathcona might well have said, "All of which I saw and part of which I was." His devotion and loyalty to the Empire was as intelligent and wise as it was ardent and powerful. The history of Canada and his personal biography during those years might almost be interchangeable terms. The Hudson's Bay Company, although organised and conducted on a financial basis, was the soul of loyalty to the Empire. The splendid courage, endurance, and persistence that characterised its entire tenure entered into the very structure of the nation.

[1] *Lord Strathcona; The Story of His Life*. Beckles Willson. Methuen and Company. London, 1902.

About the middle of the nineteenth century a man who has been termed "an uncrowned king" by some of the more enthusiastic, if not more discriminating of his followers; a man who was, at all events, an influential political leader and who especially espoused the cause of Upper Canada, opened a crusade for the acquisition on the part of the government of all the territorial rights of the Hudson's Bay Company. This man was George Brown, the founder and at that time the editor of the Toronto *Globe*. He was a member of Parliament, and he was also one of the band of great editors in which the journalism of that period found its most potent expression. This order of editorial influence was represented in the United States by Horace Greeley of the New York *Tribune*; Charles A. Dana of the New York *Sun*; and Samuel Bowles of the Springfield (Massachusetts) *Republican*, whose spirit and influence continue to manifest themselves in the high quality of that journal to-day. This dominant editorial influence still survives in the States, in the personality of the brilliant and splendidly-endowed Colonel Henry Watterson, the proprietor and editor of the Louisville (Kentucky) *Courier-Journal*, and it was evident in the New York *Evening Post*, under the conduct of Horace White, whose death (in September, 1916) was a signal loss to the American press.

There is ample authority for the assertion that George Brown's newspaper "had an influence on the populace such as no other had in Canada." It was under his administration of the Toronto *Globe* that this journal issued its first bugle call regarding the desirability that Canada should possess herself of all the wide sweep of the Hudson Bay territory of the west. This demand aroused from the Company a storm of emphatic declarations that the "Great Lone Land" was not worth the acquisition of the state; that its climate and its conditions rendered it forever useless to the interests of civilisation. Through nearly two decades had this agitation continued; but in 1869 the Government purchased the vast holdings of the Company at the price of three hundred thousand pounds and the further grant of one-twentieth of the fertile belt of land, and of forty-five thousand acres in addition adjoining various trading-posts. This transaction threw all the North-West into an excited state and Governor MacDougall was sent out to Fort Garry to still the commotion. Then came on the Rebellion incited and led by Louis Riel, the story of which is so familiar to all readers of Canadian history. The conditions became disastrous and alarming, and Governor MacDougall was not permitted to move on to his appointed post. Under these circumstances Donald A. Smith decided to go immediately to the Red River country. He was not the man to hesitate when he heard the call of duty. He was at once invested with the authority of Commissioner by the Dominion Government, and the story of his success, and of the end of the first rebellion under Louis Riel, is too well known to require extended allusion. Soon after this Mr. Smith was elected to Parliament as the first representative from Manitoba. It was to his astute knowledge, his skill as a tactician, the great confidence that he inspired, and to his ability as a Parliamentarian that the successful settlement of the affairs between the Government and the Hudson's Bay Company was primarily due. Meantime the problem of the consolidation of the Provinces became more evident as one that focussed the interest of the time. The epoch-making solution of this problem came in 1867 when the Dominion was formed.

Canada was fortunate at this critical time in having a Premier of remarkable qualities, who was the man for the hour. John Alexander Macdonald (afterwards knighted and invested with the honour of a Grand Cross of the Bath) was a Scotsman by birth whose family removed to Canada in his early childhood. With the sturdy qualities of his race he thus united the influences of Canadian environment and training, the family arriving in Canada in 1820, when the future Prime Minister was but five years of age. In his earliest youth, as a lad of fifteen, circumstances forced him into the world to earn his living. Life itself became his university. He developed in his first contact with the world that initiative, that instant perception of the situation and the facility to meet it, which so signally distinguished his statesmanship in after years. The family had landed at Quebec and journeyed to Kingston where they settled and lived until the death of the elder Macdonald in 1841, leaving the household in straitened circumstances. The Ontario of those days was very different from the smiling and prosperous Province of the present time. All Upper Canada (as it was then known) was covered with dense forests, and all means of transportation were primitive and slow. "Railways, of course, were unknown," writes Sir Joseph Pope, the authorised biographer of Sir John Alexander Macdonald, "and macadamised roads, then looked upon as great luxuries, were few and far between. The climate, too, was more severe than, owing to the cultivation of the soil, it has since become." In 1842, at the age of twenty-seven, Macdonald made his first visit to England, largely for the purpose of purchasing his law library. Quoting a letter written by him at this time to his mother, his biographer (Sir Joseph Pope) adds:

"Forty-two years passed away and again John Alexander Macdonald stood within the portals of Windsor Castle; but under what different circumstances! No longer an unknown visitor, peeping with youthful curiosity through half-open doors; but as the First Minister of a mighty Dominion, he comes by the Queen's command to dine at her table, and, in the presence of the Prime Minister and of one of the great nobles of England, who alone have been summoned as witnesses of the ceremony, to receive from the hand of his Sovereign that token and pledge of her regard which, as such, he greatly prized—the broad, red riband of the Bath."

An omnivorous reader and endowed with a winning and impressive personality, Macdonald at once became a significant and an influential figure in Canadian life. Among the creative forces of his adopted and beloved country he holds a place never to be forgotten. He first took his seat in the

Assembly of 1844; the new Parliament met in Montreal in the November of that year. Complex problems confronted the sessions of that period, in that Canada felt she had no potential voice in the administration of affairs. Every measure of the Assembly must secure the approval of the Legislative Council, the members of which were appointed for life by the governor-general, and added to this the measure must then receive the royal assent before it became operative. The conditions were also aggravated by the large majority of Canadians of French descent, sensitive and high-spirited, who rebelled against the invariable English rule of an English governor-general. These questions and other agitations made the political life on which the young member entered one of peculiar intricacy. The Canada of that day was one of undeveloped resources and of internal dissensions. It consisted only of those territories which we know as the Provinces of Ontario and Quebec. Nova Scotia, New Brunswick, and Prince Edward Island were in the same position politically as Newfoundland is in to-day, while the North-West provinces were a wilderness. With Macdonald's rise to prominence in the political world the idea of confederation began to engage the attention of all those who had at heart the good of the country. The far-seeing leader of the conservative party began a campaign for the confederation of Quebec and Ontario with Nova Scotia, New Brunswick, and Prince Edward Island, believing that the best course was to bring about this preliminary union, leaving it open to extension if time and experience should prove it to be desirable. Owing to the closeness of party divisions, successive governments vainly attempted to carry on the work of the country. It was a critical period, and the manner in which a solution for the national troubles was found will remain one of the most striking episodes in the history of the times.

Sir John Carling was the means of bringing together the conflicting elements. He was a power in the affairs of Ontario and an enthusiastic supporter of Macdonald, while he also enjoyed the friendship of the Honourable George Brown, who was recognised as the Liberal leader of Upper Canada, and who, for many years, had been the opponent of Macdonald. But the veiled and shrouded figure of Destiny hovered near. Did she bear a magic wand, concealed but potent? At all events she ordained that Brown and Carling should journey together from Toronto to Quebec on their way to attend a meeting of the Legislative Council. In their discussion of public affairs George Brown remarked: "Macdonald has the chance of his life to do great things for his country and these can only be done by carrying confederation." To this Sir John rejoined: "But you would be the first to oppose him." To Carling's surprise Brown replied: "No, I should uphold him as I feel that confederation is the only thing for the country." What a significant moment was this in the history of the future Dominion! Forces, determining but unseen, were in the air. The finely-balanced mind of Sir John Carling instantly grasped the importance of this psychological moment. "Would you mind saying to John A. Macdonald what you have just told me?" eagerly asked Sir John. "Certainly not," replied George Brown, and his companion lost no time in bringing the two leaders together. The result is well known to all; the coalition ministry was framed and carried to a successful conclusion the great task with which it had been entrusted.

From that time until his death on June 6, 1891, the energy, the genius, the influence of John Alexander Macdonald were among the most potent of the creative forces of Canada, and for the proud position that the Dominion holds to-day she is largely indebted to this great leader. One of the most important of his powers for national service lay in his ability to co-operate with strong men. When the movement for confederation was initiated the situation was extremely critical, and it was to the personal influence of the eminent French-Canadian, George Etienne Cartier (who was born in St. Antoine, Quebec, in 1814 and who died in 1873), that the support of a reluctant Province was won for the unification of Canada. Cartier was educated at the Seminary of St. Sulpice, Montreal; he was called to the bar, and as a follower of Papineau he fought against the Crown in 1837, and for some time after sought refuge in the United States. On the restoration of peace he returned to Canada and resumed his practice of law, attaining a high position, and subsequently he became the attorney for the Grand Trunk Railway. He was elected to Parliament in 1848 as the recognised leader of the French-Canadians and when, in November of 1857, John Alexander Macdonald succeeded Colonel Taché as Premier of the Province of Canada, Cartier was invited to a place in his cabinet. Later he was created a baronet of the British Empire. From 1858 to 1862 the Cartier-Macdonald ministry held its onward course, though steering its way through quicksands and tumult.

To Sir George Etienne Cartier is ascribed valuable aid in the construction of the Grand Trunk Railway and the Victoria Bridge, important influence in the promotion of education, and signal service in bettering the laws of Canada. When, in 1885, a statue to his honour was unveiled in Ottawa, Sir John Macdonald in his address said of him: "He served his country faithfully and well.... I believe no public man has retained, during the whole of his life, in so eminent a degree, the respect of both the parties into which this great country is divided.... If he had done nothing else but give to Quebec the most perfect code of law that exists in the entire world, that was enough to make him immortal...." To Lord Lisgar the Premier wrote of Cartier: "We have acted together since 1854 and never had a serious difference. He was as bold as a lion, and but for him confederation could not have been carried."

Another of the strong forces in constructive statesmanship was Sir Charles Tupper, who, almost unaided, engaged in the great struggle to overcome the opposition of Nova Scotia, his own Province, to the scheme of confederation. In this famous group of colleagues, Sir John Alexander Macdonald, Sir George Etienne Cartier, Sir Charles Tupper, and the Honourable George Brown, conspicuous ability and wonderful directive power were united with an optimistic courage, a depth of conviction in the success of important measures for the country, that rendered them practically invincible among the creative forces of Canada. Nor could any mention of this progress be complete that did not include the name of Sir Samuel Leonard Tilley, many years Minister of Finance, a worker for confederation, whose own distinction of character and tenacity of purpose determined the attitude taken by his Province of New Brunswick in her wavering and tardy decision, only crystallised into adherence by the patriotic zeal of Sir Leonard. "It is perhaps the highest of all tributes to the genius of Macdonald," says George R. Parkin,[2] "that he was able to draw to his support a group of men of the weight and worth of Cartier, Tupper, and Tilley, and retain through a long series of years their loyal devotion to him as a leader. Each in his own way a commanding personality, they were of one accord in following Macdonald with unswerving fidelity through all the vicissitudes of his fortune. Along with him they grasped and held tenaciously the idea of a great and united Canada forming an integral part of the Empire, and to that end devoted the work of their lives."

[2] "Sir John A. Macdonald," *The Makers of Canada*. Morang and Company, Limited, Toronto.

An interesting and graphic picture is preserved, in the literature of the time, of the visit of Sir John Macdonald, in 1879, to Lord Beaconsfield at Hughenden. He was received as Canada's most illustrious citizen and leading statesman. After dinner Lord Beaconsfield conducted his guest to the smoking-room at the top of the house which was hung with old portraits of former Premiers of England. The host and his Canadian guest exchanged fragments of personal reminiscences and experiences, and Lord Beaconsfield greatly interested Sir John by his brilliant description of some of the notable personalities whom, in former days, he had met at Lady Blessington's, who had a matchless gift for drawing around her the celebrities of her time. In bidding Sir John good-night, at the end of a long and delightful evening, Lord Beaconsfield said: "You have greatly interested me both in yourself and in Canada. Come back next year and I will do anything you ask me." The next year duly came, but Beaconsfield had passed away, and Gladstone was the Premier. It was during this visit that the classics were discussed somewhat at length between Beaconsfield and his guest, the Premier of England dwelling, in the most fascinating manner, upon the poets, philosophers, and orators of Greece and of Rome.

A Canoeing Party, Ontario

For nearly fifty years the influence of Sir John Macdonald was a very pillar of the Dominion. He represented a united Canada that forms so important an integral part of the mighty British Empire. Lord Lorne said of him that he was "the most successful statesman of one of the most successful of the younger nations."

On his death Canada paid him her highest honours. Queen Victoria, most gracious of Royal sovereigns, wrote a personal letter of condolence to Lady Macdonald, and caused her to be elevated to the peerage with the title of Baroness Macdonald of Earnscliffe. An impressive memorial service for the dead Premier was held in Westminster Abbey, and later his bust was placed in St. Paul's and unveiled by Lord Rosebery. Almost every large city in the Dominion is adorned with a statue of Sir John Macdonald.

One of the most important services to Canada, on the part of the Premier, had been his early recognition of the immeasurable possibilities of the North-West. As early as in 1871 he saw that the construction of a railway to the Pacific coast was a matter absolutely essential to the Dominion for the development of this portion of the country. In April of that year, while Sir John Macdonald was absent in Washington (U.S.A.) attending the proceedings of the Joint High Commission, Sir George Cartier moved a resolution in Parliament for the construction of such a road. The resolution was supported by Sir Alexander Galt and was carried. Sir Hugh Allan and Donald Smith had long held commercial relations, and the extensive and accurate knowledge of all this region that Mr. Smith had acquired was of inestimable value to the project. Into this intricate problem attending the decision and the subsequent fulfilment of it in the construction of the Canadian Pacific Railway (completed on November 7, 1885) entered a group of important and forceful men. The magnitude of the work offers material for many chapters of Canadian history. Among this group of dominant personalities stands out that of William Cornelius Van Horne (afterwards knighted) and who was particularly well characterised by James Jerome Hill who said of him: "There was no one on the whole continent who would have served our purpose so well as Mr. Van Horne. He had brains, skill, experience, and energy, and was, besides, a born leader of men." The completion of this great highway was another of the events that closely linked the life of Canada's great Premier with the forces that were creating her destiny. The first through transcontinental train on this line left Montreal on June 26, 1886, for its journey of 2905 miles through what was then an almost trackless wilderness. On the completion of the road Queen Victoria had sent a telegram characterising the achievement as one "of great importance to the British Empire."

The Grand Trunk was, however, Canada's pioneer railway and it was the first railway in the British Empire outside the United Kingdom. One of the leading factors in the varied group of the creative forces of Canada, it is one of the monumental illustrations of her claim to foresight and enterprise in thus early recognising that the art of transportation goes before and points the way for advancing enlightenment. The transportation service is, as one of the eminent officials of this line has said, "the advance guard of education." In 1914 the Grand Trunk System, led by the vision and foresight of Charles Melville Hays, completed its transcontinental lines. President Hays had predicted that the Grand Trunk would be able to handle the harvest of 1915, and his prediction was realised. His forecast for the future included steamer lines from Prince Rupert to Liverpool, by way of the Panama Canal, and further extension of lines to Australia, Japan, China, and Alaska. In fact, the Canadian prevision of unmapped possibilities of commerce that would be afforded by means of the new canal that thus connected two oceans was far more alert and engaging than that of the United States.

Beside the great enterprises involved in the conquering of nature, there were others, not less important, that contribute to the building up of human life. The claim of industry and economics is not greater than the claim of intellectual development, of scholarship, of that knowledge and refinement that leads to the highest social culture of a nation.

When the Honourable James McGill of Montreal left at his death (in 1813) a large bequest to found the university that bears his name he added another to the galaxy of Canada's benefactors and creators. Mr. McGill had amassed large wealth in the fur industry, and the college, after encountering some years of difficulty, entered in 1885 on an era of prosperity that has continually increased as the years have gone by. This era of prosperity was largely due to the securing as Principal a gifted and remarkable young man, John William Dawson, who is now so widely known to the world of science and scholarship as Sir William Dawson. For thirty-eight years he served as Principal of McGill. He found it a struggling college with less than a hundred students. He left it with more than a thousand students and with from eighty to ninety professors and lecturers. Finding it with three faculties, he doubled that number, and as within fifteen years he recognised the necessity of higher education for women, there was opened (in 1883) the Donalda Department, generously endowed by Lord Strathcona, which has since developed into the Royal Victoria College. Lord Strathcona gave, first and last, many millions of dollars to McGill; Sir William Macdonald gave to the Engineering department one million, including with this the schools of physics and chemistry, and he also equipped the Macdonald College at Saint-Anne-de-Bellevue which is incorporated with McGill. Peter Redpath, a public-spirited merchant of Montreal, presented the museum that bears his name (now rich in collections) and he also gave the Library building which houses, for McGill, the largest library in Canada save that of Parliament. These liberal gifts of Mr. Redpath were still further increased by Mrs. Redpath's generous contributions. The unsurpassed opportunities at McGill place her graduates on equality of scholarly prestige with those of Oxford and of the other great universities of the world. No consideration of the creative forces of Canada could fail to include this inestimable contribution that makes for nobler life offered by McGill University.

To the intellectual development and liberal culture of the Dominion the universities of Toronto and of Laval render priceless aid. The former is noted somewhat at length in a subsequent chapter. Laval University, founded in Quebec in 1852, by the Quebec seminary, dates back, through that institution, to its founder, François de Laval-Montmorency, the first Bishop of Quebec, who landed in Canada in 1659, and founded the seminary in 1663. This great French-Canadian university, fairly enshrined in sacred tradition and archaic history, is an object of pilgrimage to all visitors in Quebec. To its vast resources of scholarship it adds the perpetuation of the name of one of the most remarkable prelates that the world has known. A son of the crusaders, a true successor of the apostles who shared the life of Jesus Christ, a man of boundless charity, of intrepid heroism, of a life so consecrated to the Divine Service that its passing from earth in the May of 1708 cannot efface the vividness of his image nor dim the brightness of the atmosphere which enshrines his memory, he was deeply concerned with the education of his people. Monseigneur Laval specified that he desired that his seminary should be "a perpetual school of virtue." The Abbé de Saint-Vallier of France bequeathed to this Seminary in 1685 the sum of forty-two thousand francs, and Bishop Laval himself left to its maintenance his entire estate. The museums, lecture halls, and the library of Laval University are open to visitors. It is rich in historic portraits and in many fine examples of French art. On the visit of the Prince of Wales (later Edward VII.) to Canada in 1860, the heir to the British throne founded the Prince of Wales Prize, which has remained one of the features of the university.

In the equalisation of educational opportunities to an unusual degree Canada is especially strong. While the fiftieth anniversary of the consolidation of the Dominion will not be celebrated until July 1, of 1917, and while as a nation she is not yet half a century old, her educational privileges are recognised as among the best in the world. Not a single province is without its fully equipped educational system. Free public schools, high schools, colleges, and universities abound. There are already twenty-one universities in Canada. The standard of instruction is very high; the schools of applied science, law, medicine, and technical instruction are among the best in the world. They offer all late modern appliances for chemical, metallurgical, and electrical experiment: civil, mining, and electrical engineering are offered with unsurpassed opportunities for practice and research. The Royal Military College at Kingston presents a complete course in Engineering and in all branches of military science. The Royal Naval College at Halifax offers equally complete opportunities for naval training.

Not even the most fragmentary survey of the creative forces of the Dominion could fail to emphasise the notable and beneficent work of Archbishop Taché, who, born in Quebec in 1823, became identified with the Far West in 1845, where he remained, an heroic and impassioned figure, until his death, in 1894. The Archbishop's mother was a daughter of Joliet, the explorer; the same intrepid spirit that led this pathfinder on through the wilderness characterised the great prelate in a remarkable degree. At the age of twenty-two he had been admitted to the priesthood; he received his training in Montreal and was, from the first, "stirred to the soul by missionary zeal"; he eagerly embraced the call to the hardships, the most insurmountable difficulties, of the pioneer missionary. He traversed the country for four hundred miles around from St. Boniface (across the river from Winnipeg) where he was stationed; his journeys were by canoe and dog sledges; he encountered physical hardships which seem incredible for human endurance. When the slender financial support of his mission threatened to fail he pleaded that just sufficient revenue be continued to provide bread and wine for the sacrament, saying that for himself he would "find food in the fish of the lakes, and clothing from the skins of the wild animals." In his later years he was made the Bishop of Manitoba and he was present, a venerable and honoured figure, on the opening of the first Assembly of that Province in 1870-71. Archbishop Taché was one of the nearer friends and associates of Lord Strathcona, also when the latter, as Donald A. Smith, was so long the dominating personality in the North-West. The life and work of this great Archbishop of the Catholic faith are forever bound up with the history and development of Manitoba. There are other notable Catholic prelates, a remarkable group: his Eminence Cardinal Taschereau, the first Canadian prelate to become a Prince of the Church; Archbishops Bourget and Fabre of Montreal; Archbishops Lynch and Walsh of Toronto; Archbishop Cleary of Kingston; and Bishop Demers of Vancouver are all among the great religious leaders whose influence for the general advancement of the people, as well as for the progress of religion, has been wide and invaluable.

Bishop Strachan of Toronto, a priest of the Church of England, whose life fell between 1778-1867, was a strong force both in church and state. No servant of God within the entire Dominion has left a nobler record. When (in 1832) the scourge of Asiatic cholera swept over Canada, it was he who inspired courage, administered the sacraments to the dying, and sustained the survivors. His aid, both legislative and otherwise, to the cause of education, and his activity in promoting all progress in Ontario, are among the most precious records of that province. One passage from his personal counsel may well be held in memory:

"Cultivate, then, my young friends, all those virtues which dignify the human character, and mark in your behaviour the respect you entertain for everything venerable and holy. It is this conduct that will raise you above the rivalship, the intrigues, and slanders by which you will be surrounded. They will exalt you above this little spot of earth, so full of malice, contention, disorder; and extend your views, with joy and expectation, to that better country."

Nothing in all religious advancement is more impressive than the great work of the Methodist denomination in Canada. Their vital and fervent spirit has kindled the zeal of the people with the flame of the living coal on the altar. One of the remarkable contributions to the lofty order of creative forces was made by the Reverend Doctor Egerton Ryerson, the celebrated Methodist leader, and the organiser of the Public School System of Ontario. In 1841 Doctor Ryerson became Principal of Victoria College; in 1844 ne was appointed Superintendent of Public Schools in Upper Canada, and he brought to bear upon educative work the enduring impress of his ideals. "By education I mean not the mere acquisition of certain arts," he said, "but that instruction and discipline which qualify men for their appropriate duties in life, as Christians, as persons in business, and as members of the civil community." Doctor Ryerson lived until the year 1882, and he thus was enabled to see much of the fruit of his wise and untiring endeavour.

Although the Right Honourable Sir Wilfrid Laurier is still, happily, dwelling among his countrymen and lending to many notable occasions the rare distinction and the prestige of his presence, the gratifying fact that he is a factor in the life of the hour cannot constrain one to fail to express the recognition of Canada's indebtedness to his splendid services during her more recent past. A native of Quebec (born in 1841) his unqualified devotion has been given to the Empire without regard to restriction of race or language. His political career as a member of the House opened before he was thirty years of age; six years later he was called to the Cabinet; and in June, 1896, at the age of fifty-five, he became the Premier of the Dominion. When the Diamond Jubilee of Queen Victoria was celebrated, one special feature was the invitation extended to all the Prime Ministers of the British Empire to honour it by their presence. Among these Ministers Sir Wilfrid was singled out for many special attentions. He was distinguished by being made a member of the Imperial Privy Council; he was appointed a Knight of the Grand Cross of the Order of St. Michael and St. George; he was invested with honorary degrees by both Oxford and Cambridge; he was made an honorary member of the Cobden Club which awarded to him a gold medal "in recognition of exceptional and distinguished services to the cause of international and free exchange." Sir Wilfrid Laurier visited President Faure and the President of the French Republic named him as a Grand Officer of the Legion d'Honneur. In 1902 Sir Wilfrid was invited to the Coronation of Edward VII. and his presence at this imposing ceremonial reflected distinction of the highest order on Canada by his brilliant and impressive addresses made on Imperial interests and affairs. England could not but realise that in the Parliament of the vast country over the sea there were orators who would add new lustre to her national eloquence and splendid traditions.

Well, indeed, has Canada been called the country of the Twentieth Century. To no inconsiderable extent the appliances that introduce a new order of life have been either invented or first experimentally considered in the Dominion. Indeed, as if already under the spell of Destiny, these great modern miracles of communication—the railways, telegraphs, and telephones will be forever associated with the name of Canada; the country that cradled James Jerome Hill and Samuel Rogers Calloway; in which William Cornelius Van Horne and Charles Melville Hays gave the best years of their lives to building and improving transportation facilities; in which

Alexander Graham Bell initiated his experiments and where he still makes his summer home; and in which Thomas Alva Edison worked as a telegraph operator on the pioneer railway, where he printed and issued *The Grand Trunk Herald*, the first newspaper ever printed on a railway train.

In the light of the eventful period that has passed since that momentous date of August, 1914, it would seem to be a curiously prophetic glimpse that rose, like a mirage on the far horizon, before Sir Wilfrid Laurier when, in response to a toast at the banquet given on June 18, 1897, by the Imperial Institute in London in honour of the Colonial premiers, he said:

"... England has proved at all times that she can fight her own battles; but if a day were ever to come when England was in danger, let the bugle sound, let the fires be lighted upon the hills, and in all parts of the Colonial possessions whatever we can do shall be done to help her.... I have been asked if the sentiments of the French population of Canada were those of absolute loyalty towards the British Empire. Let me say ... it was the privilege of the men of our generation to see the banners of France and of England entwined together victoriously on the banks of the Alma, on the heights of Inkermann, and on the walls of Sebastopol."

Seventeen years had but passed—from 1897 to 1914—when again the banners of France and England were intertwined; and since that fateful midsummer's day what treasure and sacrifice has not Canada poured out with a courage and unflinching heroism for which words furnish no adequate interpretation. The future of the Canadian Dominion is seen, in the words of the poet, as "along the grand roads of the universe." Her citizens realise that "To-day is a new day" and the hand of Destiny is leading her on to exemplify to the world a new and a more glorious civilisation.

CHAPTER II

QUEBEC AND THE PICTURESQUE MARITIME REGION

The Maritime region of Canada embraces only, strictly speaking, Prince Edward Island, Nova Scotia, and New Brunswick; although Quebec is sometimes thought of as being included in this historic portion of the Dominion, because of its geographical situation. The city of Quebec has always been a favourite point of pilgrimage, and when Mr. Howells, in his early youth, enshrined it in a half-romantic narrative, as the scene of *Their Wedding Journey*, its attractions were heightened by his facile and charming pen. The old French city dates back to 1608, and its history, for more than a century and a half, is really the history of Canada as well. All the maritime provinces of Canada take a prominent place in poetic legend and lore as well as in historical associations. When, in 1845, the poet Longfellow wrote his tender and touching, though historically misleading poem, Evangeline, the poem focussed the general attention on Acadia (the modern Nova Scotia and New Brunswick), and particular attention on the little village of Grand-Pré, which,

"... distant, secluded still,"

lying in the fruitful valley, invited many excursions of those who delight in pilgrimages to poetic shrines. For

"Plant a poet's word but deep enough,"

and woodland or hill, mountain or shore, are thereby enchanted. The Maritime region, still vocal with the dreams and discoveries of adventurous spirits; where all pledge and prophecy still linger in the air; where impassioned endeavour, long-patient endurance, faith to break a pathway through to untrod regions with some Ulysses to inspire a faith that it is never too late to seek a newer world—how wonderful is the spell this province weaves around the wanderer!

The noble St. Lawrence is a river that fairly fulfils the purposes of a sea, with its kaleidoscopic shore lines, now bold and forbidding, now dreamy and undefined with their fleeting, ethereal beauty; and all the maritime land is pervaded by memories and associations of the brave Cabot who first sighted Nova Scotia on June 24, 1497, the date of the special festa of his native Italy—this festival of San Giovanni, when all Venice is on the Grand Canal in the fleets of gondolas; all Florence illuminated at night, a resplendent spectacle from her surrounding hills and her background of purple amethyst mountains; and when Rome, at night, disports herself in a thousand ways upon the Campagna Mystica. It was a fitting date for Cabot, the Venetian, to discover the new land. Voices unheard by others had called to him; hands, from starry spaces, beckoned and led him on. What was there in the air but

"Winged persuasions and veiled destinies,"

and all the past that came thronging to meet all the future? Cabot, Venetian born, English by adoption, was followed by several other intrepid explorers, and not to insist too much upon chronological order, what a group of wonderful names are associated with all the province of Quebec! Cartier, Champlain, Frontenac; Sir Humphrey Gilbert of the Elizabethan period, whose brave expedition was engulfed by winds and waves and went down in the great deep off Campobello.

"Alas, the land-wind failed.
   And ice-cold grew the night,
And never more on sea or shore,
   Should Sir Humphrey see the light."

But the high ideals these heroes brought did not go down nor become extinguished in the storm-tossed waters.

"Say not the struggle naught availeth!"

The struggle always avails, and leaves humanity better and farther on than the effort finds it. Then, too, came a band of holy women, the Ursuline nuns, and the sacred zeal of the novitiate lent its vital power. What is there not of spiritual nobility, of sublimest self-sacrifice, of thrilling ideals, of a truer life, associated with the early history of Canada? This is all a part of her spellbinding power; it has left its significance on the air, its impress in wave and tree and flower; its exaltation in every heart.

Quebec city is now becoming an attractive winter haunt as well for those who love out-of-door sports in the snowy carnival and who find themselves so comfortably domiciled in the Château Frontenac. The esplanade of Dufferin Terrace commands delightful views across the St. Lawrence as far as the Isle d'Orleans. The Citadel, the Parliament Buildings, the Ursuline Convent, the Basilica, and the palace of the Cardinal; together with the libraries, Laval University, the drives to the old battle-grounds, and the excursion of twenty-one miles to the shrine of Saint Anne de Beaupré, provide the visitor with abundance of interest.

The Ursuline Convent covers seven acres of ground in almost the centre of the city of Quebec. It is the largest convent on the continent, and it dates back to the July of 1639, when Marie Guyart, and three other sisters of the Ursuline order, under the protection of the Archbishop of Toulouse, were led by Divine guidance to the new country of Canada and entered on their work. Marie Guyart, the foundress of the convent, was the daughter of a silk merchant of Tours, France, and her childhood is invested with legends similar to those that are associated with the name of Catherine of Sienna. She married one Joseph Martin, but at the age of twenty-three she was left a widow, and soon became a novitiate of the Ursulines, rising to be the Mother Superior of her convent. At the age of forty, through the instrumentality of the Duchesse D'Aiguillion, a niece of Cardinal Richelieu, she came to "New France," and as recently as the August of 1911 this remarkable woman was canonised by the Sacred College of Rome and named as a saint under the title of Marie de l'Incarnation. For thirty-three years she pursued an exalted life in the convent of her founding, and died at the age of seventy-two, in the May of 1672.

A much-sought shrine is that of Saint Anne de Beaupré, easy access to which is gained by the electric railway, and in the summer it is a pleasant local sail down the St. Lawrence. The legend runs that a group of Breton mariners, in the early years of the seventeenth century, found themselves almost engulfed in the river in the sudden violence of a storm, and that they called upon *la bonne Saint Anne* for deliverance; earnestly declaring that if she would save them they would erect to her a shrine at whatever point she should bring them to land, and that this shrine should be sanctuary forever. The good saint was merciful to their entreaties, and guided them safely to land. According to their promise they at once built a small wooden chapel, very near a spring whose waters are claimed to possess a miraculous power for healing. Since that remote time three larger churches on this site have successively replaced each other, the latest of which dates only to 1878. The primitive little chapel is still preserved, even as at Assisi the Portiuncula of San Francisco is preserved near the magnificent church of Santa Maria degli Angeli.

That marvellous ministry of San Francisco (who is more familiarly known to us as Saint Francis of Assisi), which was initiated in the thirteenth century, love and sacrifice being the supreme ideals, is recalled to mind by many of the legendary incidents relating to Saint Anne de Beaupré. The mystic pilgrimage to Assisi, the "Seraphic City," is to some extent paralleled by the latter-day pilgrimages to the shrine of Saint Anne. "Any line of truth that leads us above materialism," said Arch-deacon Wilberforce of Westminster Abbey, whose passing on to the life more abundant at the date of this writing is but the larger inflorescence of his beautiful and consecrated life—"any line of truth that forces us to think and to remember that we are enwrapped by the supernatural, is helpful and stimulating. A human life lived only in the seen and felt, with no sense of the invisible, is a fatally impoverished life; a poor, blind, wingless life." Such is the deep, perpetual conviction of mankind. "The things that are seen are temporal; the things that are not seen are eternal." The mystic union of the soul with God is the one underlying and all-determining truth of life.

"Oh, beauty of holiness!
Of self-forgetfulness, of lowliness."

The latest church erected here as the shrine of Saint Anne was not completed until 1889, and it was then proclaimed a Basilica by Pio Nono. It is one of colossal space and splendour, a remarkable triumph of the Corinthian architecture, and between the two towers of the front a superb statue of Saint Anne rises above the façade. The interior is rich in paintings, sculpture, and mosaics, and on a column of onyx is another statue of the saint in whose name the church is built. It has also a Scala Santa, as has the vast Basilica of San Giovanni in Rome. Thousands of suppliants annually visit the shrine of Saint Anne. The church has a superb chasuble, the gift of Anne of Austria and Queen of France, the mother of Louis XIV. On either side of the entrance are huge piles of canes and crutches and other discarded appliances left as visible testimonials that the efficacy of prayer at this shrine enabled their possessors to dispense with adventitious aid.

Dufferin Terrace, Quebec, from the Citadel

A little book that is for sale by the Redemptorist Fathers, who occupy the monastery connected with this basilica, gives much curious information regarding Saint Anne. She is represented as being of the tribe of Judah and of the royal family of David. Her husband, Joachim, was of the same family, and of the same tribe, and the Blessed Virgin was their only child. This little record further narrates that the body of Saint Anne was originally buried in Bethlehem; but that it was brought to France by Lazarus, who, after being raised from the dead by the Saviour, became the first Bishop of Marseilles. The body of Saint Anne was then committed in burial in the village of Apt, and when Charlemagne came to celebrate the Easter feast—so runs the story—a man who was blind, deaf, and dumb came to the ceremonies, and was instantly restored. The first words he uttered were: "This hollow contains the body of Saint Anne, Mother of the Blessed Virgin Mary, the Mother of God." With the clue given in these words the hollow in the rocks was then opened and the body disclosed. This took place in the year 792, and from that remote date to the present time the church of Saint Anne at Apt has been a notable place of worship and of pilgrimage.

In the Basilica of Saint Anne de Beaupré there are some rich and massive reliquaries of gold, inlaid with jewels, in which the holy relics of the Saint are enclosed. All the gold and the jewels are votive offerings left by grateful pilgrims to this shrine who have been restored to health. It is said that there are literally bushels of watches, chains, bracelets, rings, and all manner of personal adornments that have been given in gratitude for blessings received. Large gifts of money are also among the never-ceasing stream of accumulating wealth. Twelve large chalices of gold, valued at ten thousand dollars each, have been constructed from the rings and personal articles left by the devotees. The church is fairly lined with the evidences of grateful appreciation and the tributes of enthusiasm. Each chapel is a memorial gift of personal gratitude; the altar, organ, and the electric light plant are also personal gifts, and to these there is a rather curious story attached.

Over a long period of years the newspapers of the United States printed advertisements of a widely-known patent-medicine lady who brewed her concoctions, and either by means of their intrinsic worth, or by the credulity of her customers, accumulated a large fortune. It is said that this lady made a journey to the church of Saint Anne out of curiosity, alone, but was suddenly stricken with a severe illness; that she was cured by faith, and that, through the direct influence of Saint Anne, she then became a Catholic and was baptised in the Basilica. She at once abandoned her pursuit and expressed her desire to devote her fortune to good works, in honour of the Saint; and it was she who presented the altar, the organ, and the electric light plant as well as other rich and valuable gifts.

Around the shrine of Saint Anne de Beaupré has grown up a village of some two thousand people, with hotels that accommodate hundreds of guests. There are two convents, several schools, a hospital (providing for the accommodation of the poor who come to be healed), and the monastery already mentioned. The Sisters of the Rosary have also established an academy for young women; the Sisters of Saint Francis have built a convent for their order, and the Redemptorist nuns have their own convent, while there is also a seminary for the education of priests that has about three hundred students.

The sermons of the Fathers who conduct the services in the Basilica are preached in both French and English. Sixteen priests hold continual devotions from four in the morning until nine at night. The number of annual visitors is estimated as being nearly two hundred thousand, representative of almost every nationality and language. An American publicist asked one of the Fathers whether every one who came was cured. "By no means," replied the priest; "although the miracles are many." When asked how he accounted for the failures the Father replied that he was not able to account for them; that a failure might be due to lack of faith, or to some other reason not disclosed to them. Faith is always to be reckoned with as a condition through which alone the Divine energy can flow.

In the vicinity of Saint Anne there is some beautiful scenery—Montmorency Falls, and other points of interest; Quebec, too, is almost as much frequented in winter as in summer, the bracing air being to many the very elixir of life.

Quebec Province has always kept a distinctive atmosphere of its own, due largely to the preponderance of the French-Canadian element and to climatic and topographical conditions. Advantages and privileges are constantly increasing. Macdonald College, at Saint Anne de Bellevue, founded by Sir William Macdonald, admits women on equal terms with men, and beside the School of Agriculture, it has a training institution in Domestic Science and a school for training teachers. The Department of Domestic Science is free to all Canadian girls, and students from outside of Canada pay a small tuition fee and a modest fee of some three dollars and a half a week for board-residence. On this great college Sir William Macdonald's initial expenditure was five millions of dollars. Five hundred and sixty acres were secured for the farm, of which nearly four hundred are devoted to the live stock and grain department, while the remainder is divided between vegetable, poultry, and bee culture, with a liberal share allotted to horticulture.

It is to Quebec that the middle west of the United States must look for the early history of its own great explorers, missionaries, and pathfinders; for it was from here that Champlain, La Salle, Marquette, Joliet, and others fared forth on their pioneer journeys through the Mississippi basin. Champlain died in Quebec on the Christmas Day of 1635; but his burial-place is still undetermined. The Jesuit College in which Père Marquette was domiciled ante-dated Harvard by one year, having been founded in 1635. Here Marquette made his plans for tours along the Great Lakes and down the Mississippi, with the object of converting the Indians. This Jesuit College bears the signal honour of being the first institution for higher education on the North American continent.

Something of the unique and exceptional character of the great Cardinal Richelieu, whose tomb in the Pantheon in Paris is an object of continual pilgrimage by the visitors in the French capital, seems to invest Quebec, the city of which he was the real founder. The convent and hospital of the Hotel Dieu were due to the solicitude and enterprise of his niece, the Duchesse d'Aiguillion, whose interest centred in the promulgation of religion and charities, and these institutions are still preserved as memorial monuments to her fervour. Quebec is pre-eminently a city of churches and the old French Cathedral dates back to 1647. The interior is enriched with several paintings of especial value, among them Van Dyck's "Crucifixion," which was painted in 1630, and which, in the Revolution of 1793, was purchased in Paris by the Abbé des Jardins of Quebec, and presented to the cathedral. In the sacristy are two large vaults filled with sacred relics. The vestments belonging to this cathedral are superb.

An interesting church is the Anglican Cathedral, standing in the centre of the city, to which the late King Edward VII. presented an exquisite Communion service.

For the celebration of the tercentenary of Quebec, Cy Warman, that genial poet (who has set so much of Canada to music), wrote an ode in the dialect of the habitant, of which two stanzas run:

"How you kip yourself so young,
      Ol' Quebec?
Dat's w'ats ax by all de tongue,
      Ol' Quebec;
Many years ees pass away,
Plaintee hair been turn to gray,
You're more yo'gker ev'ry day,
      Ol' Quebec.

Som' brav' men hees fight for you,
      Ol' Quebec;
Dat's w'en Canada she's new,
      Ol' Quebec;
De brav' Wolfe, de great Montcalm,
Bote was fight for you, Madame,
Now we're mak' de grande salaam,
      Ol' Quebec."

The traveller with an impassioned devotion to what he fondly calls "the quaint" may be signally gratified in Quebec. In the business section there will be found one street only four feet in width, quite rivalling the famous *via d'Aura* in Genoa, the "Street of jewellers," where one can stand in a shop on one side and almost reach his hand into the shop opposite.

The Legislative Buildings are as delightful as those in the other capitals of the Provinces of Canada; and on the brow of the high bluffs are a group of notable buildings of architectural beauty—the splendid Château Frontenac, with its view of thirty miles up and down the St. Lawrence valley; flanked by monasteries, churches, and public structures. The citadel that crowns the height is extremely picturesque to visitors who have all the enjoyment, while the Canadian Government has the doubtful felicity of keeping in due repair this enormous fortification. It was begun two hundred and fifty years ago, and reconstructed in 1823, on plans approved by the Duke of Wellington, at a cost of twenty-five million.

It is not so well known that the Duke of Kent, the father of Queen Victoria, was in command of the garrison of Quebec for several years; that the old-fashioned building in which he lived was restored by his royal daughter, and that his grand-daughter, the Princess Louise, Marchioness of Lorne (later the Duchess of Argyle), when living at Rideau Hall, Ottawa, during the period of the Marquis of Lorne's Governor-Generalship of Canada, laid the foundation stone of this restoration. Moreover, the Princess herself, with that versatility of gifts which characterised Her Royal Highness, devised the architectural plans for the new structure. Nor must the ancient gates of the old wall of Quebec be ignored in any tribute to her picturesque attractions.

Laval University in Quebec is a resort of many students, on account of the numerous manuscripts of historical value deposited there, many of them containing graphic narratives of thrilling experiences undergone in the pioneer days of the Dominion.

To turn from Quebec to the Maritime Provinces proper, they are not by any means all scenery, or historic and legendary atmosphere. Nova Scotia has large lumber interests, with fisheries, mineral wealth, and great iron and steel manufactures; and New Brunswick has ever been the home of the great timber and now of pulpwood so precious in these latter days. Prince Edward Island has a vast amount of red sandstone, and in the regions adjacent to the Bay of Fundy an enormous yield of hay is a feature of resource. The position of the Maritime Provinces is particularly noted by Mr. J. Castell Hopkins, in an extended account of these regions, and he speaks of the climatic peculiarities as one of the things with which the inhabitants must reckon. They have a great coast-line in proportion to their area. The extensive bays and harbours suggest future increase of ocean commerce and travel. "Prince

Edward Island is in reality all seacoast," writes Mr. Hopkins, "for no matter how far into the interior one may get, an hour's drive in any given direction will almost invariably discover salt water. There are bays which deserve special mention, one, the beautiful Bay de Chaleur, between New Brunswick and the Gaspé Peninsula, without rock, reef, or shoal in its ninety miles of length and forty-five of breadth, is unique in its safety to navigators, while the Bay of Fundy, between Nova Scotia and New Brunswick, with its mouth wide open to the south-west, has features which are peculiar only to this bay. Lying funnel-shaped toward the great tidal movement from east to west it gathers from the incoming tide a great deal of water that does not belong to it, and then gradually compressing it between narrowing shores, piles it up in places sixty feet in height, and this gives rise to many peculiarities. This rush of tide twice a day has formed enormous areas of marsh land and the process is still going on. The great rise and fall of water in this bay has also a climatic effect in it that keeps the air continually moving, and in the regions about its head there is probably a cooler summer climate than can be found anywhere in the same latitude."

Harbour of St. John, New Brunswick

This peculiarity unfits the climate for fruit-raising, but is especially favourable for live stock. The production of hay is very large. The water supply is inexhaustible, and water-power is always at hand to grind grain or to transform trees into lumber. The spruce and fir are found here in great abundance. The Maritime Provinces have practically no mountains, although a few heights approaching two thousand feet may be seen. Of late years the people of this region have been urged to develop agriculture to a greater extent. It is already demonstrated that wheat, barley, oats, buckwheat, and corn can be cultivated with profit; potatoes and carrots also thrive. In New Brunswick, apples, pears, grapes, and cherries do well; and every one knows of the apple orchards of Nova Scotia. The dairy industry is one of the greatest sources of revenue. Factories for the making of cheese and butter are numerous; and quite apart from the home market, the facilities for export to Europe and to the markets of the South are one special factor in the conditions for profit. Agricultural schools, a feature of the Dominion, have a particularly good representative at Truro, and the Federal Government has established experimental farms and stations throughout the Dominion, while the provincial authorities have also organised similar enterprises under their own jurisdiction. The Provincial Government of Ontario, in particular, has devoted large sums to the encouragement of agriculture, having three experimental farms, one of these being devoted to fruit.

The Central Experimental Farm of the Dominion Government is at Ottawa and there are branch farms at Charlottetown on Prince Edward Island; at Fredericton, New Brunswick; at Nappan and Kentville, Nova Scotia; at Saint Anne de la Pocatière, Cap Rouge, and Lenoxville in Quebec; at Brandon, Manitoba; at Indian Head, Rosthern, and Scott, Saskatchewan; at Lethbridge and Lacombe in Alberta; and also at Agassiz, Invermere, and Sidney in British Columbia. Sub-stations have also been established at Fort Vermilion in the Peace River District, at Grouard near Lesser Slave Lake, Grande Prairie, and Forts Resolution and Providence—all these being in northern Alberta. At the Central Experimental Farm (at Ottawa) much attention has been paid to tests, as to the growing of oats, barley, varieties of grass, and turnips and mangels. Nor has the culture of ornamental shrubs and trees been neglected; and orchards of various kinds of fruit have been planted with watchful care. Potatoes, too, have received special attention as one of the most profitable products of this region.

The picturesque attractions of the Maritime Provinces, moreover, tend to make them each year a summer resort for increasing numbers of people from the United States and elsewhere. Mail routes are well extended; the postal service is good; and the improvements in navigation have included the erection of many lighthouses on the prominent headlands and in the harbours, so that the scenic panorama at night witnessed by those on or near the coast is often most fascinating, and the presence of these aids to navigation is full of practical reassurance to those who travel by water.

Halifax is important not only as the capital of Nova Scotia, but as the leading seaport of Canada on the Atlantic coast. It has a magnificent harbour whose even depth is a joy to the navigator; it is curiously free from extremes of temperature, the coldest day of one average year being but eight degrees below zero (in February), the warmest day falling in early September when the mercury registered eighty-seven degrees. The evenings are always cool. The city has its citadel, its rocky areas, and beside its university (Dalhousie) there are colleges doing various special work, institutions for the defective classes, and several libraries, that of the Institute of Science and History being consolidated with the Library of Parliament. In the magnitude of its exports Halifax stands next to Montreal. In its imports it ranks third, Montreal and Toronto alone taking precedence of the Nova Scotian capital.

CHAPTER III

MONTREAL AND OTTAWA

Montreal, the metropolis of Canada; Ottawa, the Capital; each a city supreme in a certain individual type; within three hours of each other by rail, are closely inter-related, as are New York and Washington in the United States. In England, and in France, the Capital and the metropolis are one; but there are certain advantages to a country when its legislative centre may be kept apart from the engulfing life of its commercial metropolis. It was one of the felicitous inspirations of Queen Victoria when she chose the little village that had been known as Bytown (in honour of Colonel By, the builder of the Rideau Canal) to be the capital of the Dominion and to be known as Ottawa. For many years the parliamentary sessions had alternated between Montreal and Quebec. The foundation stone of the new Parliament Building was laid by the Prince of Wales (later Edward VII.) in 1860, when the youthful prince made his memorable tour of the Dominion and the United States. Some seven years later the first parliamentary session was held in the new capital. A most significant session it was, as it marked the date of the complete federation of all the Canadian Provinces then existent and ushered in the Dominion.

It is an anomaly that Montreal, a commercial metropolis of the most prominent and pronounced type, should be the one Canadian city that most lends herself to idealisation. One treads her thoroughfares as if under the spell of some Merlin of old, and sees the moving panorama of life as if in distance and in dream.

One is led on by invisible hands; he is haunted by voices that for centuries have been silent on earth; beckoned by some inconceivable sign and signal in the dreamy blue of the distant horizon, in whose shades phantom forms are vanishing.

"Flitting, passing, seen, and gone,"

baffling all recognition, yet beckoning by mystic flash from the ethereal realm. Was it one of these vanishers, questioned the observer, as a gleam passes in the distance, or was it instead a flash from some electric circuit, to be scientifically accounted for? One is steeped in bewilderment, for who indeed may interpret this legend-haunted air? The life of the dead centuries presses closely upon the life of the throbbing hour.

The visitor to Montreal instantly feels that anything might be possible in the strangely fascinating atmosphere of this old-world city. One has more than crossed the border line between the Dominion and the United States; one has crossed the border line of centuries. Is it 1535 or is it 1915? The twentieth century clasps hands with some dim historic period. The result is bewildering. All modern beauty of vista, of groups of sculpture, or the architectural magnificence of stately and splendid public buildings, of magnificent private residences, of cathedral and churches, of great institutions, of all latter-day conveniences and luxuries of life—all these, as one would find in New York or Paris; yet with them, as an intangible and invisible scenic setting, an impalpable atmosphere lingers, that haunting impress of the far-away past, of historic associations that persist with singular vitality; of great personalities who trod these regions where now stretch away the handsome modern streets; of intense purposes borne on the air, purposes that struggled to fulfilment, or went down to temporary defeat in darkness and tragedy—all these seem to throng about the visitor who for the first time finds himself in Montreal.

Montreal may be entered by many ways, by land or by sea; but she is very conveniently entered from New England.

It is a picturesque trip, that between Boston and Montreal, and as the sun journeys onward to the horizon line the purple valleys and the rose and amber that tinge the summits of the Green Mountains afford luxurious contrasts of colour. In the late evening the brilliant illuminations of Montreal at the west side of the Victoria Jubilee Bridge, spanning the St. Lawrence River, come into view.

In all Canada, perhaps, there is no more beautiful view than that of Montreal lying under the white moonlight with Mount Royal in the shadowy background, as seen from the railway train crossing the Victoria Jubilee Bridge. The broken reflections of the moon are seen in a wide track in the rippling, dancing waters in the middle of the river, while every lamp of the long rows that border each side of the bridge is repeated in the river below. The water front of the city is all aglow with brilliant lights; backward, in the soft, receding shadows, gleam points of light from myriad homes, and the long lines of street lamps make illuminated avenues of the thoroughfares. The moon, like a silver globe, hangs over Mount Royal, while floating clouds imprison the radiance for an instant and then, relenting, set it free again.

INTERIOR OF NOTRE DAME, MONTREAL

Interior of Notre Dame, Montreal

Nor is the view by daylight less to be remembered. The mighty river sweeps under the massive and majestic structure, while hundreds of steamers, sailing vessels, steam tugs, craft, indeed, of every description, are plying the waters of the St. Lawrence opposite the harbour, and the vast city of Montreal in its transcendently beautiful location at the base of the mountain completes a picture never to be forgotten. For miles the harbour is lined with imposing stone structures, the city's warehouses; and the numerous manufactories, with their tall chimneys sending out great volumes of smoke, stretch away on the shores of the St. Lawrence as far as the eye can reach, with their story of the wonderful commercial metropolis of the Canadian empire. The picture is one to enchain the artist and the social statistician as well. It is of itself a study in economics and commercial development.

From an engineering standpoint this bridge ranks with the foremost structures of contemporary achievements. The Victoria Tubular Bridge which it replaced was built in 1860, and was at that time considered the eighth wonder of the world; but it became insufficient to meet the increase of traffic, and in October of 1897 the work of building the present stupendous structure was inaugurated. The chief engineer was Mr. Joseph Hobson, whose ingenuity and skill contrived to utilise the tube of the old bridge as a roadway, on which a temporary steel span was moved out to the first pier, the new structure being then erected outside the temporary span. Begun in 1897, it was completed in 1899, and during its construction the enormous traffic of the Grand Trunk System was delayed very little, a remarkable fact when it is realised that while the old bridge weighed nine thousand and forty-four tons, the new one weighs twenty-two thousand tons, and while the width of the former was but sixteen feet, the width of the new bridge is sixty-six feet, with a height of from forty to sixty feet, while the one it replaced was but eighteen feet high. The old bridge was built for seven million dollars, while the new one cost two million pounds. The latter carries trains in both directions at the same time, trains with two consolidation engines and tenders, coupled, whose average weight is five thousand two hundred pounds to each foot of length, with a car-load of four thousand pounds to the foot; and a moving load on each carriage way of a thousand pounds a foot. Nor is there any limit prescribed for the speed of either railway trains or carriage and motor car crossings.

This magnificent structure is, indeed, a marvel of the age. There was a pretty scene that lives in memory which marked the date of October 16, 1901. On the very spot where the Prince of Wales (later King Edward) stood when he drove the last rivet in the old Victoria Tubular Bridge in 1860, stood their Royal Highnesses the Duke and Duchess of Cornwall and York (now King George and Queen Mary), with a group of the officials of the railway, thus linking into succession notable events separated by more than forty years.

As one of the wonderful achievements of the opening year of the twentieth century, this bridge draws thousands of sightseers, every year, to study its beauty and marvellous efficiency.

The scenes that Cartier saw fade from the eye, and one sees the solid and splendid business quarters of Montreal, the charming and enticing residential sections. Yet again an anomaly—a mountain in the heart of a city! And it is ascended, not by climbing over perpendicular rocks, but by an easy gliding car that makes its ascent as much a part of a pleasure drive as might be the drive in Hyde Park or in the Bois du Boulogne. Mount Royal suggests in some way the Monreale of Palermo, save that it is crowned by no cathedral, but from its height of a thousand feet it offers a panorama of city and river and wood and mountain ranges that is indescribable. What must be the influence on a city's life of having such a resort as this? It is in itself a prospect of unique and unrivalled beauty; it is a playground for all forms of recreation, *al fresco*; it is spiritual sanctuary. Again, the mystic vanishers beset one's footsteps, and signals beckon from the vast azure sea of the air. The sunset splendours glow and deepen over Westmount, Montreal's most beautiful suburb, which climbs up the mountain side, with such views, such charm of outlook, as one might well travel many a league to find.

It is again in that realm where nothing is but what is not, that one is led to that haunt of the student and the antiquary, the Château de Ramezay, built more than two hundred years ago by Claude de Ramezay, then governor of Montreal. And if the American Congressional Commission, comprising Franklin, Chase, and Carroll, who sat there for days and nights arguing, pleading, insisting that Canada should unite with the thirteen states in their rebellion and defiance of King George, had prevailed, had the Canadians yielded, what would the course of history have been? How would its trend of events have contrasted with the present? It is an interesting and curious speculation not without historical value of its own.

The Antiquarian and Numismatic Society of Montreal acquired the Château de Ramezay in 1895, after the building had passed through several vicissitudes of ownership, to make of it an Historical Portrait Gallery and Museum. One finds here a copy of the old painting in oils of the first Ursuline Monastery in Quebec, which was built in 1640, and destroyed by fire a year later, the original work being in the Ursuline Convent in Quebec. In the foreground of the picture is the house that was occupied by Bishop Laval in 1699. A large number of interesting old portraits are here, the gifts of the descendants or adherents of the sitters themselves; and coats-of-arms, antiquities, documents, and other matters of interest make up a valuable historical museum.

Montreal is enshrined in legendary lore. The Ile de la Cité, in Paris, is hardly more entangled in mystic story than is the metropolis of the Dominion. The tale that has come down the ages that the martyred preacher Saint-Denis walked from the heights of Montmartre, near Paris, to the Ile de la Cité, carrying his severed head in his hands, does not more challenge one's confidence in its authenticity than do many of the legends that haunt the imagination of the visitor in Montreal. About the middle of the seventeenth century a permanent settlement was founded in La Place Royale, near where the old Customs House now stands. Upon a warehouse in close proximity is placed a tablet with an inscription to the effect that on this site stood the first manor-house of Montreal, which from 1661 to 1712 was the seminary of St. Sulpice.

The story of the settlement of La Place Royale is one of the mystical tales to be found in the Relations des Jésuites, and it tells that Jean Jacque Olier, an Abbé of France, suddenly experienced a deep religious re-awakening, and gave himself with ardour to devising and carrying out new projects in connection with the education and training of young priests in St. Sulpice, Paris. Hearing of the settlement on the island of Montreal he conceived the idea of founding a mission there. The Sieur de la Dauversiére, of Brittany, had conceived a similar project, and the two men met, by chance, as strangers at Meudon. Although they had never seen each other before, they fell into each other's arms and related their plans; they obtained the aid of Madame de Bullion and other influential leaders at court, and formed a society known as the Compagnie de Notre Dame de Montreal. It is further related that about this time a young nun, Jeanne Mance, had a vision in which she was called to go to the same place and found a convent. A French writer records that then a miracle took place: "God, lifting for her the veils of space, showed her while yet in France the shores of the island and the site for Ville Marie, at the foot of the mountain." The little company landed from the St. Lawrence on May 18, 1642, and at the first religious service held, Father Vimont said, "You are a grain of mustard seed that shall rise and grow till its branches overshadow the earth. You are few, but your work is the work of God. His smile is upon you."

Thirty years later the first streets were laid out in Montreal. Religion and education went hand in hand. In 1721 the population had increased to three thousand; steam navigation was initiated in 1809 by the second steamboat built in America (the first being that of Robert Fulton which plied on the Hudson in 1807) and the steam river traffic between Montreal and Quebec was thus begun. Navigation across the Atlantic from Canada opened in 1831; the first railroad was successfully started in 1836; and Montreal was incorporated in 1832. The Lachine Canal had been completed in 1825. From the first, Montreal has been prosperous, and the present metropolis, rapidly nearing a population of three-quarters of a million, with its nine miles of river front, its fifty public parks, its admirable municipal improvements in all modern appliances, stands as a monument to the faith and devotion of its early founders led to the wilderness as by vision.

Montreal has an Art Gallery, of Greek Ionic architecture, built of Vermont marble, the entrance hall lined with Bottichino marble, with handsome staircases, and numerous salons. The collection of pictures and sculpture is already an interesting one, and an annual Loan Exhibition is made possible by the generous enterprise of the citizens, many of the private collections being very rich in artistic treasures. Nor is music neglected in Montreal. The organ recitals at Christ Church Cathedral are famous far beyond the city.

Women's work in Montreal is a very prominent and valuable feature of the city's life; including much social service work and the promotion of guilds of various orders. The Canadian woman, indeed, plays an important part in the entire life and progress of the Dominion. The churches of Montreal include many of great beauty, such as Notre Dame, St. James' Cathedral, Christ Church Cathedral, and others. The Grey Nunnery, covering an entire block, and the Royal Victoria Hospital are impressive buildings; and the banks and office structures of the city are in many cases very imposing and seem to duplicate the stately and impressive architecture of London.

There is no Canadian industry that is without representation in Montreal markets, and her manufactures have a world-wide repute. Montreal is the greatest grain port of America, taking precedence of New York in the quantity of grain handled at her port.

Situated on an island thirty-two miles long and from four to eight miles wide, at the junction of the St. Lawrence and Ottawa rivers, Montreal is a seaport, although a thousand miles from the sea; for the construction of a thirty-foot channel enables the largest ocean vessels to sail to her docks. The Canadian canals enable the steamers of the Great Lakes to sail to the harbour of Montreal, where they transfer their cargoes to the ocean steamers. Montreal has, indeed, almost unrivalled facilities by both rail and water. Her harbour is under the control of a Board of Commissioners appointed by the Government of the Dominion, and twenty-seven millions of dollars had been spent in providing the most approved modern facilities up to the beginning of 1916, with nine millions more for the same purpose already available. Both her export and import trade have been increasing so rapidly that even these liberal endowments are taxed to the utmost.

With this commercial supremacy, the City of the Royal Mountain offers educational advantages and scientific culture of the highest order. The great value of the McGill University is not only the distinction of its intellectual position, or the high quality of its work, but also its guarantees of equality of educational opportunity to all whose career comes within the sphere of its influence. The princely endowments of the late Lord Strathcona and of Sir William Macdonald provided a foundation whose far-reaching value can hardly be estimated, and the university has been singularly fortunate in the character and endowments that have graced her staff of professors. While McGill offers special training of the most advanced type in preparation for the various professions, and for the acquirement of technical qualifications, she has never yielded to any purely utilitarian standards. She has held to the ideal that Education is primarily for the soul herself, and not, as said the Grecian philosopher of old, "to be undertaken in the spirit of merchants and traders, with a view to buying or selling." It is the glory of McGill that she sends forth, not only culture and trained skill, but men prepared for the duties of citizenship, and the obligations, the privileges, the responsibilities that await them as members of society.

Montreal City

McGill celebrated in 1904 her seventy-sixth anniversary, and in the lofty and glowing address made on that occasion by Principal and Vice-Chancellor Peterson, we find him saying—

"Manners are formed and personality is built up in the school of life,—even the student school. Honesty, purity, reverence,—all the moral virtues, in fact,—are just as important for the youth of the country as are learning and scholarships. We want to have a hall-mark for McGill men by which they may be known and recognised the world over. It lies with our students themselves to set the standard. 'How truly it is in man,' as Mr. Gladstone said to the students in Edinburgh, 'in man, and not in his circumstances, that the secret of his destiny resides. For most of you that destiny will take its final bent towards evil or towards good, not from the information you imbibe, but from the habits of mind, thought, and life that you shall acquire during your academic career. In many things it is wise to believe before experience; to believe until you may know; and believe me when I tell you that the thrift of time will repay you in after life with an usury of profit beyond your most sanguine dreams, and that the waste of it will make you dwindle, alike in intellectual and in moral stature, beneath your darkest reckonings.'"

There was one little incident in the scientific history of McGill that is not without its special interest to-day in the safe-guarding of human life. This was the first application of wireless telegraphy to the operation of moving trains. Many people now believe that in the wireless control of moving trains lies in the future the most effectual protection against railway accidents. It was in 1902, just six years after Marconi made his successes in England, that the experiment was first tried. Professor Ernest Rutherford, now of the University of Manchester, and Professor Howard T. Barnes, both of the Macdonald physical laboratory of McGill, were invited to accompany the American Association of General Passenger and Ticket Agents, who in that year held a convention in Portland. The Grand Trunk provided a special train from Chicago to Portland, and on this train, when moving at fifty miles an hour, signals were exchanged with a given station, and with the comparatively simple apparatus installed it was found possible to keep the train in communication with a station for a distance of eight or ten miles.

Ottawa was obviously created to be the capital of the Dominion. Her interesting history, initiated by the choice of Queen Victoria, the glory of whose long reign is a priceless possession of the Dominion, attracts careful study; and the first view over the charming city and its equally charming environment, is one to linger for a lifetime. The majestic beauty of her Parliament Buildings

"Set on the landscape like a crown;"

towers and bastions and buttresses clinging to the height on which they are built above the river; and the exquisite outline of the turrets and high-pointed tower of the magnificent Château Laurier all silhouetted against the western sky—

"Dim in the sunset's misty fires,"

offer a pictorial enchantment to linger in the memory. This young city, with hardly more than half a century's life behind it, has made itself a distinctive point in the States as well as in the Dominion.

"Have you seen Ottawa? Have you stayed in Château Laurier?" are interrogations not unusual among us in the States when Canada is discussed. Is Ottawa, with its artistic Château Laurier, the Carcasonne of the newer world? For surely no guest of the Château Laurier quite dreams of classing it among ordinary hotels; in it he tastes a flavour of something a little apart, of life in an artistically appointed palace which he enters from his railway train through a brilliantly lighted marble corridor reminding him of the entrance to Bertolini's on the terraced hills of Naples. The Ottawa Grand Trunk Station itself, built of white marble with its pillared façade, is like a Greek temple, and the richly decorated corridors and salons of the Château are as reminiscent of Venice as of France. This magnificent hotel was of course named after Canada's great statesman, the Right Honourable Sir Wilfrid Laurier, G.C.M.G., whose bust in marble adorns the entrance corridor. The decorations are of the François I. period; the building is absolutely fireproof, and the luxurious furnishing suggests that of private palaces rather than of an hotel.

One of the most interesting places in Ottawa is the Archives, a handsome stone building completed in 1906. The extensive records of Canadian history under the able and courteous administration of Dr. Arthur Doughty, Keeper of the Archives, are made accessible to scholars and research students; and this building has become one of the haunts of the savant. Numerous glass cases are filled with valuable manuscripts and documents; historic souvenirs abound; the library contains over twenty thousand books; and there are many beautiful paintings and engravings in the various rooms, illustrating important epochs in the history of the Dominion and also including many portraits of value and interest.

Ottawa—showing the Parliament Buildings and Château Laurier

The Experimental Farm, three miles out of Ottawa, covers nearly five hundred acres of land, and it is one of the chief attractions, offering, as it does, so much efficient instruction in the seeding, culture, and harvesting of agricultural products, and the care of live stock. Not far from this Farm is the Royal Astronomical Observatory, built in Romanesque style, with a central octagonal tower under a revolving hemispherical dome, containing the telescope. The Observatory comprises an astronomical library, photographic and lecture rooms, and a reading-room.

Ottawa is a growing city and is one of the beautiful capitals of the American continent with the population now approaching the one hundred and fifty thousand mark. There is much of old-world ceremony in the city.

Rideau Hall, the residence of the Governor-General (at the time of writing, the Duke of Devonshire, who succeeded His Royal Highness the Duke of Connaught and Strathearn), is a rambling grey stone structure, with ample grounds, comprising some eighty-five acres. The gracious character of all ceremonial courtesies and hospitalities at Rideau Hall are deeply appreciated by the people of the Dominion. The Duke of Devonshire is the head of one of the greatest of English families, the Cavendishes, and his appointment was a popular one with Canadians. The Duchess of Devonshire is the daughter of a former Governor-General of Canada, the Marquis of Lansdowne, and is no stranger to Canada.

In an address given by the Duke of Connaught before the Canadian Club, his Royal Highness thus alluded to the position of Governor-General of the Dominion:—

"I do not know of a prouder position for any Englishman to hold than that of his Majesty's representative as Governor-General of Canada. When my late brother, King Edward the Seventh, asked me to accept this high post, an offer which was renewed after his death by our present gracious Sovereign, I felt great doubt as to whether I could do justice to so high a position. I had no doubt that I should be a friend of the Canadians to-day as I was forty-three years ago. Since I have been in Canada the last year and a half, I have felt more and more that I have been able to gain the keen sympathy and, I venture to say, the affection of the whole Canadian people. I am sure you will believe me when I say that I never spent a happier year and a half. To Englishmen who have not been in Canada, I say the sooner they go the better. It is moving with leaps and bounds."

The Parliament Buildings occupy a commanding site near the park in which the Château Laurier is built, thus sharing the advantage of all the lovely grounds. The Rideau Canal, with its locks, joins the Ottawa River in this park, under the very shadow of Parliament, offering a picturesque feature as it passes to the Rideau Lakes. The extensive Library of Parliament is, happily, open to the people, and its generous hospitalities and rich resources have been of themselves a signal attraction to scholars and literary workers. Fortunately the greater part of this library escaped destruction in the fire of 1916 that partially destroyed the Parliament Buildings, although as they will be restored with increased facilities, the calamity was not wholly evil in its results.

The Library of Parliament is built upon the lines of some of the famous old chapter-houses in England attached to a noble cathedral. The interior is circular, with a dome of forty-two feet in height, a vaulted roof and rich carvings. It is an interior rich in the revelation of all that is best in the realm of thought, all that touches human interests and makes for those nobler ideals which are the real resources of life.

The beauty of the Parliament Buildings in the early dawn has been celebrated by an Ottawa poet, Duncan Campbell Scott:

"Fair, in the South, fair as a shrine that makes
   The wonder of a dream, imperious Towers
Pierce and possess the sky, guarding the halls
   Where our young strength is welded strenuously;
While, in the East, the star of morning dowers
The land with a large tremulous light, that falls
   A pledge and presage of our destiny."

CHAPTER IV

TORONTO THE BEAUTIFUL

Toronto, city of education, culture, religion; a city of homes with all that makes for the beauty and the happiness of family life; Toronto, with her noble University whose enrolment of students exceeds in number that of Oxford, her conservatories of music, her impressive cathedrals and churches, her splendid Parliament Buildings, and her classic Public Library with its numerous branches—the capital of the rich province of Ontario, this beautiful and inspiring city of Canada provides, indeed, an ample basis for the enthusiasm and devotion of her citizens. No city could be more advantageously located, seeing that she commands the blue waters of Lake Ontario. Toronto is the centre from which radiate several of the most picturesque excursions into the western continent. The world-wonder of Niagara Falls is in her near neighbourhood. From Toronto all the summer "playgrounds" of Canada may be reached with the utmost convenience and readiness; or the tourist may make that picturesque sail down the St. Lawrence; or, again, would he be like Wordsworth's *Stepping Westward*, he may take train and embark at Sarnia for the tour of the Great Lakes, ending at the terminal of Fort William, whence again he may wander into all the scenic glories of Canada.

At Toronto the holiday-maker may board the luxurious train for Huntsville, where he takes the steamer for that idyllic cruise by the chain of lakes that lands him at the fascinating Hotel Wawa; or gives him access to any one of a myriad resorts in the unique Lake-of-Bays region. Algonquin Park, the Muskoka Lakes, all these "Highlands of Ontario" which are attracting throngs of summer wanderers, are within easy reach of Toronto, to all of which, indeed, the city is the gateway, and the distributing centre as well. The playgrounds of the Dominion are much appreciated by the great nation lying on her southern border. New England and the West have long been increasingly familiar with the allurements of a Canadian summer; and now the southern states, on and near the Gulf of Mexico, are sending out for information of the facilities for vacation sojourns amid the parks and lakes and shining rivers of Canada. Those far-famed Canadian resorts, comprising not only the Lake of Bays, Algonquin Park, and Muskoka, but Timagami, Kawartha Lakes, French River, Lake Nipissing, and Georgian Bay, all lie north of Toronto, and these resorts, some of them over eighteen hundred feet above sea-level, with their invigorating, balsam-laden air, are a revelation to the visitor from the heated South.

The Southerner finds himself especially enthralled by Canada's long summer days and lingering twilights, with their ethereal and almost unearthly beauty of amber lights and evanescent shadows, a beauty that has hitherto been rather exclusively associated with Scandinavia, the land of the midnight sun. What an hour for a twilight paddle across some crystal lake, in turning homeward after an idyllic day. Canada has been fortunate in keeping her wilds singularly unspoiled, for practically only one railway line extends into all these romantic regions, that of the Grand Trunk System, which has been the means of the multiplication of delightful summer hotels and rustic camps. These Canadian resorts (whose range of prices is so moderate as to amaze the people from the States) are as socially delightful as they are in scenic charm. They are characterised by the refinement of courtesy and generous hospitality that is the hall-mark of the Dominion.

Toronto is one of the most accessible centres of the North American continent, being only three hours from Buffalo, one night from New York and Boston, and fourteen hours from Chicago.

Does all this enumeration of her charms only have to do with getting away from them? The citizen of this beautiful city on the lake will assert that there is another equally spellbinding range of charms to be enjoyed without wandering far away from Toronto itself.

The harbour of Toronto is one of the most beautiful of any of the water-front cities. It has a rather curious configuration formed by a picturesque island of more than two thousand acres that forms a species of breakwater. In the summer the waters near the island are alive with craft. Every kind of sailing boat, canoes, and yachts, as well as motor and steam launches, may be seen riding the waves. The island itself is utilised in much the same fashion as Coney Island in the New York harbour, as a resort for popular amusement. With this inland sea of Lake Ontario at its doors, with its fine architecture, its development and culture of the arts, professions, and industries; with such picturesque treasure as that of the Rosedale ravines, the Humber valley, the Don River, and the gentle hills, Toronto is well calculated to be one of the embodied inspirations of the Dominion.

It is claimed that there are more homes, each with its green lawn and its garden—homes owned by their occupants—within the thirty-six square miles that comprise Toronto than in any other city on the American continent. Toronto is truly a thing of life in its expansion. The construction of streets and buildings is in constant progress and the residential limits are being carried many miles into the country. Within the past decade the city has crossed two rivers, marched up a hill, and clambered over two ravines, all of which give the residential region an aspect of romantic beauty. The architectural charm of the city impresses the stranger; especially the cathedrals of St. James and St. Michael and the University of Toronto, that great Norman pile, dignified and with its old-world atmosphere. Surrounding it are the colleges—Victoria, with its Gothic dining-hall and residences; St. Michael's, Knox, and Wycliffe. Soon Trinity will join the ranks of college settlements. McMaster, the Baptist University, is at the northern edge of the campus, and not far away are the great medical schools, the School of Science, the Conservatory of Music, the University Library, the Dental College, and the many college residences. The University of Toronto is perhaps the largest English-speaking University in the British Empire, and the year 1916 found two thousand five hundred of her sons fighting for the Empire. The Royal Ontario Museum, with its Oriental and Indian collection, lies to the north of the campus, and the great General Hospital as well as a special hospital for children are adjacent. Many of the churches are of real beauty—St. Paul's Anglican, a structure which cost one and a half million dollars; the Eaton Memorial on the hill; the Metropolitan Methodist, owning ground estimated as worth over two millions; and the parish church of St. James, with its tower over three hundred feet in height. The Margaret Eaton School of Literature and Expression is an institution of great value, attracting students from all parts of the Dominion. As a theatrical and a musical city, Toronto shares with New York, Boston, and Montreal many of the most noted dramas and musical entertainments. As a musical centre herself, Toronto ranks fourth among the large cities of the continent; and she has an annual average of four thousand musical students. Her own Mendelssohn Choir is not only conceded to be the finest in America, but one of the best in the world.

Nor are the graphic arts neglected in Toronto. There are already two leading organisations, the Ontario Society of Artists and the Canadian Art Club. A College of Art was founded in 1912; there is a Women's Art Association, an Arts and Letters Club, which has issued a very creditable Year Book of Canadian Art, as well as a Heliconian Club, composed of women engaged in artistic and literary work, and who, presumably, quaff the living waters of Helicon to reinforce their energies.

In her Public School System, with an enrolment of thirty-five thousand pupils, Toronto employs many of the most advanced educational methods of the day.

If the visitor in Toronto were to ask for what is perhaps the most really significant factor in the city's life, and one which is likely to be missed by the surface observer, the answer would be that this factor would be found in the Public Library System, so splendidly administered by the Chief Librarian, George H. Locke. A Canadian, a native of Toronto, Mr. Locke was allured for a few years by Harvard University and the University of Chicago; but fortunately for his own city, he has chosen to devote himself to her development and culture through the medium of library work, in a manner whose original genius for relating literature to the needs of the people, and more especially to the youth and the children, is making itself felt in the Dominion as well as in the city.

In many aspects of his manifold and remarkably adjustable system, Mr. Locke creates his own precedents. In any survey of the processes in many of the noted libraries of the past, the chief aim, if not regarded as the chief duty, of the keeper of books has seemed to be that of protecting them from popular contact. The books were to be safeguarded from too familiar approach as are the works of art in the great galleries and museums. In every case they did not, it is true, imitate the methods of the Laurentian Library in Florence and chain the books to the desks, but something of the spirit of the stern custodian was in them all. Mr. Locke at once outlined his policy on the basis of his conviction that books were made for the people, and not the people for books, and that opportunities for more knowledge and greater intelligence should be provided. More especially he held that books had indispensable messages for the youth of a great city. The adult readers were welcomed and accorded every possible opportunity and privilege; but the children were not to be merely welcomed, they were to be enticed by the very attractiveness of the surroundings to come in from the highways and the byways to the feast of literature provided so lavishly for them.

Assisted by a staff of one hundred young women whose enthusiasm leapt up to meet his own, young women with wit and initiative of their own as well, all of which their chief especially encouraged on their parts, the work went forward. "If you think you have a good plan," Mr. Locke says, in effect, to his staff, "try it. Don't come to me about it. If it is successful, then let us talk it over. If it is not, bury it quietly and don't put up any monument to it."

The Central Library, with its fourteen branches, works as a unit; yet not as the unit of a machine, but in a unity of spirit and purpose inclusive of many individual variations. One feature of the system of the highest value is that of the open shelves. Nothing so educates the child, in all that most essential development of what Matthew Arnold so well terms the humanities, as the habit of browsing at will among books. From the official report made by Mr. Locke for the year 1915 the following extract is taken, as it illustrates clearly one novel and invaluable feature of the work—

"The work with the children, which showed such a remarkable increase last year, has shown even greater results, and we see new possibilities for the coming year. This department is decidedly aggressive in its methods, and no phase of public social service in this city has awakened such wide interest. The Story Hour, already popular, was given a decided help onwards by the series of lectures which the Children's Librarians arranged for during October and November, when Miss Marie Shedlock, of London, England, spoke to five delighted audiences on 'Story Telling.' That part of the Story Hour which is devoted to Canadian historical characters is really a National Movement, for it supplies to the children, many of whom are of foreign parentage, a Canadian historical background, something much needed in a new country with its great problems to be solved by those who now are but children. This year there were 12,671 children in the Story Hours and 249,260 books were circulated among boys and girls."

The "Story Hour" is a semi-weekly feature of the library work, and one which has developed unmeasured ardour on the part of the youthful auditors.

Another signally refining and helpful influence is that of the culture of flowers; a garden plot, or beds of flowers, being a feature of the grounds surrounding each of the fourteen libraries. The children are encouraged to aid in this care of flowers, and seats placed in the gardens enable summer readers to pursue their work amid this beauty, and in the invigorating air.

The "J. Ross Robertson Historical Collection," housed in the Reference Library, is as a gallery of Canadiana of the utmost value to the student of the history of the Dominion. The collection numbers already three thousand two hundred and twenty-nine pictures, and in the year of 1915 alone, it was visited by more than twelve thousand people. These pictures tell the story of the development of Canada from the forest, lake, and prairie, with tribes of wandering Red Men, into the land of fruit, grain, and manufactures. Mr. Robertson has proved a real benefactor to the entire province as well as the Dominion, for students come from all parts of the country to study this collection.

Toronto is constructively much like London, in that a number of separate communities are federated to form one city. In nearly every one of these separate and component parts a branch of the Public Library is established, taking the name of the specific centre, such as Wychwood, Dovercourt, and Yorkville. The latest of these branches, that at Wychwood, is a perfect architectural reproduction of the Shakespearean period, thus celebrating the tercentenary in 1916 in a tangible manner, and its Elizabethan charm attracts numerous appreciative visitors. One typical instance of the library spirit is that of taking a primitive and discarded little church, fitting it up with books, and with light and heat and flowers (for in every library interior beautiful flowers are an unfailing ornament) making of this a small branch in an undeveloped part of the city, and forming it into a notable centre of joy, helpfulness, and inspiration.

In addition to the University of Toronto, and in close alliance with it, is University College, a state institution, in which languages and the liberal arts are taught; and this notable university system in Toronto is inclusive of a number of other affiliated institutions, in which the students may avail themselves of the university examinations and degrees, among which are the Toronto College of Music and the Conservatory of Music. There are four university museums, the Mineralogical and the Geological, the Archæological and the Biological; and there is also a Gallery set apart for Palæontology. A stately and impressive building, the School of Domestic Science, presented by Mrs. Massey Treble, is the centre of instruction as useful as it is important. No visitor in the Dominion can fail to perceive how Canada is especially a home-building, home-conserving country. If one were called upon to define the Canadian nation in a phrase, it would be that of a home-building people. That the home, in all the purity and sanctity of family life, is the unit of civilisation is an article of faith in Canada.

The Royal Astronomical Society of Toronto is an association of much importance in the scientific world. In May, 1916, it had the honour of being addressed by an astronomer whom it is no exaggeration to term the most brilliant figure of the age in interstellar physics. This was Doctor Percival Lowell, whose brilliant and original investigations have thrown great light upon the evolution of the planets, and whose especial discoveries (as they may now be claimed) of the conditions on Mars have arrested the attention of the entire scientific world. It was on this theme, including aspects of Mars developed in observations made as recently as in January and March of 1916, that Doctor Lowell addressed the Society.[1]

[1] Dr. Percival Lowell died November 13, 1916, at Flagstaff Observatory, Arizona, U.S.A.

The population of Toronto is already over the half million mark, the city directory for 1915 recording a population of 534,000, and the number is said to increase on an average of thirty thousand a year. It is a great manufacturing city, which has been able to harness a waterfall, even the mighty cataract of Niagara, into its daily service. Is it that the twentieth century calls from the fabled past those genii and magicians who can command and control the forces of Nature? The result would almost confirm that fascinating speculation. Apparently the Torontian is more fortunate than one individual who is said to have been enabled to send the broomstick to fetch water, but forgetting the incantation necessary to stop it, he was drowned. Toronto apparently knows the secret of controlling her almost unrivalled waterpower. There are in and about Toronto more than nine hundred factories that number over sixty-five thousand employees, with an annual pay-roll of twenty-nine millions, representing a capital of seventy-five millions. The electric power from Niagara Falls is supplied at moderate rates, and thus the extension of manufacturing plant is encouraged to the advantage of the city itself.

The illumination of the Toronto streets by night is a feature of no little interest. The use of hydro-electric power has permitted the lighting by means of cluster lights, a system of unique beauty and incomparable service, and of great decorative effect as well. This power is supplied from the main station located at Niagara Falls, on the Canadian side, which itself is supplied directly from the cataract, with a high voltage of electrical energy.

The annual Canadian National Exposition held in Toronto during the last week in August and the first in September is considered to be almost a barometer of the progress of the world in general. Its promoters point with pride to the fact that this Exposition was the first to introduce the dawn of the Electrical Age to Canada; the first to introduce to general knowledge Marconi's wireless telegraphy; the first to demonstrate the uses of the telephone, and the advantages of the electric car service, and has thus, for a long series of years, made itself an important factor of contemporary progress.

The Bigwin Inn, Lake-of-Bays, Ontario

This Exposition is held in a natural park of some two hundred and sixty acres, sloping from the blue and sparkling waters of Lake Ontario, with a water front of nearly two miles in extent. The grounds are made a very "garden-city," with wide, paved streets and walks; with vistas of emerald turf enriched with shrubs and flowering plants and trees, amid which the permanent State buildings, graceful and rich in architectural detail, reveal themselves to great advantage. This Exposition is justly held throughout the Dominion as an annual focussing of the latest inventions and appliances, as a gauge of productive power in every direction, and it draws over a million visitors to the city every season.

As the Capital and metropolis of the rich and important province of Ontario, Toronto can hardly be adequately considered without some outline of the activities of the Province as well. The Parliament buildings occupy a prominent site in the city, and the Commissioners who are lodged in their various departments represent every important industry and interest in Ontario. Among these interests are the Good Roads Association, the Vegetable Growers, the Game and Fisheries, and the Women's Institute of Ontario, under the head of the Minister of Agriculture. Ontario has its Agricultural College at Guelph with the Macdonald Institute for girls in which homemaking as well as housekeeping is taught and which is the inspiration centre of the Women's Institutes of the province. The system of travelling libraries is of unsurpassed aid in the disseminating of information. The Women's Institute and the Farmers' Institute co-operate to the mutual advantage of each. Among the topics discussed in the former are "Discipline for Children," "Problem of the Farmer's Wife," "Furnishing a Living-room for Comfort," "Old-Fashioned Hospitality," and "The Value of Pleasing Manners." The activities of this Institute radiate an influence and suggest a series of standards that is little less than invaluable in its effect on the general rural life. The Institute has a membership of more than twenty-five thousand women; they represent some eight hundred and fifty branches; and their influence easily reaches twice the number of the membership. Courses of lessons in Domestic Science are given in stated centres; special instructors in cooking, dairying, poultry-raising; and topics relating to household labour of all kinds are assigned for discussion from time to time, the meetings always drawing large and eager audiences. The entire instruction is eminently practical, and in one Report made to the Minister of Agriculture the programme of lessons offered as typical included "Invalid Cookery," "Table Seating and Serving," "How to Spend the Winter Evenings," and "Wholesome Reading for Boys and Girls." It will readily be seen how extremely valuable is such a range of discussion as this, in a comparatively new country, where each household must so largely depend upon its own resources. "The strength of the Empire is in the homes of her people," said one lecturer, and the opinion is wide-spread. This Association further urges that its prevailing spirit shall know no distinction of class or creed; that it shall reach and include, with cordial, gracious welcome, every woman who is inclined to come into it. The motto of the Institute is, "If you know a good thing, pass it on." The Ontario Vegetable Growers' Association is another energetic organisation, whose aim is to "plant and make things grow."

The importance of social welfare is very fully recognised in Canada. "We are not here simply to make a living, to spend all our days in work," states one leading member; "we are here to enjoy life, and I believe that God intended that every one should enjoy a well-rounded life, with time for recreation and for mental and spiritual development."

In the prominence given to social service in the Dominion, a new and distinctive profession is opened, and one especially fitted for educated and cultivated young women. Various spheres of work are open, as those of assistants to city pastors, and as nurses, park attendants, health inspectors, police matrons, school inspectors, and as officials in the many charitable and educational institutions. Friendly visiting is not the least of these many channels for aid to social betterment, and for the extension of sympathies and the promotion of the higher life.

CHAPTER V

THE CANADIAN SUMMER RESORTS

Canada is Nature's pleasure-ground. The ineffable spell of beauty enchants the entire Dominion. It is not difficult to recognise the sources of her poets' inspirations. The wanderer in all this bewildering loveliness can say with the singer:

"I bathe my spirit in blue skies
   And taste the springs of life."

How Lampman has painted the very atmosphere in the lines:

"I lift mine eyes sometimes to gaze,
   The burning skyline blinds my sight;
The woods far off are blue with haze;
   The hills are drenched in light."

Never was there beauty of Nature that so transmuted itself into vitality. The air is the very elixir of life. It is the infinite reservoir from which untold measures of energy may be drawn and stored up for the future. One does, indeed, "taste the springs of life" in actual experience.

The colossal scale of the summer resorts of Canada suggests the haunts of the Titans. The Maritime Provinces have long been a recognised locality for vacation days; but the region of central Canada, from Lake-of-Bays and Algonquin Park to Minaki, on the lakes east of Winnipeg, opens a new world to the summer visitor. It invites the seeker after health, rest, sport, or artistic enjoyment; it offers ideal conditions for the writer or the student, as well; but all this terrestrial paradise requires a clearly-defined geographical presentation in order to be at all adequately comprehended. In a country stretching over three thousand seven hundred miles from coast to coast; and in which the pleasure grounds already opened to easy accessibility by rail or steamer are thousands of miles in extent, a clear idea of their relative aspects in geographical space is an initial requirement. Canada is a Wonderland, but she is not an untraced wilderness.

Take, for example, Lake-of-Bays! Poetic, bewitching, star-crowned Wawa! The instant devotion inspired by this fascinating fairyland is, like beauty, its own excuse for being. As the visitor steps, in the brilliant sunshine of a late afternoon, upon the beach at Norway Point he finds himself within two hundred yards of the hotel. Here is a splendid dock with shelter rooms and baggage rooms, and here are porters from the Wawa, and his impedimenta having been handed over he turns to look at the oncoming sunset over the lake and over wooded islands, the colour-scheme changing in the flitting, opalescent lights, the cloud-shadows drifting over the green of island trees and vegetation, with a fringe of pine and balsam along the shores of the lake offering their refreshing shade for the saunterers and the bathers. The dancing pavilion is not far away at one end of the long piazza, and strains of music from the orchestra are floating out on the wonderful air. On a plot of verdant grass a group of white-robed children are dancing like a very fairy ring; and the western sky which the Wawa fronts is aglow with the sunset splendours.

Or, perchance, one arrives in the morning (for there are three steamers a day) in the pure, transparent light which plays such optical tricks with distance. There may be illusions similar to those that beset, and delight, the visitors to the Grand Canyon in Arizona. One stands on the brink of that titanic chasm and seeing an enticing point apparently close at hand he remarks that he will just step over to it. "How far do you think it is?" questions the habitué with secret delight; "that point is two miles away from us," he continues with due enjoyment in his companion's discomfiture. Something of the same illusions of the air beset one at Norway Point, on which the Wawa stands. This point is a favourite with an increasing number of summer colonists as the numerous cottages and picturesque camps suggest.

Not the least of a summer's enjoyment here is the charm of the trip. It is very easy, but it is also very picturesque. North from Toronto at a distance of some hundred and forty-six miles is the pretty little village of Huntsville, nestled among lakes and hills. Here begins the Lake-of-Bays region. The locality is one of the loveliest in Ontario; the lakes are dotted with islands and connected by winding rivers, with luxuriant growth of woodlands; the surface of the water is covered with lilies, the hills are dark with their sombre pines, and the entire landscape is fascinating. At this point the traveller is transferred from the railway to the waiting steamer on which he gaily steps for a sail on this unique series of lakes. The steamer glides to the end of one and enters a river; and the craft pushes on through it while branches of trees and tangled vines sway so near, on either side, that they may be almost grasped by the hand. What will happen next? one mentally questions. How will a steamer ever thread this wildwood? For apparently there is but an unmarked stretch of woodlands ahead, and even the steam launch of an enchanted journey can hardly be expected to navigate forests. Like most difficulties, however, this one comes to a satisfactory solution when another lake that has concealed itself behind a grove is now revealed and the steamer sails on.

But when she meets solid land how is she to negotiate the portage? It is then that the genius of the lamp appears, which one has but to rub in order to attain to the realisation of any of his earthly desires, and the touch on the lamp, as Aladdin holds it up for the passengers, produces, not the Amazon nor yet the Mississippi, but a mile of railroad, the shortest railroad in the world, bridging the portage between the lakes. Into the cars throng the passengers for the swift transit around the hills to the lake and the other steamer waiting. "Lake-of-Bays," indeed! Lake of a myriad bays, for the entire shores are indented with the inlets bordered by firs that mirror themselves in the water. It is through all this shining pathway that the tourist makes his triumphal progress and arrives at length at Norway Point. When one realises that all this Wonderland is, after all, only nine hours from Buffalo, one sees how easily accessible from the States are Canada's most charming summer districts. The romantic journey would almost be worth the taking even if one remained but a single night. For the beautiful hours of life are not over when they have passed; they linger in memory; they pervade all the quality of life.

It is in the climate that the very concentration of vitality lies, and a night's sleep at Norway Point seems to transform one's entire being with a renewal of life. What a view it is at night from the upper piazza when the powerful searchlight of the hotel is turned over lakes and woods and clustered islands; and the evening steamer coming in, gay with flags and pennons, with snatches of music and light laughter borne on the evening air. The searchlight on the hotel, the lights on the boat, flash their signals back and forth. For a moment the visitor is again on the Swiss lakes where boats and inns call to each other in signals of light. For some years past the custom, familiar to the sojourners in Geneva, Lucerne, and Vevey, has been adopted as one of the novel and amusing features at the Wawa. Of all the fair lands ever dreamed, is that which is revealed (or is it half created?) under the swiftly moving wave of light, that flashes its high illumination over the lakes, near and far, that gleam like silver. The searchlight brings out the forests in their dark and massive shadows, revealing, too, the numbers of little boats and canoes, with their firefly lights, dotting the lake.

Behind the hotel there rises a densely wooded bluff, some two hundred feet high, from whose summit alluring views attract the lingerer on the hillside. On this height is the reservoir that supplies the hotel, the altitude giving great momentum to the running water. The grounds comprise some three hundred acres—everything is on a generous scale in Canada—and over these grounds are scattered pergolas and rustic seats that offer their enticing ease to the strollers in the open air, who perhaps agree with Walt Whitman that it is in open space in which "all heroic deeds are conceived, and all great poems, also."

It is not surprising that hotels and cottages spring up around these lakes, and that campers find here a favourite haunt. An immense new hotel, the Bigwin Inn, has been completed on Bigwin Island, the enterprise of one of the foremost citizens of Ontario. The Bigwin is something novel in design, the dining-hall occupying one building (with entrancing piazzas and balconies towards the lake) while other buildings house the private rooms for the guests, the Social Hall, Office, and dancing pavilion, though all these are connected by covered corridors. The Bigwin will be one of the greatest summer hotels on the continent, and its establishment is one of the evidences of the increasing popular recognition of the charm and beauty of the Lake-of-Bays country. The hotel is picturesquely situated on Bigwin Island, a tract of two-and-a-half miles in length, densely wooded, and with easy approach. The swift communication rendered possible between The Bigwin and The Wawa, by means of motor boats and steam launches, will enhance the enjoyment of each. The new hotel will be a temple of festivities and gaiety. The dancing pavilion has every late luxury of device for the dancers, and for those interludes of "sitting out" a dance for which the revel itself is made. There are palm corners; there are balconies overhanging the waters until one might well believe himself in Venice; and there are supper rooms, card tables, and provision for necessary music as well as for the onlookers.

The steamers of the Lake-of-Bays Navigation Company will make the Bigwin one of their ports of call, thus assuring a triple service every day, and rendering easy all arrivals and departures. The steamer-landing is near the hotel, and the entire island furnishes the grounds for the Inn. The pretty Italian custom of building the dining-rooms of the hotel so as to overhang the water is one of the noteworthy features of the Bigwin. At Bertolini's, in Naples, a similar effect is attained by the glass-enclosed terrace, in the air, so much in use for afternoon teas and festive occasions. At the Bigwin the *salle-a-manger* actually projects by some feet above the water, and its circular form and artistic architectural design render it a unique spectacle from the decks of the steamers as they traverse the lake. The Inn, which will open at the end of the War, will accommodate six hundred guests.

The evolution of summer resorts would alone make up almost a social history of the past three-quarters of a century. It is a far cry to the days when, in the United States, Saratoga and Niagara Falls, with a small contingent at Newport, held the exclusive fashionable prestige for summer life. New England had its North Shore, to which Boston largely transferred itself when the summer opened. The White Mountains have always retained their clientele composed for the most part of people to whom the seclusion and pure air ministered rather to the carrying on of their studious pursuits than to the abandonment of them. Newport came to have a formidable rival in Bar Harbour. The opening of luxurious railway facilities to the Far West, and the provision of beautiful hotels in Colorado, at the Grand Canyon, in California, the Yellowstone Park, and other localities have made all those regions a land of summer. There are few, now, that are not familiar to the travelling public, and so the unparalleled summer resorts of Canada open a new range of attractions and experiences.

Apart from the two dominating hotels, the Wawa and the Bigwin, the Lake-of-Bays offers numerous other centres for vacation days in smaller hotels, cottages, and camps. Grunwald, perched on the west shore of Lake Mary; Dwight Bay, Point Ideal, Bona Vista, Britannia, and many other inviting nooks are discovered.

And when the season at enchanting Wawa is over? Then, again, the sail through Peninsula Lake, through Fairy River and Fairy Lake, to the wharf at Huntsville again, where the train awaits the traveller. Alas! for the perfection of connections. One has no excuse for lingering longer. Yet so early in the September days, to many sojourners the best of the season is yet to come. North of the Lake-of-Bays is Algonquin Park. This government reservation of nearly two million acres, with the comfortable and commodious Highland Inn perched on a high terrace looking out on another of the great lakes over the islands and dense woodlands, is to many visitors the most alluring place for out-of-door life in the whole of Canada. The Highland Inn offers much that is not set down on the bills. To find in this sportsman's paradise hotel accommodations that satisfy the typical demands of twentieth-century civilisation; to find homelike rooms, with books and papers and magazines in plentiful profusion; with a writing-desk well stocked with stationery near one's elbow at every turn; spacious piazzas on which to dream; an hotel under the same management as the palatial Château Laurier, the magnificent Fort Garry in Winnipeg, and the hardly less imposing Macdonald in Edmonton—to find these things is to be at once assured of the perfection of every detail. The traveller, only too ready to take the goods the gods provide, accepts this felicitous dispensation as a part of the boundless benevolences of the universe. If he is a sportsman, the world is indeed at his feet. He may secure his canoe and his guide and fish all day in any one of the many lakes; as there are two thousand in all, he may be said to have a range of choice. In the life-giving air, two thousand feet above sea level, he may enjoy indefinitely long tramps, studying, at close range, the wild animals in the Park. For more than twenty years they have been protected from harm by the law that forbids carrying firearms within the reservation limits; and the mink, the beaver, an almost innumerable variety of birds, with squirrels and the graceful and friendly deer are found in abundance in Algonquin Park. The camp sites are unsurpassed and the hospitalities of the campers are as ready as they are ample. The gypsy kettle is always swung, the camp fire is burning, and the lovely nymphs of the lake and woodland who flit about in picturesque garb are ready to offer the impromptu guest almost any order of refreshment at a moment's notice.

The true camper, like the poet, is born and not made. It is an instinct, a gift, a grace, to adapt oneself to the simple life of the woodlands, which is, however, not without its creature comforts. Lady campers may invite one, with traces of housewifely pride, to glance at the interior of their spotless tents; an interior little used save for sleep or for shelter in sudden storms. They take pride in the beds of springy balsam well covered by blankets; and the little tables with a few books and a chair or two. A bed of balsam boughs; a breakfast of trout freshly caught in the lake, with coffee made over the camp fire, combined with youth and health and keen interest in the world in general, and what more could one ask? And if one is not acclimated to the system of domestic life as ordered by the livers in the open air, then he may enjoy in the Highland Inn all the regulation viands and appointments of the highest civilisation, with his breakfast of grape-fruit, cereals, delicious coffee not made over a camp fire; trout, hot cakes, and the wonderful maple syrup of the land of the Maple Leaf. With these he will have his matutinal paper, with the latest news of the universe, that has come up from Toronto at night, and for the day before him relays of attractions, each more delightful than the other, beckon to him.

In the vast woodlands one may encounter many happy couples strolling, not invariably side by side, for there is no surplus space beyond the width required for the single pedestrian. As they fare forth in true Indian file, He calls to Her, "Come on"; or occasionally, by way of special conversational brilliancy, he exclaims in a friendly tone, "Are you there?" They are possibly making their way over a portage. The guide has the canoe, reversed, on his head. As they wind along intricate paths, He goes in advance, and She faithfully follows. There is all the charm of conversational entertainment when He looks sideways over his shoulder and exclaims, "Getting on all right?" She would be ashamed to confess she was not! When their canoe-trip was projected that morning She, who did not know a canoe from a constellation, was quite in rapture. As a tenderfoot, as yet unprofited by the proximity of the wilderness, She descended from her bower equipped with a parasol for the sun, an umbrella for possible rain, a handbag duly supplied with pencil, notebook, violet water, and various feminine conveniences; a volume of her favourite poet in her hand that He may read aloud to her, and a novel for her own private delectation, in case He should be oblivious of poetic ecstasies and like a mere man prefer to smoke and ... dream. But He, who has seen the wilderness before in the course of his august career, and to whom canoeing is no mystery, regards Her with unaccustomed severities and austerities. "You can't take those things," he laconically observes, with one finger designating her numerous impedimenta; "upset the canoe." Poet and novelist, to say nothing of lace-trimmed parasol, are banished; and She receives the first intimation of an idea that there is some necessity of equilibrium connected with canoeing.

Between the two extremes of the campers in the open and the guests of the Highland Inn, Algonquin Park offers another mode of living that has caught the fancy of the public. This is the provision made by two log cabin camps which the Grand Trunk System has built in picturesque places in the Park. Nominigan Camp ("camp amid the balsams") is seven miles from the Highland Inn, and is reached either by the stage, which makes the trip every day, or by the more romantic way of canoeing over the lakes, and walking over the connecting portages. The site of Nominigan Camp is one worth going far to see. On the shore of one of the most beautiful lakes it was ever the happiness of man to behold, with a vista of hills and woodlands, the spot is wildly beautiful. And the camp itself; imagine a large central log house with abundance of rooms, and great fireplaces in which to burn logs and sit and wonder; with radiator heating also, and electric light, and bathrooms with running water; with a large dining-room and admirable food; with a great salon where every one may gather; and with several log cottages adjacent where families or parties, or the single traveller, can have sleeping rooms, coming to the central house for meals; the high standards of comfortable and refined life maintained and yet offering this idyllic freedom—could there be a more inviting combination? It is no wonder that an eminent guest who had passed some time at Nominigan wrote:

"To put a camp of this kind deep in the heart of the wilderness, and touch the wild life of the forest and lake with a most acceptable bit of civilisation in the form of grate fires, running water, bath-tubs, and inside toilet arrangements is decidedly a feat worthy to be spoken of when summer resorts are mentioned. To likewise supply a crowd of seventy-five guests with such an excellent table as we found provided for us, and to serve it so acceptably as to make one for a moment forget that he was beyond the bounds of civilisation, was likewise a feat of which the management should be proud."

Sir Arthur Conan Doyle and Lady Conan Doyle were guests at Nominigan in the summer of 1914, and the creator of "Sherlock Holmes" proved to be as ingenious in entering into the diversions of the locality as he is in the field of romance he has made so especially his own. Lady Conan Doyle, who developed a genuine gift for fishing, caught an eight pound salmon trout. Equal in beauty is Camp Minnesing ("Island Camp") on the shore of Island Lake.

Between the Highland Inn and the Nominigan and Minnesing camps there is daily stage connection, and it is thus easy to unite both the comfortable living in a well-ordered hotel, in touch with daily papers and several daily mails, with constant excursions into the wild territory, with canoeing, fishing, or walks and tramps through the interminable forests. Of all the Canadian parks, Algonquin Park is the most accessible from the United States and Eastern Canada. At the Algonquin Park station one may take a train in the morning for Rock Lake, a distance of twelve miles, where there is a famous fishing region for black bass, and where boats and canoes and all necessary outfit may be obtained. In Cache Lake the black bass also abound. At White Lake are salmon trout, and a canoe trip over one or two other of the smaller lakes brings the angler to Little Island Lake, noted for its speckled trout. But there are some two thousand lakes in the Park, so your choice of fishing grounds is unlimited.

Not the least among the interests of a sojourn in Algonquin Park is a visit to the home of Mr. G. W. Bartlett, the Superintendent of the Park, whose house is within a stone's throw of the Highland Inn. Among his treasures is a remarkably fine collection of wild animals and birds, prepared by the art of the taxidermist, and the government of Ontario has also inaugurated a "Zoo," which has already a small collection and which will be constantly increased.

The amateur photographer finds great interest in this Park as the animals, accustomed only to kindness, are easily approached, and the "bits" of forest scenes, of silver-shining waters, of giant rocks jutting out from the hillside, offer unlimited material for the artist to compose. Landscapes for the asking surprise the eye; and if Algonquin Park is the more obviously and more familiarly known as the sportsman's paradise, it is none the less the happy hunting-ground of the artist. The colour effects are something with which to conjure. The scarlet glow of the sunsets suddenly make a towering rock seem to leap into the air to a height undreamed of; while over the still, solemn pine trees the sky turns to flame; rocks and jutting hillsides take on the effect of colossal sculptures; the clouds resolve themselves into spectral angels watching over the world, and the forests take on a grace of line that holds the gazer with its wonderful spell of beauty.

From June until into September the days are long in the Algonquin Park country; they dawn in rose and wane in gold. The air is all vitality with its filtering through millions of acres of pine and balsam and spruce; the sunshine of the days is radiant; the moonlit nights are cool. Wandering through Algonquin woodlands one seems to hear borne on the air the poet's haunting lines:

"Along the sky, in wavy lines,
   O'er isle and reach and bay.
Green-belted with eternal pines,
   The mountains stretch away.

Below, the maple masses sleep
   Where shore with waters blends,
While midway on the tranquil deep
   The evening light descends."

This wonderful Park is very popular for its summer camps for girls and for boys, located on the lakes in close contact with the hotels. Here young people can be sent under the supervision of college men and women, thus enjoying all the freedom and wild charm of the summer life with every protection and safeguard thrown about them. Camp Minne-Wawa is one of these; a summer camp for boys and young men established in 1911 by Dr. Wise, of the Chair of English Language and Literature at the Bordentown Military Institute, New Jersey, assisted by a staff of notable educators. The aim of this culture is described as that of "Right Thinking and Character Building." The Minne-Wawa is on the Lake of Two Rivers in the southern portion of the park. The trains make a special stop for this camp; and the tents, all on raised platforms, with the natural life, the physical and intellectual training, and the careful supervision of Doctor and Mrs. Wise; with the provision, too, that the selection of applicants is restricted to those whose conduct is that of gentlemen—all these conditions render this a valuable and interesting feature of vacation life in Algonquin.

The Timagami region is one of great scenic beauty and it is also of special interest to the geologist. Through rail service from Buffalo to the station of Timagami renders the journey an easy one from the States, while the district is also in still closer touch with Toronto. The lakes and the surrounding hills are of the Laurentian formation. There is very little disintegration, and therefore little mud or sand. There is rock; there is water; and very little shading between. The crystal clearness of the water is famous, and one can gaze into it for a depth of from twenty-five to thirty-five feet. The atmosphere is so clear and dry that conversations can be carried on over a mile of distance. The echo phenomena all about these islands rivals that of the Leaning Tower of Pisa, or as under the dome of the Taj Mahal. "Anywhere between the islands you can get as many as six distinct repetitions of the echo," writes an *habitué*, and adds:

"Some August night when the moon is sailing through fleecy clouds and the planets shine like points of light in the crystal depths below your canoe, let a clear baritone voice roll out a flood of song among Timagami's islands, and you might think the gods themselves had awakened, and that every rock and islet was the home of some musical spirit voicing the theme of the night in a thousand silvery, reverberating melodies."

SIR ARTHUR AND LADY CONAN DOYLE AND PARTY

Sir Arthur and Lady Conan Doyle at Party

Very engaging is all this country of the Highlands of Ontario made so easy of access. Allandale (always associated with its alluring lunch-room), Barrie, the pretty town on a crescent of Kempenfeldt Bay, busy Orillia, with its numerous beautiful residences, on to Gravenhurst at the foot of Lake Muskoka, the journey is one of perpetual delight. Muskoka wharf is but a mile from Gravenhurst, and the trains run directly to the steamer.

The Canadian lakes are a marvel in themselves. The entire country is literally and lavishly strewn with them. Their abundance modifies the climate perceptibly. They range from lakes 300 miles long and 600 feet deep to the small lakelets hidden away in the trackless forests. There are at least nine lakes more than 100 miles long, and there are more than thirty-five over fifty miles long. Many of these are still further elongated by the bays that indent their shores, and they are so connected by rivers that almost continuous canoeing for scores of miles is sometimes practicable, with only occasionally a mile or two of portage. In connection with such a multitude of lakes there are some very interesting geological facts.

In the Muskoka region there are more than one hundred hotels, from the Royal Muskoka, accommodating three hundred guests, to those of the simplest, yet entirely comfortable order that can receive only fifteen or twenty guests with prices often as low as six dollars a week. The month of September in the Muskoka Lakes is particularly delightful. It is estimated that there is an annual transient summer population of not less than thirty thousand every year of people from both the States and the Dominion. Many of the romantic islands in the lakes are owned by wealthy people who have built charming summer villas upon them. There are between four and five hundred of these islands, the largest of which consists of over eleven hundred acres, and on many of which any one is at liberty to build. The generous attitude of the Ontario Government is always a fact with which to reckon. There are very beautiful places in this Muskoka district: the "River of Shadows" (apparently a subterranean forest, so perfectly is every leaf and branch mirrored in the water), the Moon River, and the Falls of Bala. It is of the strange, wild beauty of Muskoka that Lampman wrote:

"When silent shadows darken from the shores,
   And all thy swaying fairies over floors
Of luminous water lying strange and bright
   Are spinning mists of silver in the moon;
      When, out of magic bays,
The yells and demon laughter of the loon
      Startle the hills and raise
The solitary echoes far away;

O Spirit of the sunset! in thine hand
   This hollow of the forest brims with fire,
   And piling high to westward builds a pyre
Of sombre spruces and black pines that stand,
   Ragged, and grim, and eaten through with gold.
      The arched east grows sweet
With rose and orange, and the night a-cold
      Looms, and beneath her feet
Still waters green and purple in strange schemes,
Till twilight wakes the hoot-owl from his dreams."

All these Highlands of Ontario are a part of the vast Laurentian range and they are characterised by a singular type of rugged and stately beauty. They are densely wooded; and the luxuriant maples in all their golden-green, that wonderfully vivid emerald with a hint of gold caught from the sunshine in the summer, and their brilliant scarlet and amber in the early autumn; the fragrant balsams; the giant hemlocks; the tall pines that almost lead one to question George Eliot's assertion that "Care is taken that the trees do not grow into the sky," for the Canadian pine seems almost to pierce the sky—all this marvel of forest, with the shining lakes and sunlit glades, renders the Highlands of Ontario one of the wonders of the world. From Buffalo and Toronto to North Bay on Lake Nipissing, this entire region is traversed by the Grand Trunk System carrying summer wanderers through this enchanting scenery—hills, and lofty peaks, and woods, variegated with the silver expanse of lakes and flowing rivers; and if, perchance, one is travelling by night, it is rather delightful to raise the heavy curtain of the large window of a Pullman sleeper and watch the stars, and the sky, and the often weird effects of chiaroscuro. They not unfrequently suggest artistic creations. By night or by day it is all a spellbinding land, the celestial heavens glittering by night, the sunshine flooding the world with illumination by day; and silver mists, and ethereal shadows lurk in the deep pinewoods. To the initiate there are magic guides in all these haunts, unseen save of him who hath the "spirit-gifted eyes." The light of all the constellations that have ever looked down on earth since the morning-stars sang together is in these Canadian skies. For always is it true that

"The Muse can knit
What is past, what is done,
With the web that's just begun."

Not only the romance of Canada, but the tangible realities of her prosperity are disclosed to the eye of the traveller. Farms in a high state of cultivation; comfortable, alluring farmhouses, with their lawns, and gardens, and parterres of flowers, and a rustic seat here and there are in continual evidence. The refinements of life, from the neatness and grace of rural homes to the beautiful little railway stations with their attractive architecture, their plots of greenery, their brilliant beds of flowers, are impressive to the onlooker, and do more to convey to travellers a true concept of the character of the Canadian people than can be fully estimated. The gratification of one's sense of beauty in these charming little way stations along the route adds immeasurably to the enjoyment of the journey.

Then, too, what can be said of that sail among the thirty thousand islands in the Georgian Bay? In colour and idyllic charm this sail rivals the famous cruise among the Ionian Islands:

"The Isles of Greece, the Isles of Greece,
  Where burning Sappho loved and sung,"

and all the summer resorts of this region, Minnecoganashene, Sans Souci, Rose Point, and various nooks of verdant charm are peopled by their summer lovers.

The Great Lakes, shared alike by the Dominion and the States, offer a delightful cruise between Sarnia (Ontario) and Duluth (Minnesota) with calls at Fort William and Port Arthur, and a further excursion to the Falls of Kakabeka, a cascade higher than that of Niagara, which are near Port Arthur.

Lake Nipissing and the French River are attractive grounds for the camper and the canoeist; but they are not suited to the "tenderfoot." It is amazing that a region which can be reached with ease is yet so absolutely a place where the lover of Nature in her wild solitudes can absolutely secure a vacation from relentless Time! In the Lake Nipissing land he may elude the postman and the telephone. Doubtless by 1920, some invading airship will drop a voluminous mail at his feet when he is out in his canoe; but at the present time the sojourner here is immune from cables, telegrams, Marconigrams, long-distance telephones, special deliveries, messenger boys, and all this incubus of what we call civilisation. If radiograms fall upon him they must needs come from the solar system alone. Emerson, even in the prehistoric period of the nineteenth century, declared solitude a thing impossible to find.

"When I would spend a lonely day
Sun and moon are in my way,"

he complains. The lingerer camping out on the French River has no green-shaded electric reading-lamp at his elbow; no electric bell summons his servitor. He "catches" his breakfast in the deep waters of the lake; he concocts his matutinal coffee over a camp-fire. No ingenious victrola enchants his evening with the lyric melody of Melba or Caruso; but instead, the strange cry of the loon echoes startlingly through the silences. And so it falls out that the hardy devotees of the chase and the camp hail this region as their El Dorado.

Unlike the Nipissing, Timagami, as before noted, may be considered to be the earthly paradise of those to whom the necessities of life consist in the modern luxuries; those who would quite sympathise with John Lothrop Motley; who remarked that if he had the luxuries of life he could get on very well without the necessities.

Nibigami, "country of lakes," is a new outing ground in Canada now made accessible by the Canadian Government Railways; and all this hitherto unknown wilderness is enlisting the devotion of thousands of hunters, of fishermen, and hardly less of the artist and student.

Three hours east of Winnipeg is Minaki, the "Beautiful Country" of the Indians, at which station passengers may disembark to step into a steam launch for a sail of twenty minutes to Minaki Inn. This is a large and charmingly appointed hotel, accommodating three hundred and fifty guests, with its annex, Minaki Lodge, affording rooms for seventy-five in addition, located in a natural park of fourteen acres, every room having its own outlook over lakes or woodlands. With its spacious piazzas, its artistic furnishing, its admirable management, it is little wonder that the Minaki Inn has leapt into popular favour, not only for season guests, but also for travellers en route for the Canadian Rockies, for Jasper and Mount Robson Parks, or Prince Rupert, and for all those who find the Minaki a restful place at which to break the journey. The hotel is woodland embowered and lake mirrored. It is supremely comfortable.

Around the lakes on which the Inn is placed is a large and constantly increasing number of cottages, very artistic in architectural detail, built by wealthy people of Winnipeg and elsewhere for their summer homes. They are by no means primitive in construction; the latest devices in heating, lighting, and household conveniences as well as luxurious furnishings are in evidence; and at night from the piazzas and balconies of the hotel the circle of these friendly illuminations around the lakes is fascinating to the gazer.

View in Jasper Park

Jasper Park, lying west of Edmonton, in the foothills of the Rockies, is another National reservation included among the Playgrounds of Canada; and it has an area half as large as that of the kingdom of Belgium, comprising some 4400 square miles. The Government will keep this in its natural state for all future time, so that, as the country becomes more settled, and the features peculiarly Canadian become obliterated, Jasper Park may reveal to coming generations the nature of the primæval wilderness. Jasper Park is invested with historic interest, as it was the scene of the fierce commercial conflicts between the Hudson's Bay and the North-West Trading Companies. It is also rich in Indian legend and tradition.

Jasper Park is, however, not filled with game as is Algonquin. It is said that a century ago it teemed with bear, mink, beaver, elk, and caribou—but since that time the resident Indians have devastated the animal life; and when they learned that the Dominion was about to take over the entire tract for a permanent reservation, they embarked upon a wholesale slaughter of the animals. The Park is now made by Government decree a safe and friendly region for the wild game, and it is thus confidently hoped to gradually increase the animal life of the preserve.

The flora of the Park is so varied and so unusual as to make it an important locality to the botanist. Not only is there an infinite variety of flowers, many of which are not found elsewhere on the continent, the aquilegia, the mampanula, the moon-daisy, and endless variations on the chrysanthemum; but also the strange grasses, mosses, lichens, and curious shrubs, all combine to enlist and hold the curiosity of the student of nature.

The steel highway has brought this Alpine region, on the western border of Alberta, into easy and swift connection with the travelling world. Already the Grand Trunk Pacific is projecting hotels of the same exceptional character as those with which Algonquin Park is so well provided. At present there is the unique feature of a "tent city," which renders a sojourn of any length one that is entirely comfortable and provisioned with the amenities of life. It is one to rather enhance, indeed, the ordinary experiences of travel. The sleeping tents (as separate as rooms in an hotel) are all fitted with board floors and are equipped with comfortable beds and every convenience. There is a large central marquee for the dining-room, and all this comfort, to say nothing of glories of scenery undreamed of, is offered at the almost nominal rate of two and a half dollars a day. The town site commands a magnificent view of Athabasca Valley. The Athabasca river expands, at intervals, into lakes, of which Brule Lake, Jasper Lake, and Fish Lake are notable. At the juncture of the Athabasca and the Maligne rivers stood formerly the headquarters of the North-Western Fur Company; while the old Jasper House, the Hudson's Bay Company's post, now in ruins, was in close proximity. The site is now defined only by a pile of stones and by several graves, with mouldering crosses, that suggest the close of the drama of earthly life for those who lived and toiled here, unconsciously aiding to build up the future. The very atmosphere is pervaded by a sense of heroic effort.

One of the delightful excursions for sylvan wanderers is that of the trail to Maligne Lake, a beautiful sheet of water some thirty miles distant; and in Maligne Canyon, only eight miles from Jasper, are two comfortable shelter-houses for the free use of all tourists; each house divided into three parts, with one large room for ladies, one for gentlemen, and a central hall fitted with a range and other conveniences, where impromptu cooking may be conducted with successful results. These shelter-houses provide one more illustration of the way in which the tourist is safe-guarded all over the Dominion, even in what would seem her most impenetrable localities. So swiftly are modern conditions of comfort on their winged way that the refinements of life fairly spring up in the wilderness and almost every conceivable need or requirement of the traveller is anticipated.

The Canadian summer resorts are destined to play an important part in sociology. They attract sojourners from widely separated localities and promote interchange of views, of valuable knowledge, of ideas, of sympathies, that form an interchange of the utmost significance in its influence and determining effect upon the general international life. The summer allurements of the Dominion are to be increasingly appreciated by the civilised world, as they open up new realms teeming with new inspirations.

The beauty of Banff and Lake Louise is already known to the tourist, but it is, rather especially, the wonderful region opened to travel by the extensions of the Grand Trunk System that is so unusually spellbinding. The grandeur of these majestic mountain-peaks; the valleys and plateaus amid the gleam of lake and river; the brilliant foliage; the rich scheme of colour of purple and vermilion cliffs; the glint of blue waters through overarching trees—Ah! Land of the Maple Leaf, how fair is thy heritage!

CHAPTER VI

COBALT AND THE SILVER MINES

The famous Cobalt Silver Mines naturally focus the interest of the capitalist and the financier in any tour across the great Dominion. While British Columbia and the Yukon have been called the "Wonderland" of Canada, not alone for their mineral possibilities, but for a great wealth of other natural resources besides, and because many millions of dollars have been extracted by placer miners from rivers and streams, yet Ontario is found to exceed all other provinces, so far as yet developed, in the volume of mineral production. The Klondyke gold discoveries in the Canadian Yukon became a romance which has fairly rivalled the Tale of the Golden Fleece. Yet when in the year 1903 the copious and apparently unmeasurable deposits of silver-cobalt ores containing an extraordinarily high percentage of silver were discovered in the district of Cobalt (not far to the west from Lake Temiskaming), this event sent a thrill of sensation through the world of mining and mineral interests that left little to exceed, in romantic ardour, in the poetic legends of the Yukon:

"Steeped in eternal beauty, crystalline waters and woods."

Cobalt, Ontario

Since the discovery of silver in 1903, Cobalt has produced $130,000,000 worth of the white metal. Dividends totalling over $60,000,000 have been paid to shareholders of twenty-four mines. One company alone has distributed among its shareholders in dividends nearly $15,000,000.

In some of the Cobalt mines the ores that contained such phenomenal quantities of silver have been depleted, and ores of lower grade are now being worked, so that a much larger mass of ore, more machinery, and a larger force of working-men are now required to produce the same amount of silver.

The geological intervention of radioactivity is believed by physicists to have a determining influence upon the development of subterranean resources as well as upon the surface features of the earth and the formation of mountain chains. Vitality is another ever-increasing phenomenon, but the bewildering abundance of life that confronts the student of nature is no more inciting to research than the mystery of metals deposited far in the ground. The natural resources of Canada are so vast that even yet, as Dr. W. J. A. Donald asserts, "the greater part of three million six hundred thousand square miles of the Dominion is still *terra incognita* as regards its mineral resources, or even its geological features."

During the present war all enterprises are, more or less, and, indeed, largely, in abeyance in the Dominion; but the present is always compact of the future, nor can any strictly dividing line be drawn. "Even in the midst of the greatest tragedies," said Sir Clifford Sifton in his address before the Canadian Club of Montreal on January 25, 1915, "while we are trying to do our duty in the greatest crisis of life, we still must speak, act, think, and do in reference to the ordinary affairs of life; and the better we think and act and do in regard to these affairs, the better we shall act in these crises and the better we shall discharge our duty." Canada will never be numbered with those nations regarding whom the words were said of old, "Where there is no vision the people perish."

There is no lack of vision in the Dominion. The splendid loyalty of Canada, not only to the Empire, but to the cause of righteousness, is beyond all estimate in words; as the Right Honourable Sir Robert L. Borden has so finely expressed, there can be only one conclusion regarding the present tragedy of conflict. "To overthrow the most powerful and highly organised system of militarism that ever existed must necessarily entail terrible war and perhaps a protracted struggle. We have not glorified war or sought to depart from the paths of peace; but our hearts are firm and united in an inflexible determination that the cause for which we have drawn the sword shall be maintained to an honourable and triumphant issue."

This is the spirit of the Dominion. But all conflicts must have an end, and when the end of this struggle comes there is a marvellous future awaiting the Dominion. The future of a nation as well as that of an individual is not merely, nor even mostly, to be mechanically surveyed. It is not a definite geographical region with boundaries that can be located and crossed with a clear knowledge of the line of demarcation. The future is something that is created by men's thoughts. It is made, not found; it is constructed, not discovered. And thus, even while all internal industries are somewhat in the grasp of an enforced pause, yet new plans and projects for the future are in order. The mineral resources of Canada are incalculable. But that they will form one of the most remarkable factors in her future prosperity and importance is a practicable certainty.

It was somewhere as early as 1846 that the veins of silver were discovered in the region adjacent to Port Arthur on Lake Superior; and twenty years later that ore was actively producing silver which it continued to do until 1903. On a small island, near Thunder Cape (known as the Silver Islet), was the most famous and the richest of these mines, and the ore, interlined with veins of quartz and carbonates, was found in a wide area. It traversed a large belt of diabase, and only where the vein transversed the diabase was it richly infused with silver. Otherwise, it bore galena alone. As early as 1884 the mine had carried to a level of nearly two thousand feet, and it was estimated that not less than three million two hundred and fifty thousand dollars worth of silver had been extracted from it.

When the Cobalt silver mines began to be worked, Canada took her place as the third silver-producing country in the world; and this distinction must be largely attributed to the richness and copious output of these particular veins.

Cobalt is about 330 miles north of Toronto, on the Ontario Government Railway, and four hours south of Cochrane. At Cobalt the mines are clustered all around and beneath the town, a lake in the centre having been drained to facilitate the search for ore. To the south-east these mines are distributed over a distance of four miles. While the Cobalt silver district proper is comprised within this area, other mines, and productive ones too, have been found in the farther outlying country. London is the chief silver market of the world. Much of the bullion shipped from Cobalt is sent directly there, and London is also the basing point of prices.

The vast mills of Cobalt, transforming the crude ore into bullion, and the hydraulic plant on the top of a hill, where one man manipulates power sufficient to wash down huge rocks and to uproot and send down large trees and stumps, open out to the uninitiate a new idea of the way in which man contrives to control Nature and force her to do his bidding.

At Cobalt the "silver sidewalk" is not only an actual and visible spectacle, a solid surface on the level ground of shining silver from one to three feet in extent, but it is an indication of untold possibilities. Still, up to this time, the richness of the veins has been found to be rather in their number than their depth. These deposits are found in association with the pre-Cambrian rocks which, according to the geologists, belong to the Huronian and the Keewatin formations, through which a later diabase has been intruded in the form of a sill. This is not held to be necessarily the source of the ore deposits, but rather the means of opening the way for their introduction from other sources. A large majority of the productive veins, some eighty per cent., in fact, occur solely in the Huronian formation. The remaining twenty per cent. is divided between the Keewatin and the later diabase. As has been said above, these deposits are not especially deep, most of them being found below the sill within a depth of two hundred feet. The ores from all the Cobalt region include white arsenic, cobalt oxide, and nickel oxide, as well as the fine silver, and not infrequently a semi-refined mixture of the cobalt and nickel oxides.

If silver were the magnet that first drew the attention of the miner, the prospector, or the capitalist to Cobalt, it is not the only encouragement to the settlement of all this beautiful region. A few miles out from Cobalt is the pretty suburb of New Liskeard on a sheet of the bluest water, sparkling in the sunshine and the transparent air; where numbers of artistically designed cottages have sprung up; where the business street reveals a thriving trade; where one or two newspapers are published; and where the seeker after the occult may find his palmist and his mental healer as well as his dentist and his physician. Electric cars connect this idyllic little village with Cobalt, and motor cars dart about in a way which suggests that this region is by no means outside of the cosmopolitan luxuries of life. The country is one of great scientific interest. The geologist may find new data; the botanist and ornithologist new fields for observation.

Cobalt is recognised as a permanent silver camp, and as one of the richest on the entire American continent. At first the stories told of silver paths, brilliant and shining in the sunshine, were regarded as part and parcel of the usual myths that spring up in mining camps. But the "silver sidewalks" were there. They were the most palpable of facts. A hundred miles to the north of the town of Cobalt, on Porcupine Creek, the prospectors found gold. Specimens of the alluring yellow ore may be seen in glass cases in the corridor of the King Edward Hotel, Toronto. In that city many of the miners may be met, for mining is now a scientific pursuit rather than merely an industry, and whether the miner takes his ease in cosmopolitan centres and gives his mines "absent treatment," after the convenient fashion of Christian Scientists, or whether he is less remote from his interests, does not seem to affect the results in a vital manner.

During the year 1915 thirteen mines in Northern Ontario produced gold, and many of these are now making alterations and additions to their plants which will enable them to largely increase their output.

The following table shows the steady advance of the Porcupine gold camp since its discovery in 1910:—

Year	Value of Production $
1910	35,539
1911	17,187
1912	1,730,628
1913	4,284,928
1914	5,203,229
1915	7,580,766
Total	18,852,277

To find this possibly incalculable wealth in the densely wooded wilderness is a continually increasing surprise. The Porcupine district, as well as the Cobalt region, is reached by the Temiskaming and Northern Ontario Railway, a line of two hundred miles in length, built by the Province of Ontario, and furnishing connection between the Transcontinental line from Quebec to Winnipeg, north of the lakes, and the cities in the southern portion of the provinces of Ontario and Quebec. The construction of this connecting line led to the discovery of Lake Timagami (one of the popular summer resorts), and about thirty miles north of the lake the first indication of silver was accidently found by a workman who hurled his hammer at a scampering rabbit and hit a rock instead, chipping off a layer that disclosed a vein of almost pure silver. This initiated the famous La Rose mine, taking its name from the man who made this fortunate throw of his hammer, and within the succeeding four years this immediate region was capitalised at some five hundred millions. While the Cobalt silver mines, then, owe their discovery to this employee on the line, the engineers prospecting for the grade of the Grand Trunk Pacific accidentally uncovered vast coal-fields in Alberta.

This Temiskaming and Northern Ontario Railway connects the Grand Trunk System at North Bay with the Canadian Government lines at Cochrane. The opening up of all this country has not only resulted in the exploiting of these famous mines, but has brought to knowledge the existence of the largest tract of pulpwood in the world. The belt of these forests extends from Ontario to Quebec and westward to the prairies of Manitoba, a thousand miles of almost unbroken woodland.

The hydraulic mechanism used in prospecting for ore is one of the marvels of inventive genius. One man can operate the powerful lever that turns on a torrent of water against trees, huge stumps, vast rocks, and sends them rolling down the hillside. All obstruction, indeed, the very hill itself, is washed down. The twentieth century will always stand out as a remarkable era for the invention of mechanism to harness and utilise power hitherto undreamt of for practical application. These inventions are securing the increasing spiritual liberation of man. When he is enabled to harness the powers of the ether; to send the lightning on his errands; to bridle a force that no man ever saw or touched; when he can cause the waves of the ether to serve his chariot wheels, he has indeed transformed the world in which he finds himself.

There are rumours of a recent invention made by Mr. Asa Thurston Heydon in the Yukon that may largely revolutionise the mining industry. It was in the middle 'eighties that Mr. Heydon began studying the primitive divining-rod, the use of which he was inclined to believe was based upon some germs of scientific truth. He thought it possible that some natural law lay hidden in the garments of superstition. For thirty years he experimented and observed. This research has led him to what he believes is a series of discoveries, one of which is his invention called the clairoscope, which is the diviner for substances that are in the earth. Fitted with one or another substance attached, it turns to that which corresponds with the given thing attached. He calls the instrument the clairoscope and the result obtained the clairum. The clairum, Mr. Heydon explains, is the counterpart of the spectrum. The latter is limited to the luminous, the former to the non-luminous, rays. The spectrum exemplifies one pole of the spherical organisation of energy, and the clairum exemplifies the opposite pole. Mr. Heydon's researches are based on his conviction that everything, organic and inorganic, from electrons to the mighty universe itself, is surrounded by a sphere; that these spheres blend and combine "in accordance with the laws of force-centres," but that in all combinations "they retain their identity as do rays of light." This interesting speculator holds that the non-luminous rays are constant, changing only from attraction to repulsion, and that they are the radii of the spheres. He believes that the distinctive energy that operates the clairoscope is a higher dynamic energy; nothing less, indeed, than that vital force which is characteristic of all life. "A name must be found," he says, "for this vital force which is rhythmically circulating throughout the universe, forming the pulse of existence. The dream of the alchemist is founded in the nature of things," continues Mr. Heydon, "and will be realised when mankind shall have discovered the simple process of polarising and depolarising electrons at will. This will induce the polarisation of the correlated material sphere, and an electron of the desired element will awaken from its slumbers."

To what degree Mr. Heydon's theories will bear the test of his future investigations it is impossible to conjecture; but it is already true that the clairoscope is being used to some extent to locate minerals and has proved useful.

To descend into a mine, down to a three hundred and fifty feet level, and see the strange panorama of life that is before one's eyes, is a novel experience. Into the cage steps the little party, and the downward journey begins. All is dark save for the lamps of the miners, affixed to their caps, and the lights that are swung give a fitful and weird illumination. Through the narrow aisles on every level push-carts are passing, and the visitor must pack himself into as little space as possible as he stands against the wall to let the traffic pass by. Everything is dripping; one walks in mud and water, and sees the glisten of the wet walls. The air is cold and damp. It seems inconceivable that men can work under such conditions, yet the visitor is assured by some of the workmen themselves that they prefer this labour to any of the employments open to them on the surface of the earth. This subterranean world incites curiosity, interest, and still the onlooker is not sorry when he finds himself again in the air and sunlight above.

On the hills about Cobalt are perched attractive cottages and bungalows, and the quiet, pleasantly social little town bears no trace of the traditional atmosphere of the mining-camp of that peculiar order that has been most vividly derived from the pictures in the novels of Bret Harte.

CHAPTER VII

WINNIPEG AND EDMONTON

The traveller whose imagination had vaguely pictured Winnipeg as a fur-trading station somewhere toward the North Pole would be aroused from such reveries by the spectacle of this brilliant and cosmopolitan centre, with its beautiful architecture, its broad boulevards, the magnificent Fort Garry Hotel on the site of the ancient fort, and the civic centre in the Free Exposition building, where specimens of all the great products of the Canadian West are displayed. Winnipeg, which in 1870 had a population of two hundred and fifteen people, in 1917 records its quarter of a million. It grows at such a rate that it is unsafe to prophesy to what degree these figures may be increased in the immediate future. A representative of Baedeker, who had been sent to the United States to prepare a volume on its western regions, complained to a fellow-voyager on the ocean steamer, when returning to his own country, that it was mathematically impossible to cope with the Far West with any accuracy. "Why, I prepare the exact population of a town—Seattle, for instance—and before I can get my report into print the population has doubled." This was naturally a tangible grievance, and one which was extremely difficult for the statistician to meet. Possibly the same baffling problem of accuracy confronts him who would record the population of Winnipeg.

From the tower of the Fort Garry Hotel there is revealed a scene hardly to be compared with any other on the continent. The spectator can see broad boulevards, many of which are a hundred and thirty-two feet in width; an electric railway, operating hundreds of cars, whose service is said to be the most perfect of that of any city in the States or in Canada; streets paved with asphalt and macadam; extensive parks, where equipages not less fine than those of Hyde Park or the Bois de Boulogne, are seen rolling along the smooth, winding roads; churches, numbering nearly two hundred; the University of Manitoba; the art school; and the unexcelled beauty of miles of residential regions, laid out in those graceful curves and crescents so familiar in the West End of London—all these are indicated in this great centre of commercial, industrial, and social life.

To those who had thought of Winnipeg as being remote, if not inaccessible, it is rather surprising to find that this metropolis of Western Canada is but twenty-seven hours from Chicago and but forty-five hours from Washington. At the time of the Chicago Exposition of 1893, one of the most popular routes between Boston and that city was through the Hoosac tunnel, on which the passenger boarded his train in Boston at seven P.M., and arrived in Chicago at seven the second morning after—a journey of thirty-six hours, which no one at that time regarded as being too long. Nor does it require the memory of that traditional being, the "oldest inhabitant," to recall that when the Pennsylvania Railroad succeeded in reducing the time between New York and Chicago to twenty-five hours, it was then held to be much more of a marvel than is now the eighteen-hours' journey of the Twentieth-Century Flyer. Winnipeg is forty-eight hours from Montreal, fifty-three from Quebec, and only forty-five from New York. No city on the western continent is more splendidly equipped than Winnipeg for business enterprises, great conventions, and large convocations of all orders. Besides the spacious and superb Fort Garry Hotel, she has more than fifty other guest-houses and one of the largest departmental stores on the continent; she has parks covering more than five hundred acres; she has more than twenty banks; and in a single year these banks did a business of almost one billion seven hundred million dollars. All the grain business of the Canadian West centres in Winnipeg. In the magnificent Union Station of white marble, costing some two millions of dollars, there are twenty-seven railway tracks, long distance and local, all of which radiate from the city. The Winnipeg River offers unmeasured facilities for power, a total of sixty thousand horse-power being already developed, which is sold to manufacturers and other consumers at the cost of production. There are over four hundred successful factory plants in operation, employing twenty thousand factory workers. Thus told in bald statistics alone, the story of Winnipeg is singularly impressive; but these facts and figures are but the mere skeleton of the story of Winnipeg. In this northern metropolis the polarity of life in general is changed.

Union Station and Fort Garry Hotel, Winnipeg

A signal aim in this city is the culture of beauty. In the laying out of streets and avenues the question of vista and the composition, so to speak, of the landscape has received unfailing consideration. All the country about is finely wooded, and with its rolling declivities offers cool and shaded nooks and spaces for summer outings. Here and there are lofty elms, and occasional wooded areas of many acres in extent. These are a surprise to the traveller whose conceptions of this region have been those of a bare and more or less desolate prairie land. The nature of the soil of the neighbourhood is a factor of determining importance. The clay belt begins at Cochrane, the junction of the Transcontinental line with the Ontario Government Railway, and it extends for three hundred miles to the west, affording a tract with plentiful water and with every productive condition. The provision of population for this clay belt is now a foremost question in Canada and engages the attention of both the Province of Ontario and of the Transcontinental Railway. The generation that cleared the bush lands has almost passed away, and the present settlers have different ideas of pioneer life. One age does not repeat itself. The continual invention of machinery that liberates human life has its dominating influence, and all signs of the times point to new methods of entering on new settlements. The British settlers who arrive are not accustomed to the clearing of timber-lands, yet this clay belt has probably resources to sustain a population of from one to two million people, and the climate is no more severe than that of Quebec or of northern Maine. The transformation of this region of wilderness into a well-populated country would provide a much-needed link between Eastern and Western Canada.

The distances, as we have seen, between Winnipeg and other of the great centres both in the Dominion and in the United States are by no means appalling; and with the splendid railway facilities now provided by the new Trans-continental route between Winnipeg, Toronto, and Montreal, by way of Cochrane, Cobalt, and North Bay, across New Ontario, and through the Highlands of the same Province, a route that only opened on July 13, 1915, this region is abounding in attractions for the new settler.

There are two sources of revenue which are of unmeasured value; one is that of pulpwood which can be advantageously disposed of, and the other that of employment in constructing government roads. Another inducement will be that of the "ready-made farm." This scheme has been utilised to some extent in Alberta and in New Brunswick as an inducement to colonists. Thousands of these farms, on which buildings have been erected and a small area placed under cultivation, with stock and farming implements furnished, have been placed at the disposal of settlers, each for a small cash payment, and with the conditions of subsequent payments made most liberal and lenient. In Ontario the scheme has not yet been worked out in detail; but the government of the Province is favourable toward adopting a similar system, building a house and barn and clearing ten acres on a farm of a hundred and sixty acres, as well as advancing a limited sum of money for the purchase of stock. The Ontario government also propose arrangements for assisting the farmer in marketing his pulpwood.

All these conditions of the surrounding country are of vital importance to the city of Winnipeg. The settlement of wild lands, the development of industrial resources, centres of population springing up in new sections—all these directly contribute to the growth and importance of the metropolitan centre. The civilisation of Canada has proceeded more rapidly in the transformation of the wilderness into populated lands than did that of the western part of the United States. Four years after the formation of the Dominion (July 1, 1867) Canada had extended across the entire continent. By the conditions of the time, both in applied inventions and in the degree of progress achieved by man, Canada has escaped the disadvantage that the long efforts of pioneer life entail upon a nation. The new towns and cities begin with well-paved streets, electric lighting, and electric transit.

Winnipeg, since 1899, has owned and operated its own water system, which is the hydro-electric power plant. The architecture is largely of a permanent nature, the designs following the latest developments of taste, skill, and efficient construction. Much of it compares favourably with the best architecture of New York or Washington. The blocks of handsome residences; the architectural taste of the public buildings; and the constant series of lawns, with their flowers and plants, leafy shrubs and luxuriant trees, make the city one of exceeding beauty and attractiveness. Churches, schools (and they are among the best in Canada), theatres, and lecture halls abound; the libraries are particularly enlightened and helpful and their growth and extension are only comparable with the library developments of St. Paul and Minneapolis, of Los Angeles and other young cities of the most advanced degrees of progress. "The world of books is still the world," wrote Mrs. Browning; and the community that renews its resources from the best that has been thought and said in the world, as it is conserved in literature, will be that which is the more efficient in all that makes for human advancement. Familiarity with the best literature has the most potent of influences for good taste, good manners, high ideals of conduct, mutual courtesy, and self-respect.

Canada cannot afford to ignore Matthew Arnold's wise warning not to mistake material achievement for civilisation. In its true and full significance, civilisation means "the humanisation of man in society; his making progress there towards his true and full humanity. We hear a nation called highly civilised," Mr. Arnold proceeds to say, "by reason of its industry, commerce, and wealth, or by reason of its liberty or equality, or by reason of its numerous churches, schools, libraries, and newspapers. But there is something in human nature, some instinct of growth, some law of perfection, which rebels against this narrow account of the matter. Do not tell me, says human nature, of the magnitude of your industry and commerce; of the beneficence of your institutions, your freedom, your equality; of the great and growing number of your churches and schools, libraries and newspapers; tell me also if your civilisation—which is the grand name you give to all this development—tell me if your civilisation is interesting."

Carlyle, as Matthew Arnold reminds us, once wrote to a younger brother who thought of emigrating to the United States: "Could you banish yourself from all that is interesting to your mind, forget the history, the glorious institutions, the noble principles of old Scotland—that you might eat a better dinner, perhaps?"

Mr. Arnold hastens to disclaim any sympathy with the idea that young men should not emigrate; it was the term "interesting" that caught his eye in Carlyle's counsel, and it is for that element that he makes his eloquent plea. It is that element, moreover, which the young and splendid city of Winnipeg may well reckon as one of its fundamental characteristics. In the *Journal Intime* of M. Amiel, the reader finds him saying that "the human heart is, as it were, haunted by confused reminiscences of an age of gold; or, rather, by aspirations toward a harmony of things which every-day reality denies to us." In all the appointments of wealth and luxury, M. Amiel made an effort to realise or to approach this ideal, and thus finds in this order of life one form of poetry. Society demands distinction and beauty as a component part of human nature's daily food.

Obviously, a new country cannot offer archives of long centuries of history, nor ruined castles, nor an assortment of myth and tradition. These may and do have their part in that atmosphere of interest which is the nurture of the intellectual powers; but the Future is no less stimulating than the Past; prophecy is not less alluring than history. The art of life itself is the finest of all the fine arts and to the seeing eye may invest a city with as much fascination as is to be derived from the galleries of the Louvre or of the Vatican. The spiritual life of all the ages is preserved in libraries, and the youngest of cities may well be heir to the records of this life. "No matter how poor I am," said William Ellery Channing; "no matter though the prosperous of my own time will not enter my obscure dwelling—if the sacred virtues will enter and take up their abode under my roof; if Milton will sing of Paradise; and Shakespeare open to me the worlds of imagination and the workings of the human heart; if Franklin will enrich me with his practical wisdom—I shall not pine for intellectual companionship, and I may become a cultivated man, though excluded from what is called the best society in the place where I live."

It is not only noble art and beautiful architecture combined with historic and social traditions that appeal to all that is best in life. What could more readily appeal to the imagination than that visible expression of faith in the future of the Great Dominion, the completion of a new great transcontinental line making possible direct transit across Canada from ocean to ocean? What could more appeal to the imagination than the marvellous invention of the wireless control of moving trains as has been already described in a previous chapter?

What can, indeed, be a feature of greater interest than the practical creation of a new world; the power of man conquering and transforming the domain of Nature? Do not Romance and Poetry spring up here anew? Science and the Muses have a subtle basis of understanding. James Russell Lowell has interpreted this mutual comprehension in the lines:

"He who first stretched his nerves of subtle wire
Over the land and through the sea-depths still,
Thought only of the flame-winged messenger
As a dull drudge that should encircle earth
With sordid messages of Trade, and tame
Blithe Ariel to a bagman. But the Muse
Not long will be defrauded. From her foe
Her misused wand she snatches; at a touch
The Age of Wonder is renewed again,
And to our disenchanted deity restores
The Shoes of Swiftness that gave odds to Thought;

The Cloak that makes invisible; and with these
I glide an airy fire from shore to shore."

Winnipeg has an interesting centre in the Industrial Bureau and permanent Exposition and Public Service Building, located in the leading business street and contributing in many ways to the swiftest means of unfolding industrial opportunities and to the most liberal development of the city. Both the Dominion and the Province of Manitoba, beside all the railways centering in Winnipeg and thirty western Boards of Trade, have installed attractive and extensive exhibits of the natural resources, so extensive, indeed, as to be practically complete in their revelation to the visitor of every variety and quality of the country. The manufacturing interests of the city are represented by eighty-five practical exhibits of articles "made in Winnipeg." There is also a museum with a large collection of mounted birds and wild animals of Canada; and there are historic relics and curios; as well as collections of economic minerals and other exhibits of various interest. Winnipeg has also, in this building, the first Civic Art Gallery in Canada, and it is wisely made free to all. In connection with the Gallery is an Art School where painting and drawing are taught. In this Public Service centre is a Convention Hall that will seat four thousand people and a smaller lecture or banquet hall seating about four hundred. There are also other accommodations for meetings, large or small gatherings, as may be, that are so numerous in business, social, industrial, or educational activities. Over seven hundred meetings were held in this building within the first ten months after it was opened. Adjoining Convention Hall is the Central Farmers' Market, where citizens conveniently find the produce of farm, market, or garden. The Industrial Bureau, which has its quarters in this building, is a thoroughly representative one, incorporated under Provincial Government Charter, with a directorate elected from appointed representatives of twenty-nine public bodies of the city, grouping together the best talent, administrative, professional, educational, and industrial, which could be brought together for the work of public service. The Bureau organisation is non-partisan, non-sectarian, and has no axe to grind other than that which concerns the benefit of the whole community. It is the Civic Bureau of Information for citizens, visitors, and outside inquirers.

The Fort Garry Hotel is a social centre of Winnipeg. Its imposing architectural effects render it a landmark in the panoramic view of the city. Its walls, of buff sandstone, rise to a height of fourteen stories, and the copper roof and lofty pinnacles are transformed to molten gold when the sun shines on them. The majestic structure is an adaptation from the period of François I., with something reminiscent of the old chateau in Touraine and Normandy. In the standards of elegance and beauty in all entertainments, these Grand Trunk hostelries—the Château Laurier, the Fort Garry, the Macdonald of Edmonton—all introduce standards of polite life that are of incalculable benefit to the community and which have hardly before been approached in the Dominion. In elegance and refinement, both of appointments and of service, these hotels rival, if indeed they do not almost excel, the choicest luxuriance and beauty of Paris and New York. One block to the east of the Fort Garry is the magnificent Union Station in which the Canadian Northern and Grand Trunk Pacific centre, and which has every convenience and device up to date; and between the station and the Fort Garry Hotel is a wide boulevard with a double row of trees in the centre, and a little park, under the very shadow of the house, has its picturesque approach through the ivy-clad ruins of the old gateway to the fort; an historic reminder of the time when, a century ago, this entrance was built by the Hudson's Bay Company in a turbulent period. The contrast between the sense of peaceful though intense activity, under the brilliant sunshine over the broad, beautiful streets, whose smooth pavement is a joy to motorists, with that time when savage assaults must be defended by the forces within Fort Garry, is a contrast to incite a train of speculative reflection. There were "sceptred spirits" in those days whose heroic deeds shine through all the years between their time and our own. The history of the Hudson's Bay Company is, in itself, one of the most thrilling chronicles of the Dominion.

From the windows and balconies of the Fort Garry Hotel the view is magnificent—St. Boniface, with its splendid cathedral group, Assiniboine Park, and the Legislative Buildings, with two rivers winding away into the vast spaces of the prairie—all make up a panorama never to be forgotten. The interior of this alluring house is singularly charming to the eye. The furnishings are rich and yet have that air of simplicity that appeals to the artistic sense—grey marble floors with soft rugs and the main dining-room all in cream and gold. The foyer and loggia connecting the banquet and ball rooms suggest the ancient cloister with their vaulted ceilings and the mediæval lanterns for electric lights. The café has marble wainscoting, suggestive of some old baronial castle, while in the grillroom there is oak panelling that would delight old England. There are three hundred rooms, two hundred and thirty-five of which have private baths while the others have easy access to bathrooms. What a contrast of living is thus revealed between the fastidious and luxurious life of the twentieth century and that of the primitive days of a hundred years ago when the old Fort Garry occupied the site of this hotel!

For fully fifty miles west of Winnipeg extends a belt of land some 300 miles in width, provided with good water found at reasonable depths, which is the marvel of the world for grain raising. This Red River Valley is the great wheat-producing region of the continent, and the journey of nearly eight hundred miles from Winnipeg to Edmonton reveals vast fields of golden grain, while along the route the colossal elevators loom up in the level expanse like some colossal fortifications.

Winnipeg has been from the first a predestined centre of commerce. It is the metropolis of the transcontinental lines and is the one supreme gateway through which all travellers and all traffic from ocean to ocean must pass. No other city on the western continent has such an absolute monopoly of all transit from the east to the west, or the reverse.

Edmonton, the capital of Alberta, most attractive in its beauty of locality, stands on the bold bluffs of the Saskatchewan. The railway bridge spanning this gulf is one of the finest on the continent, with its imposing piers of hewn stone, over a hundred feet in height, with trusses of steel. Two bridges at the level of the river provide for other traffic, with the novel arrangement that heavy vehicles are lifted and lowered from the surface of the bluff to the river by means of colossal elevators. The elevator is a municipal institution, and municipal ownership is the general rule in Edmonton, the city owning and operating the trolley lines, the electric light plant, the water-works, and the telephone system. Edmonton would be the earthly paradise of the disciples of Henry George, for it is a single-tax town. The University of Alberta with its splendid campus of three hundred and fifty acres, fronts the impressive capitol, of cream-hued sandstone, which stands on the Edmonton side of the river.

The capitol is four stories in height, with classic portico and a dome surmounted by a tall lantern, while the building is rendered still more beautiful by its artistic approach; wide terraced steps, with balustrades, ornamented with heavy bronze lamps, the effect of which, when lighted at night, is not without reminiscences of Paris. The Hotel Macdonald has a charming situation on the high bank of the river, within a few minutes' walk of the centre of the town. The traveller enters by the spacious court and covered loggia, passing thence into the great rotunda, with its floor of pink Levantine marble and its ceiling of solid oak. Adjoining this is a lounge, opening on a terrace 50 feet wide, overlooking the river, and the palm-room (octagonal in form, with its dome decorated in Wedgwood designs), as well as a beautiful dining-room, a café, and other public rooms. As one walks through all this magnificence in the place so recently occupied by Indians, hunters, and trappers of the frontier trading posts, he begins to realise something of that almost incredible rapidity of growth and development that characterises the great North-West.

The Canadian Women's Press Club in Edmonton is an organisation that delights the heart of the modern woman, to whom her clubs are the very breath of being; and its President, Mrs. Arthur Murphy, is well known to the world of letters under her *nom de plume*, "Janey Canuck." Mrs. Murphy is one of the most famous of Canadian writers, and has contributed much to the general knowledge of the Dominion. Her work has received very high praise. "She has opened a new path in Canadian literature," says an eminent critic, "and her *Open Trails* and *Seeds of Pine* will inspire many other writers."

Mrs. Murphy is the wife of the Rev. Arthur Murphy, D.D., who at one time was the chaplain to the Empress Frederick. Her work has attracted much attention in England, and *The Bookman* of London, in a critical review of her books extending into several pages, said:

"The work of 'Janey Canuck' has the optimism of the true lyric; the song of the open road. The refrain of the windswept spaces was never set to a better tune.... It is not style that matters in the work of 'Janey Canuck' any more than it matters in the work of Walt Whitman—a kindred philosopher. She comes scattering seeds of gladness in our mist, and lo! our gloom is gone like a black cloud that breaks before the April sun. She is the philosopher of gladness and content and common sense, a philosophy as durable as Bergsonism."

Mrs. Murphy has been honoured by King George by the decoration that entitles her to be known as a "Lady of Grace," an appropriate title, indeed, for so gracious a lady.

Edmonton is the gateway to the Yellowhead Pass; and the beauty of its location, the charming nature of its people, and the vastness of the territory of which it is naturally the centre, all conspire to incite dream and prophecy of the future of this young city of University ideals and marked intellectual and literary quality.

CHAPTER VIII

ON THE GRAND TRUNK PACIFIC

One of the most enchanting pleasure trips that can be enjoyed on the North American continent is that from Winnipeg to Prince Rupert through regions of scenic glory

"Where all wonder tales come true";

where one journeys to the accompaniment of a bewildering series of surprises that open vistas of new interests and enjoyments never dreamed of before. It is one of the signal charms of a journey through regions of majestic beauty and of scenic enchantment that it is not over even when it is past. Such a trip is a treasure laid up in life for future enjoyment without limit.

It is only some five hours from Edmonton before one begins to enter on this wonderland of romance. It is so new that the world of travel has not yet realised the marvel and glory of this trip. When it is stated that even the first surveying for this transcontinental line began only in 1910, it will be readily seen that in this region is opened up an absolutely new part of the world to general travel. The anomaly of traversing these primeval wilds in a train so luxuriously appointed as are the limiteds on the Grand Trunk Pacific appeals to the comprehension of man's conquest over nature. To travel in the comfort of these commodious coaches, equipped with a richly-furnished drawing-room, an admirable dining-car, an observation car with a spacious balcony platform at the rear and fitted with writing-desks, stationery in abundance, books, magazines, and newspapers, is to enjoy a journey on a flying hotel.

"Here is a train worth while!" wrote Sir Arthur Conan Doyle after the conclusion of the extensive trip that he and Lady Conan Doyle enjoyed over the Dominion: "it is the latest word in comfort, in luxury, in safety, in speed. The dining-car is never taken off. The observation car is a pleasant club. The road is as smooth as polished marble, with heavy rails well ballasted, no smoke or cinders.... It has the highest maintenance of track and rolling stock.... It runs on a marvellous line, destined to a mighty future."

MOUNT EDITH CAVELL AND CAVELL LAKE

Mount Edith Cavell and Cavell Lake

The entrance to the Wonderland begins, as was said, some five hours from Edmonton. The best plan is to leave this thriving young capital of Alberta by a late evening train, and waken in the morning to find one's self in a region where the peaks to the south of the Yellowhead Pass begin to appear on the horizon. He who understands the romance of railroad travel will raise the heavy blind of the windows of his lower berth or his drawing-room, so as not to miss the strange panorama of the night. Indeed, if we compare the romance of a night on shipboard with that of a night on a flying railroad train, the latter is incomparably the greater. The first requisite is an added relay of pillows—all that one wants, and all that one does not want, so to speak—pillows on which to prop one's self up to the proper angle of altitude that he may lie at ease and watch that marvellous moving panorama of forest and glade, of starlit sky, or of the hills flooded with moonlight; with flitting gleams of shining silver as the train glides past lakes, or along the course of a winding river. It is the realm of fäery, where nothing is but what is not. Is there a moon? There are a dozen moons! There is one in the south, but a moment later it appears in the far east—no well-regulated moon would career about in the heavens in so erratic a manner, therefore there must be another; and when, at the next glimpse, it again appears at some different point of the compass, one's conviction that the earth must have as many moons as Jupiter is reinforced. The vast forest solitudes are all strange; to waken suddenly and find one's self flying through these unreal regions is an experience never to be forgotten. It is an experience entirely lost save to one who unveils his windows to the mystic scenes rather than sleep in the darkness of drawn blinds. The elusive fascination possible to the nights on a railway train is a chapter of life in itself. It recalls to one the dictum of Socrates that all exact inquiry into such matters as the movements and nature of the sun and the moon should be excluded from too close investigation!

From Winnipeg the traveller speeds over fields of emerald or fields of gold, according to the season; the harvest time is a world of gold and resplendence; and ere the grain ripens it forms an infinite expanse of tender green. The economist would see in these far-reaching fields of growing grain a theme for his statistics and practical deductions as to their contribution to the world's wealth; but the eye of the pleasure-traveller regards them solely in the light of æsthetic effect. Wheat or oats, grass or anything else, it is all one to him as long as the colour scheme enchants his eye. As he approaches the mountain region the scene is etherealised. Away on the horizon are illuminated points, but whether on earth, or in the heavens, who can tell? One begins to enter into the atmosphere that pervades mountain solitudes. It eludes all analysis, but it is the most potent of impressions. The gateway to the mountains prefigures itself as the portal to some trackless spaces not of earth. The peaks shine with a celestial light. Snow-capped, catching the morning sunshine in dazzling splendour, they rise as a very wall beyond which mortal may not pass. Is the wall as impenetrable as it seems? How can a railway train dash itself through the palisades of bewildering mountain peaks, clustered in their shining splendour? And what world lies beyond?

The grandeur grows more impressive. And as among the problems of life, so among mountains, there is usually a way out. In this case it is the Yellowhead Pass. In the preliminary survey and construction of the railroad this Pass was chosen by the skilled engineers who at once recognised its striking characteristics, for it permitted the railway to take its line across the Rocky Mountains at the lowest altitude of any transcontinental line on the continent. The swiftly flowing waters of the Athabasca River mirror the towering peaks above. The Pass grows wider; again, there is a narrower curve as it deftly penetrates its way between the vast heights. The tourist has of course betaken himself to the outside platform of the observation car. Here is a spacious balcony, with projecting roof to shield from sun or wind; a space ample for some sixteen seats, which offers a moving picture that reveals the handiwork of Nature as distinct from that of Art. Here the traveller sits, with all the majesty of the mountain contours about and above him.

This Yellowhead Pass had been, for some generations, the great natural highway of the fur trade. The Hudson Bay post was established here as early as in 1800, and the name of a yellow-haired trader, known to the Indians as "Tête Jaunne" (otherwise Jasper Hawes), led to the present name of this historic spot. One cannot but dwell a little on the Yellowhead Pass itself, as one of the special features of the trip; not merely a passage-way to traverse, but as a region rich in novel points of beauty, never twice the same, but varying with every atmospheric change and from every new angle of vision. Traverse the Yellowhead Pass by day in the brilliant sunlight; or on one of the marvellous moonlit nights, when every peak rises in silver sheens; when the stars look down as if they were great globes of light near at hand, and the walls of sheer rock are so softened under the mystic light as to be no more mere rocky precipices, but the field of the weird dances of the Brocken. Gnomes and sprites emerge from some unseen caverns; the cliffs tower into the sky and bring the stars down to earth, so as to make them seem as accessible as electric lights. There are projecting balconies far above where perhaps the Spirits of the Solitudes congregate.

The eastern approach to the Yellowhead Pass is guarded by the Boule Roche and the Roche à Perdrix Mountains, these marking, also, the entrance to Jasper Park. The fabled Valley of the Cashmere is hardly less familiar to the great tide of summer travel than is this Yellowhead region. In a preceding chapter (on the summer resorts of Canada) the pleasure resources of Jasper Park were somewhat suggested, and Mount Robson Park will doubtless also become one of the great favourites of the world. The great natural reserve of Jasper Park comprising 4400 square miles is one that for all time will be preserved in its absolute integrity. No spoliation will be permitted. It is not only a national but a continental pleasure-ground for all time. Mountain-climbers will find here the fullest scope for their prowess. More and more will the Mountaineering enthusiasts of Britain be allured to Canada instead of to Switzerland—a part of the great Empire, calling with a thousand voices to every trueborn Briton. To many visitors the best use they have for a mountain peak is to look at it rather than to ascend it. Why tramp about when the eye registers all its supreme splendour and the tourist may luxuriate in the shaded portico outside his camp and revel in the changeful panorama of colour and beauty? Or he may stroll in fertile valleys, brilliant with flowers; he may ride, or drive, along good trails with new enchantments meeting him at every turn.

Two beautiful lakes, Pyramid and Patricia, are in the very shadow of Pyramid Mountain, only four miles from Jasper station. At this station are the Park superintendent and his staff, who are ever ready with help and information and who effectually banish from the mind of the tourist any fear of strangeness or solitude. While hunting is not permitted in Jasper Park, the angler may, if he likes, fish all day in the clear lakes. They are well stocked with trout. The complete ban upon hunting or any use of firearms is a great safeguard to the wanderer through woods and valleys, making accidents of this nature impossible. Maligne Cañon and Maligne Lake have been already discussed in the chapter already alluded to on summer resorts, but no description could convey any idea of the spectacular beauty of the excursion leading past Lakes Edith and Beauvert, through dense forests of spruce and cottonwood, with the walls of the cañon rising 300 feet in height on either side. Here is a trip of thirty-five miles from the cañon to Maligne Lake, that sheet of pure, emerald water—an excursion amid such magnificence of beauty as to defy adequate description.

Jasper Park is now enriched by the presence of an imperishable monument that will endure throughout the ages; one to which thousands of travellers, in the years to come, will make their pilgrimage as to a shrine. It is a memorial that not only lends its glory to the Dominion, but to the entire continent as well; for not unaccompanied by faithful hearts from her great sister nation across the border shall Canadians seek this mystic altar to which every wind wafts aromatic fire. For it is a shrine consecrate to all that is noblest in womanhood, all that is most heroic and divine in our common humanity. The Dominion, the States, are at one in their reverent appreciation of the greatness of simple fidelity to duty. He who keeps faith with his ideals is the true hero. It is he who enters into the fellowship of the mystery. He may go down to death in apparent darkness and defeat; he rises in eternal glory. For to be spiritually-minded is life and peace, even the life eternal.

It is fitting that Edith Cavell, who gave her life for her country; who died the death of the martyr rather than betray her trust, should be commemorated with a memorial whose monumental grandeur exceeds that of any Egyptian king or Assyrian monarch of remote antiquity.

A marvel of glory is this mountain peak now christened Mount Edith Cavell. It rises in solitary majesty out of this morning-world, lifting its head into the faint, transparent azure of ethereal spaces, while its base is rooted amid the rocky fastnesses of the great range. The naming of Mount Edith Cavell is the tribute of the Dominion to one great-souled woman, and thus to all that makes for the greatness of womanhood. On its precipitous slopes may be read by all who have the inner vision the scroll of human fate.

The peak is calculated to enchain the eye by its towering height and faultless symmetry. Did Nature herself design and fashion it for its strange destiny? Was it indeed reserved for its present consecration? Who may know? Life is a chain of sequences divinely ordered. It lieth not with man to direct his steps.

"The shuttle of the Unseen powers
Works out a pattern not as ours."

In the matter of naming new places in Canada the Geographic Board is the governing body. It was at their meeting in Ottawa in March 1916 that the decision was made that this peak should immortalise the name of Edith Cavell. The suggestion had previously been made that the name of Mount

Robson should be changed to that of Mount Cavell, but this would have been so inevitably confusing all over the world that it was thought wiser to select a peak hitherto unnamed. To Dr. E. Deville, the Surveyor-General, the Geographic Board therefore made this announcement much to the gratification of that well-known official. Thus is a woman's life of simple faithfulness to duty lifted into immortal resplendence. What a monitor suggesting unfaltering devotion to great issues will Mount Edith Cavell remain to the throngs of passengers on this Grand Trunk Pacific line, who will watch for its appearance on the horizon, and gaze, with steadfast view, until it fades in the far distance. For several miles can it be seen, and what traveller will gaze on this height without feeling it to be one of the spellbinders of the Dominion? or without finding himself involuntarily recalling those wonderful lines of Emerson?

"Inspirer, prophet evermore!
    Pillar which God aloft hath set
    So that men might it not forget;
It shall be life's ornament
And mix itself with each event.
      By million changes skilled to tell
      What in the Eternal standeth well!"

Brulè Lake, in Jasper Park, is an expansion of the Athabasca River, and the railroad line follows the east bank of the lake. Canada would be the paradise of Undine, the water sprite of La Motte Fouqué's famous story, for rivers broaden into lakes, and lakes connect themselves by a chain of rivers, until the continuous possibilities for inland navigation appeal to the geologist as a problem of the ages to be solved. Many theories are evolved; even as they are in Arizona, as to the origin of that apparently impenetrable mystery, the petrified forest.

At the station of Miette Hot Springs another excursion may beckon to some travellers in that up the valley of Fiddle Creek, which flows into the Athabasca River. There are a number of basins encrusted with yellow from the sulphur that abounds in the water, which has strong medicinal properties, and which ranges from a hundred and eleven to a hundred and twenty-seven degrees in temperature.

Then, too, there are the Punch Bowl Falls, reached by an attractive trail from the station known as Pocahontas. Jasper Park extends to the boundary line which marks the division between Alberta and British Columbia; and crossing this boundary the traveller finds himself in another of Canada's gigantic reserves, that of Mount Robson Park, with Mount Robson itself as the centre dominating the entire region. The train stops at Mount Robson station, and one seems to enter a new world in this near approach to that king and monarch of the Canadian Rockies, the peak of Mount Robson towering upwards for 13,068 feet in the clear air. Of his first view of this peak Lawrence J. Burpee, F.R.G.S., writes:

"... Almost without warning it came. We rounded the western end of the Rainbow Mountains and looked up the valley of the Grand Fork. 'My God!' some one whispered. Rising at the head of the valley and towering far above all the surrounding peaks we saw a vast cone, so perfectly proportioned that one's first impression was rather one of wonderful symmetry and beauty than of actual height. Then we began to realise the stupendous majesty of the mountain...."

It is not only that Mount Robson is supreme in the range of the Rockies in Canada, but it is one of the notable mountains of the world. In its peculiar beauty of form and proportion it is hardly surpassed by any known peak. It has many aspects and phases—it is clearly seen in brilliant sunshine, it is dimly discerned when it enwraps itself in clouds and ethereal mists, it is seen again by resplendent moonlight—and one finds each phase has its own enchantment. Its glistening crest is visible for twelve miles after the train pulls out from the station. Its colossal glacier tumbles masses of ice-fields down into Berg Lake at the foot, and these masses of ice continue to drift on the surface of emerald water that holds its colour in the same strange way as do the waters of the Gulf of Corinth.

The Alpine Club of Canada has made excursions to these places, and of one quest on Berg Lake a member writes:

"... I shall not soon forget that first day when we came up the trail and, looking through as far as the eye could reach, saw countless blossoms— brilliant crimson Indian paintbrush, pale pink columbines, and mauve asters, their stems imbedded in the softest and greenest of foliage and moss; nor another day, when on the side of Rearguard, we came upon a garden of blue forget-me-nots.... Whilst we lingered amongst the flowers that first day, an avalanche crashed into the lake and the big waves came rolling across until they reached the shore above which we were standing, while broken ice floated out as miniature icebergs upon the milky blue surface of the lake. And Lake Adolphus, across the Pass—I could not find a word to describe its indescribable blue. Seen from camp or through the trees from the side of

Mount Mumm, it was absolutely lovely. Then there was the Robson Glacier, in plain view of camp and only a few minutes' walk distant, a never-ending source of interest, with its ice cave and its seracs and crevasses."

As the train sweeps on the tourist sees, from his comfortable seat on the platform of the observation car, a myriad rocky pinnacles silhouetted against the heavens. The peerless grandeur of these peaks, snow-crowned and glistening with glaciers; of emerald lakes at the foot mirroring overhanging crags; of unmeasured wastes of windswept snow-fields; of ethereal solitudes and depths unfathomed, in the wild gorges, where, for all the eternities, only the stars have looked down; and the isolated grandeur of Mount Robson itself lifting its glittering summit into the skies—all this amazing wonder enters with new force and richness into life itself. Half a century ago Milton and Cheadle christened it "a Giant among Giants, Immeasurably Supreme." The first ascent of Mount Robson was made only as recently as in 1909 by the Rev. George Kinney and Mr. Donald Phillips, their final success being the outcome of a trial of twenty days, during which they were continually baffled and driven back by adverse and seemingly impossible conditions. But the difference between success and failure may be accurately defined as persistence of energy. He who gives up, fails; he who does not give up, succeeds. It is only a question of time and of tenacity of purpose. Two unsuccessful attempts to ascend to the summit of Mount Robson had been made in 1907-8. There is a trail leading to the north side of Mount Robson, along the Grand Fork River, skirting the shore of Lake Helena and up through the Valley of a Thousand Falls, with the celebrated Emperor Falls within view, and thus on to Berg Lake and to Robson Pass. The trip to Berg Lake can be made within one day, and it is an excursion into regions of such marvellous beauty that can never be translated into words. In all this bewildering sublimity the spellbound gazer can only question, with Robert Service:

"Have you seen God in His splendours? heard the text that
   Nature renders?"

Such fantasies of combination, too, as meet the eye: castles, towers, fortresses, that glow like opal and ruby and topaz; walls of sheer glaciers rising in dazzling whiteness like a spectral caravan; formless solitudes fit only for the abode of the gods! The spirit of the mountains is abroad on her revels; ice peaks 10,000 feet in the upper air are her toys; the winds are her Æolian harp; the Valley of a Thousand Falls is her theatre for pastime. Neither the Swiss Alps, nor yet that mysterious chain of the Tyrol, haunted by drifting cloudshapes and vocal with rushing waterfalls, can compare with the colossal scale of this splendour of all the Mount Robson region. It is the encountering of an entirely new range of experiences. It is Service again who interprets one's emotional enthusiasms in the stanzas:

"Have you gazed on naked grandeur where there's nothing else
   to gaze on?
       Set pieces and drop-curtain scenes galore,
Big mountains heaved to heaven, which the blinding sunsets
   blazon,
       Black canyons where the rapids rip and roar?
Have you swept the visioned valley with the green stream
   streaking through it,
       Searched the Vastness for a something you have lost?
Have you strung your soul to silence? Then for God's sake go
   and do it;
       Hear the challenge, learn the lesson, pay the cost.

"Have you known the Great White Silence, not a snow-gemmed
   twig a-quiver?
       (Eternal truths that shame our soothing lies),
Have you broken trail on snow-shoes? mushed your huskies up
   the river,
       Dared the unknown, led the way, and clutched the prize?"

Strangest of all, in these stern mountain solitudes, with their glittering crevasses of ice, there are sheltered valleys all aglow with myriads of flowers in brilliant and gorgeous hues; and here, at sunset, peaks touched to gold and crimson are seen looming up in the transparent air against a background of intensely blue sky, a spectacle to inspire both painter and poet with its unearthly beauty.

To traverse such a region as this amid the luxury of the appointments of the Grand Trunk Pacific's transcontinental trains seems at first an anomaly; nothing is primitive save the forests primeval; nothing wild but the scenery. It is all a new universe, somewhere between the once familiar earth and the dream of Paradise—something by which to set the compass of life to a new polarity.

An intrepid mountain climber, Miss Mary L. Jobe, F.R.G.S., made a wonderful quest into these Canadian Rockies recently, and explored a region 100 miles north-west of Mount Robson. Of one scene there Miss Jobe writes:

"A massive white peak shot into the blue from a walled fortress of rock. Two colossal rocky towers stood guard over a file of lesser peaks; multi-coloured masses of granite, glacier-hung, glowed with irridescent tints, while down a valley rushed a foaming river to meet the cascades of colour pouring from the mountain...."

Between Mount Robson and Prince George (from which young city a railway will soon be completed linking it with Vancouver) the route on to Prince Rupert follows the Fraser River, the waters of which are a chrysolite green, the furious current flecked with foam, while the Fraser, at one point, transforms itself into a lake, seven miles wide, with that easy power of compassing transformation scenes, lightning changes, so to speak, of which the rivers of the Dominion appear to hold the secret. When a Canadian river grows tired of running, it immediately turns itself into a lake. When a Canadian lake becomes tired of staying in the same place, it at once proceeds to become a river. Just what species of genii control the wilds of Canada has not yet engaged the attention of her statisticians. The great Fraser River has its headquarters in the Yellowhead, and flowing through a broad valley, watering large fertile tracts of land, it makes its progress to the Pacific 800 miles away. The view of this wonderful river from the railroad, as the line passes high above the swirling waters, is a magnificent one. The Fraser has a beautiful bend at Prince George, turning sharply to the south, while the railway proceeds through another smiling valley, the Nechako—a valley which is rich in plateau lands favourable for agricultural uses, and along whose course are numberless sylvan scenes that lend to it great beauty. Vanderhoof, the gateway to all the region of lakes of British Columbia, is the capital of the Nechako Valley. The railway again enters into the mountains, the Coast Range, in the Bulkley Valley, and for a distance of 200 miles, between Smithers and Prince Rupert, the view is diversified by mountain peaks. The Nechako and Bulkley Rivers water fertile valleys of more than 6,000,000 of acres, easily cultivated and offering a scenic setting unparalleled in the world. Hazleton is a prosperous and growing centre with an assured future. From this city the railway route follows the Skeena River, which also has a trick of widening at intervals. The splendid train glides on and on, and is it on the air that one seems to hear echoed:

"There's a whisper on the night-wind, there's a star a-gleam to
  guide us,
And the wild is calling, calling ... let us go!"?

The onward route is enthralling. There comes in sight La Riviere au Shuswap, a tributary of the Fraser, with a vanishing view of three peaks close together, far up the valley, as the train rushes past. For it is not every mountain that can have a station to itself, as has Mount Robson, thus giving the passenger time to see its wonders with no little satisfaction. Before the junction of the Bulkley and the Telkwa Rivers is reached, the railway passes Lakes Decker and Burns; and at the junction of the rivers mineral deposits of copper, silver, lead, and coal have been discovered that promise rich leading. Hudson Bay Mountain is a prominent peak, 9000 feet in height, and in this mountain also silver and silver lead, copper, and anthracite coal are found; and the Hudson Bay Glacier lies only four miles from the railway track, easily reached on horseback. The train runs close to the shore of Lake Kathlyn, a lake filled with a black-spotted trout, and Hudson Bay Mountain is repeated in the lake as in a mirror.

Charles Melville Hays

Bulkley Gate is something to see, if one may judge by the contagious enthusiasm of the young train agent who proceeds to announce it, with the pride of a showman displaying his wares. By just what necromancy a railroad system magnetises every employé, from the most important officials to the youthful recruit, with its own courtesy and unanalysable charm in all the relations of service, may not be revealed; but the result is very much in evidence.

In all the hotels of this line, as well as upon railroad lines, the duty, grace, and charm of courtesy of manner are constantly inculcated. To make the service the best on the continent seems to be the ideal of the staff through every grade and department. Bulkley Gate proves itself quite worthy of its young champion—a wonderful gate indeed, formed by a dyke that formerly crossed the valley, and at last gave way before the power of the river. The Skeena and the Bulkley Rivers unite near Hazleton, and in close vicinity is the Rocher Deboule Mountain, which is known as the Mountain of Minerals. It is extremely rich in copper ore, large quantities of which have already been taken from it. All along the picturesque and turbulent Skeena River are quaint Indian villages, with the totem poles of their tribes. Here also mountain peaks are much in evidence, and in the spring of 1916 one of these, 9000 feet in height, was chosen to bear the name of Mount Sir Robert, in honour of the Premier of the Dominion, Sir Robert Borden. A large glacier, which seems to be at least a mile in width, has been named Borden Glacier, and both the peak and the glacier can be seen from Doreen station.

Thus is the entire route one of exceptional beauty and never-failing interest. From the first to the last there is not a dull moment. And in crossing the wonderful bridge that connects Kaien Island (on which Prince Rupert stands) with the mainland, the traveller finds something to enlist his enthusiasm for science as well as that enlisted for nature. This bridge is nearly a thousand feet in length, and includes six spans, two of which are of two hundred and fifty feet each. The engineers encountered great difficulty, because of the furious racing of the water through the channel, so that at times the divers could not descend. The conditions not unfrequently reduced the working hours to little more than three out of the twenty-four.

The construction of the Grand Trunk Pacific that extended the western lines of the Grand Trunk System from Winnipeg to Prince Rupert was an epic story of the Dominion. For it was really one of the determining events of British Empire history, as well as an exceptionally potent factor in the contemporary development of Canada. It has not only changed the map of the country, but also takes its place in international advancement. To open a new and vast territory whose splendour of scenery, incalculably marvellous resources, and climatic conditions are such as to invite and sustain immigration is an achievement that brings to bear a signal influence upon the peoples of the entire European continent and even upon the Orient. It was at once the opening of a new realm for human life. Education and culture are invited to enter. It is hardly possible for the mind to grasp, or for the imagination to picture, all the possibilities of the future that are initiated by so great an enterprise. The Indian trail, the packhorse, the canoe, gave way to the steel tracks, the luxurious trains of vestibuled cars laden with civilisation advancing into the wilderness. A great Canadian railway is not built to meet the recognised demands of settlement. It has to act as pioneer and create the conditions that make settlement possible. Its construction is, literally, the manifestation of belief in the things not seen. It is a creative power prospecting for paths of national destiny.

The story of that reconnaissance through hundreds of miles of an apparently impenetrable wilderness is one to haunt the imagination. It is a story of hardships and of heroisms. Emerson declares that

"The hero is not fed on sweets."

The pathfinder shares the usual experience that invests heroism.

It is to Charles Melville Hays that the conception of thus extending the Grand Trunk System is primarily due. Mr. Hays was endowed with the "seeing eye." He was gifted with that penetrating order of comprehension that swiftly discriminates between the possible and the impossible, and sets the key of achievement accordingly. He was not infelicitously called "the Cecil Rhodes of Canada." With that same brilliant capacity to conceive new combinations that build up new orders of life, Mr. Hays had that tenacity of purpose which alone renders such conceptions available, and he had an even larger power than that of the Empire builder in Africa for relating his dream to definite conditions.

It is recorded that there came a morning in Canada when the Dominion awakened "to experience a thrill of excitement from the Atlantic to the Pacific." For the newspapers had announced that a new Transcontinental railway was to be undertaken, and that the Grand Trunk System was the initiator of this stupendous scheme. It seems that Mr. Hays himself had conveyed to the press merely this laconic statement overnight, and it was the spark that incited a very conflagration of discussion. There was an instantaneous public clamour whose geographical limits were only defined from Halifax and Vancouver, from Dawson to Hudson Bay. But when the morning dawned, and the startlingly interesting news incited the pursuit of the President of the Grand Trunk System for fuller information, that distinguished official had already boarded his steamer and was fairly off on the high seas for Europe. The man at the head of a railway system that, by the addition of its new western lines, attains to no less than 8115 miles in extent, with its inestimable potentialities of service, may well be accorded rank among the notable figures whose genius and courage have helped to shape the destiny of the Dominion.

In the work of constructing this great trans-continental road, Mr. Hays called as his lieutenant, in 1909, Mr. Edson Joseph Chamberlain. Mr. Chamberlain was Vice-President and General Manager of the Grand Trunk Pacific for three busy years, and after the tragedy of the *Titanic* in 1912, he was called to succeed Mr. Hays as President of the Grand Trunk System.

The chief engineer in charge of the construction of the Grand Trunk Pacific was Mr. J. B. Kelliher. With him went a party of gentlemen to make the preliminary exploration after the surveyors had made their pioneer report on the possibilities of the route. While they had secured a general impression of the topography, the problems that remained were intricate and manifold.

HUDSON BAY MOUNTAIN AND LAKE KATHLYN, BULKLEY VALLEY

Hudson Bay Mountain and Lake Kathlyn, Bulkley Valley

"In order to obtain a faint idea of the prospect that confronted those entrusted with the reconnaissance," writes Frederick A. Talbot,[1] "conceive a vast country rolling away in humps, towering ridges, and wide-yawning valleys as far as the eye can see, and with the knowledge that the horizon can be moved onward for hundreds of miles without bringing any welcome break in the outlook. On every hand is the interminable forest, a verdant sea, except where here and there jagged splashes of black betoken that the fire fiend has been at work. The trees swinging wave-like before the breeze conceal dangers untold beneath their heavy, blanket-like branches.... Here is a swamp whose treacherous mass stretches for mile after mile.... There is a litter of jagged rock ... here a maze of fallen tree trunks, levelled by wind, water, and fire, piled up beneath the trees to a height of ten, fifteen, and twenty feet in an inextricable mass, over which one has to make one's way...." Mr. Talbot graphically describes that silence of the trackless solitudes: "Not a sound beyond the sighing of the wind through the trees, the rifle-like crack of a dead, gaunt monarch as it crashes to the ground, or the howl of a wolf." At night the party slept in sleeping-bags; they had scant provisions, too, because to carry an adequate supply would have been an impediment to progress; and after the quicksands, the impenetrable forests, they would suddenly encounter some mad river or vast lake; and at one cache where they arrived, famished and weary, they found that wild animals had broken in and destroyed the store of dried fruits, fish, and canned food they had expected to find. What a story is this record of pioneer work for the selection of the route and the discovery of the most favourable Pass for the construction of the Grand Trunk Pacific! There were many possible Passes investigated before the decision was gradually arrived at, by the process of elimination, to choose that of the Yellowhead. The number was first reduced to four; the Wapiti, Pine River, Yellowhead, and Peace River, and then Mr. Hays decided on that of the Yellowhead.

[1] *The Making of a Great Canadian Railway.* London: Seeley, Service and Company, Limited.

"Our engineers have secured so easy a grade through the Yellowhead Pass," said the Chairman of the Board of Directors, "that when the traveller takes the trip he will be no more conscious of crossing a big mountain range, except for the magnificent scenery, than he would be when he travels by the London and North-Western or by the Great Eastern Railway."

One interesting fact in connection with the enormous enterprise of constructing this road was the installation of temporary telephone facilities, linking together the long line of construction camps that trailed from Winnipeg to the coast.

Something of all this wonderful story comes fragmentarily to the passenger whose interest is aroused by the splendid construction of the road, on which no effort was spared to secure permanence and safety. One feature that is always a noticeable one to the traveller is that of the "milestones," so to speak; the tall signs clearly inscribed with the figures registering the miles as they are so rapidly passed over.

Not only flowers and glaciers, sunsets and tumbling cataracts, rocky pinnacles and frowning ramparts, enchant a journey unrivalled on the continent, but in the palace-train, whose cars are a series of drawing-rooms in their luxurious appeal, there are varied opportunities for studies of humanity, human interest, and sympathies as well. For example, in one corner is an aged French Abbé, absorbed in his breviary and in a richly bound volume which reveals itself as the meditations of Fénelon. The air of detachment and scholarly isolation that he contrives to throw around himself forbids even much speculation as to whence he came or whither he is going—as if even one's mental questioning might be an intrusion.

At one little station, as the train stops, its resplendent comfort contrasting strangely with the primitive life of the newly-fledged village, there enter a man and woman who have been attended to the very steps of the vestibule by a throng that apparently represents the entire population of the town. They are all singing, and the man and woman linger in the vestibule joining in the song. The man is in the uniform of an officer of the Salvation Army; the woman, sweet-faced and smiling, is also costumed in this order, with the usual Salvation Army bonnet projecting over her serene and pleasant face. The refrain of the song floats out on the air:

"Yes, we'll gather at the river,
That flows by the throne of God."

There is something in the time, the place, the isolation in the new and just-opened country through which the train is passing, the on-coming darkness, and the penetrating cadence of the trite and familiar melody that touches every heart. Every one joins in the melody; and as the train begins to move, the outer throng withdrawing into safer distance, the man and the woman still leaning from the door of the vestibule, there is a waving of hands, and a chorus of farewells from the vanishing group left behind, and the train flies on to the benediction of song that still pursues it on the air:

"God be with you till we meet again!"

The man and the woman catch up the line; they are singing with melodious voices, the magnetism enchains the passengers, and the cadence echoes again through the railway car:

"God be with you till we meet again!"

It was one of the little episodes that transcend conventionalities and make strangers into friends. The darkness is coming on; various nationalities, various individualities—the elaborately outfitted English tourist, the Reverend Abbé, the pioneer settlers, the stately official on some mission of Government, the college Professor with one eye on the landscape in scientific scrutiny—yet all meeting for the moment in a sense of their common heritage as children of the Divine Father.

Later it was learned that the Salvation Army officer and his sweet Scotch wife were none other than Commissioner and Mrs. Charles Sowton, who were on their way to open meetings in the little Indian village of Metlakatla, near Prince Rupert, going on later to Vancouver and Victoria. The Salvation Army is one of the features of the great North-West. A new territory had been created, and Commissioner Sowton was appointed to superintend all the activities of the army in the country west of Port Arthur. For more than thirty years the Commissioner had been engaged in Salvation Army work, during which period he and Mrs. Sowton had been stationed in the British Isles, Norway, India, and the United States in turn. On their arrival in Victoria on this trip, Commissioner and Mrs. Sowton were given an official reception, the Mayor and the City Council joining with the people of the City to welcome these faithful helpers of humanity. In Vancouver, also, a large meeting was held in the Pantages Theatre in their honour, Mayor Taylor presiding and many representative citizens being present.

Nor did the passengers on that particular train fail to make friends with the wounded Canadian soldier, a brave youth who had lost one arm in service at the front, and thus crippled for life was returning to his home at Prince Rupert. To one passenger who was deeply touched by his courage, his youth, and his patriotism, he was moved to show a little talisman that he carried in his pocket, an envelope containing the prayer written by Lord Roberts for the soldiers at the time of the South African war:

"... If it be Thy will, enable us to win victory for England, but, above all, grant us a better victory over temptation and sin, over life and death, that we may be more than conquerors through Him who loved us, and laid down His life for us, Jesus, our Saviour, the Captain of the army of God."

To his new friend the lad handed his signed card of "Self-control; The Sake of Others, and for Love of Christ and Country," the promise to abstain from all intoxicating liquors, and to do all in his power to promote good habits among his comrades. And there was his little card of personal prayer:

"Almighty God, Grant me Thy power, and keep my heart in Thy peace, help me to avoid evil, and be with me in life and death, for Jesus' sake."

And the two, strangers but an hour before, were drawn near as sharers of a common hope, a common faith in the Divine care and leading.

On the arrival at Prince Rupert the populace came out to meet the young soldier. In him they honoured all Canadian soldiers who were offering their lives that their Empire might live and that the freedom of humanity from Prussian tyranny might be preserved. There was more than one band of music at the station, and musicians, soldiers, and people joined in the war song:

"When my King and Country call me and I'm wanted at the front,
    Where the shrapnel shells are bursting in the air;
When the foe in fury charges and we're sent to bear the brunt.
    And the roll is called for service,—I'll be there!

"When the Kaiser's lines are broken and his armies out of France,
    When the Belgian desolation we repair;
When the final muster's ordered and the bugle sounds 'Advance'
    May the God of Battles help me to be there!

"When for me 'Last Post' is sounded and I cross the silent ford,
    I've a Pilot who of 'mine fields' will beware;
When 'Reveille' sounds in Heaven and the Armies of the Lord
    Sing the Hallelujah chorus,—I'll be there!"

No literature relating to the terrible struggle could have brought home such an intense realisation of the significance of the war, and the indomitable courage and splendid loyalty of the Dominion, to the passengers on that Grand Trunk Pacific train as did these personal contacts and experiences. Canada is not a military nation. She desires to follow the paths of peaceful progress and noble development. She has no enmities toward any race, but she sees clearly the utter demoralisation of the entire world if militarism and armaments are not exterminated. "The people of the British dominions are animated by a stern resolve that there shall be no such outcome," said Premier Borden in an address before the New England Society, "and they believe it possible to create a well-ordered world whose harmony shall be based on a mutual respect for common rights."

INDIAN TOTEM POLE, ALASKA

Indian Totem Pole, Alaska

The wonderful journey, whose majestic splendour so impressed itself upon individual life that, in a sense, it could never be over, had its termination at Prince Rupert. There, again, one may watch the rose and flame of dawn and the glory of colour from terraced heights over-looking sea and land; and in all the play of colour reflected from a thousand waters he may almost find prefigured the twelve gates of the Heavenly City that were all of pearl; and the foundations of the wall which were garnished with precious stones—jasper and sapphire, emerald and chrysolite, and last—an amethyst!

CHAPTER IX

PRINCE RUPERT AND ALASKA

Mrs. Carlyle declared that when Robert Browning's poem of *Sordello* appeared she read it through twice with the deepest attention, but that at the conclusion of the second reading she was utterly unable to determine as to whether "Sordello" was a tree, an island, or a man. Somewhat of the same bewilderment has beset many people of late years in regard to any mention of Prince Rupert, the young seaport of the great North-West. One citizen of the United States to whom a rather unusual degree of cosmopolitan travel had been allotted by the Fates that appointed his not undistinguished destiny, and who enjoyed the well-earned admiration of a host of friends as being pre-eminently entitled to speak with authority on many abstract matters for which those less erudite cared little and, alas! knew less, assured his votaries, on inquiry, that Prince Rupert was a town somewhere in the "Dolomites" and that its title should be spelled with a final "z"; while another cheerfully relegated Prince Rupert to the maritime provinces of Canada. Still another, who was nothing if not historical, connected the name only with that of the son of Frederick, Count Palatine of the Rhine, who was created Duke of Cumberland in 1644 and who so distinguished himself in scientific pursuits that he was rewarded with a tomb in Westminster Abbey (somewhere about 1682). His portrait, painted by Sir Peter Lely, is in the National Portrait Gallery at London. Not to prolong mere pleasantries, however, the Prince Rupert whose citizens forecast for it the future of the "Liverpool of America" is really the terminal of that vast and splendid new transcontinental highway, the Grand Trunk System.

Prince Rupert was really created in Boston (U.S.A.), for before the dense forest covering the rocky island with an almost impenetrable growth was felled, the town was laid out by Messrs. Brett and Hall, one of the most distinguished firms of landscape architects in the United States. As a result it is one of the most charmingly designed cities of the entire northern continent. The scenic setting of Prince Rupert is one of incomparable beauty, with its ineffable glory of sea and sky, its hills and cliffs, with terrace above terrace, a scenic setting that suggests, and even rivals, that of Algiers, or Naples, or Genoa, in that unique order of picturesque loveliness investing the cities that rise from terraces above blue seas, with architectural splendours silhouetted against the sapphire sky.

Kaien Island, upon which the main part of the city will stand, comprises some 28 square miles lying 550 miles north of Vancouver. From the magnificent harbour the island rises imperiously, dominated by its central peak, Mount Hays, which towers to some 2300 feet in the clear air, with a grandeur of outlook that the artistic genius of Messrs. Brett and Hall admirably utilised in a way that insures the young city so novel and delightful a background. From Mount Hays the view over the harbour, the islands, and the far waters of the Pacific, and over lakes, forests, and rivers on the mainlands, is a view to be included among the noblest scenic delights of the world. No more romantic panorama discloses itself from Amalfi, Hong Kong, or from the Acropolis of Athens. Nor is Prince Rupert icebound and stormbound in the winter, for the Japanese current that washes the shores insures an open harbour all the year round. The entrance to the bay is singularly commodious and is usually free from fog. The harbour of Prince Rupert has every claim to be considered one of the finest in the world.

The task on which Messrs. Brett and Hall entered was a novel one. It was nothing less than the creation of a city seen in ideal vision. On the actual site was a waste and wild of rocks and stones, of tangled undergrowth and huge stumps of trees that had been felled. The mountain, also, had to be reckoned with, and even if the Boston landscape experts had possessed that traditional faith which is said to be able to remove mountains, they did not wish to remove Mount Hays. Like Mount Royal, in stately, splendid Montreal, the mountain was the most picturesque of assets. Here and there some giant tree had escaped the fate of its companions, and stood as if contemplating their fate. The uncompromising debris, the rocky sub-stratum, the abounding mass of loose stone, all combined to present difficulties. "Prince Rupert! A town hewn out of solid rock," has since that day been the description of the new city, quoted with appreciative interest.

How did Messrs. Hall and Brett attack the problem? It was a complexity of topography that baffled, if it did not defy, solutions. But Nature yields, perforce, to the necromancy of genius, and the initial achievement was to create a series of planes, planes level, planes inclined, and they then discovered that the trend of all these was, naturally, from north-east to south-west. Nature smiled upon them to the degree of establishing the means for all these planes to be, approximately, parallel in direction. Doubtless these landscape creators (being Bostonians) congratulated themselves in true Emersonian phrase on the truth that:

"... the world is built in order
And the atoms march in tune."

This stupendous work was first entered upon by the architects in January of 1908, the preliminary hydrographic and topographic surveys having been made in the two previous years by a large engineering force under the direction of James H. Bacon, the Harbour Engineer of the Grand Trunk

Pacific. The planes being appropriately parallel allowed rectangular systems of blocks for building, thus offering the best facilities for traffic; and the lie of the land permitted the splendid, spacious avenues with charm of vista and vast perspective, in combination with curving streets of limited crescents, so attractive for the residential part of the city. Beside Mount Hays Park, other plaza reservations were made, squares and playgrounds being especially considered. Along Hays Creek was a wonderful natural park which was utilised, and there has perhaps seldom been a combination of art and nature more artistically blended.

For the most beautiful residential section the eastern end of Kaien Island was selected. Connecting this residential region with the business section was a broad highway called Prince Rupert Boulevard, which also formed a link in a circular drive of twenty miles, extending around the island. There is a superb view obtained from here over Lake Morse and Lake Wainwright, and in this transparent air, under a glowing sky, this view alone would be a signal inspiration to painter or poet. For Prince Rupert is one of the most ideally enchanting places to be found on any shore; and one of the notable drives of the world, hardly even excepting that picturesque and romantic pilgrimage route between Sorrento and Amalfi, is found in Prince Rupert Boulevard in its connection with Lake Avenue. These shores of all the marvellous North-West are only comparable with those of Italy in their ineffable charm.

It is not alone, however, for the romance of beauty that Prince Rupert is notable. This brilliant young city is destined to be a traffic centre of great proportions and of cosmopolitan importance. It will inevitably become the emporium of Alaska and of all the great Northern region. The port is but thirty miles south of the Alaskan boundary, and it is thus the natural starting-point for Dawson, Nome, and other of the Alaskan and Yukon centres. From Prince Rupert to New York or to Boston or to Chicago there is now this direct line through Edmonton and Winnipeg, and thus it cannot but become a great international port. Prince Rupert is four hundred miles nearer to Yokohama than is Vancouver, and it is six hundred miles less than by way of San Francisco. Since the completion of the Grand Trunk Pacific this route has offered the shortest and most direct route to the Yukon and to Alaska. The first train over the new extension of the Grand Trunk from Winnipeg to Prince Rupert arrived at this port on April 9, 1914, a date not unimportant in the history of progress in Canada, as it initiated conditions which inaugurate an entirely new era in its prosperous development.

This romantic young city has the distinction of having had more time and money devoted to its design than has perhaps ever before been bestowed upon a town seen only in vision. Henri Bergson might almost point to it as an illustration of his creative evolution. Before the opening of the town site, plank sidewalks and roadways, sewers and water mains, and other municipal facilities for the sanitary welfare and the comfort of ten thousand people were constructed. At the present time in this city, which only celebrated its ninth birthday in January 1917, there are already seven thousand inhabitants. There are three daily newspapers, the *News*, *Journal*, and *Empire*. There are five banks, branches of the Bank of Montreal, Canadian Bank of Commerce, Union Bank of Canada, the Royal, and the Bank of British North America. Two clubs, the Prince Rupert and the Pioneer, have each attractive houses of their own, and include in their membership the leading professional and business men of the city.

The harbour is equipped for the most modern and exacting requirements. It might well be called the harbour for the ships from the Seven Seas. The Grand Trunk Pacific Steamship Company have also established a splendid service between Skagway, Prince Rupert, and Seattle, the *Prince Rupert* and the *Prince George* providing all the comforts of the best ocean liners, and offering scenery on the voyage that is so resplendent a feature with its perpetual surprises. Prince Rupert has an exceptionally high order of population, people of education, refinement, energy, and enterprise. Churches abound; the schools are the pride of the city; the social life is interesting and especially distinctive in having so large a preponderance of cultivated people.

The fishing industry at Prince Rupert is already one of the most important and the cold storage plant is one of the largest on the continent. There is a vast cannery interest, for the salmon pack of the Skeena River has established itself with the public as being of a finer order than salmon caught farther south. Prince Rupert is already the acknowledged centre of the Skeena salmon fishery, there being twelve manufactories on the river, employing twelve hundred boats in constant service and more than five thousand labourers, women as well as men working in this industry. The halibut landed at the port in the first nine months of 1916 amounted to 11,667,300 lbs.

Prince Rupert has, also, another important commercial asset in its pulpwood. Untold quantities of valuable timber are at its very doors. Mining industries, too, are forecast, as it is believed that there is much rich ore in the adjacent region, and a smelter is already projected. All these, however, are held as subordinate in any case to the commercial possibilities of the city which promise an undoubted destiny. The Skeena River is one of the invaluable assets, increasing all traffic conveniences for fruit-raising and agricultural production, and offering a waterway delightful for excursions and explorations. The completion of the Grand Trunk Pacific has brought the eastern portion of the United States and Alaska forty-eight hours nearer to each other through Chicago, and has greatly enhanced the commercial interests between the two countries. The climate of Prince Rupert has a remarkably even temperature, averaging in summer about seventy-seven degrees, and the coldest record in any winter (this one being exceptional) was that of eight degrees below zero. As a rule the winter temperature does not reach so low a degree. The climate thus permits much out-of-door life and is perhaps not an altogether negligible factor in the easy grace of social intercourse. The town has the beginning of a library, and more than one magazine and reading club. "To open a door, to widen the horizon, this is human service of the highest order." The creation of Prince Rupert is well calculated to rank high in this service.

JUNCTION OF SKEENA AND BULKLEY RIVERS, BRITISH COLUMBIA

Junction of Skeena and Bulkley Rivers, British Columbia

One of the interesting features of this town, which is one full of surprises lying in wait for the alert and expectant traveller, is the great dry dock of the Grand Trunk Pacific and Ship Repair Company, which has cost something like three million dollars, and was completed in 1915. This ship-building and repair plant is virtually three docks in one; and it can handle a ship of twenty thousand tons displacement and a length of six hundred feet, drawing thirty feet of water; moreover, it can deal with three ships at a time. It has derricks that can lift out, for repair, boilers weighing sixty tons, and after passing them through the shops replace them in the ship. It also furnishes power, light, compressed air, with wharf and storage space. The dock, in conjunction with the machine and the repair shops, can handle any class of work, wood or steel, boilers or any kind of mechanism. During its construction over a hundred and fifty men were employed, with a pay-roll that ran to some twelve thousand dollars a month. The inestimable convenience of such a plant for vessels in these waters in need of repair can hardly be overestimated.

In June 1915 the great enterprise was undertaken across the harbour opposite Prince Rupert of clearing seven hundred acres for residential use. Within three months one hundred acres of this was prepared, but from causes connected with the war, and temporary conditions of finance, the entire completion of the work is delayed for a time. In Prince Rupert the site for the magnificent terminal station is already cleared; and when the war shall be ended and conditions in the Dominion resume their prosperity, these buildings will be erected. The telegraph service of Prince Rupert is admirable. There is a direct service establishing through communication with the East, and the rates between Prince Rupert and Vancouver have been reduced to one dollar for a ten-word message. There is direct communication by telephone with Hazleton, Skeena Crossing, and with the mine of the Montana Development Company at Carnaby.

The civic affairs of Prince Rupert are well administered. The city has adopted the single-tax plan. It owns its electric lighting and power, its telephone and water systems. The fire department is equipped with the most modern appliances. It has twenty-one miles of planked roadways; it has five miles of plank pavements for pedestrians; and has already three miles of sewers. Five parks aggregate nearly a hundred acres of reservation for the city's recreation.

The lumber industry in British Columbia is one of the utmost importance as the northern part of the province alone produces an annual output of some twelve million feet. The southern portion of the province also makes considerable shipments. The Forestry Department of the Provincial Government of the Dominion report that there is available, in Prince Rupert district, twenty-five million acres averaging over fifteen thousand feet to the acre. In addition there is a tract which will be available for commercial purposes, within the next half century, of an area of seventeen million acres. About half this timber is spruce, red cedar and hemlock come next in order, and there is perhaps ten per cent. of balsam and yellow cedar. The cannery repairs and boxes required for the salmon pack and for the halibut trade make enormous demands on lumber. This branch of commerce was completely transformed by the completion of the Grand Trunk Pacific. It enabled Prince Rupert to compete on an equal basis with many other points, for a direct railroad line running through the centre of the Prairie Provinces to Winnipeg, and especially a railroad that has a better grade and shorter haul than any other with which it competes, places Prince Rupert on a fortunate basis with regard to markets.

It is hardly possible to estimate the future that lies before Prince Rupert. As tributary resources it has an ocean and an Empire. To its port will come the ships from all countries. They will bring products from the East, of the various far-off continents, and they will sail away laden with lumber and the rich exports of the vast North-West. Never was a city more skilfully planned. The Dominion Government's Hydrographic Survey had made a complete survey of Prince Rupert Harbour and its approaches, discovering that from the entrance to the extreme end, a distance of fourteen miles, it was entirely free from rocks or obstructions of any kind, and that the depth afforded ample anchorage. The Provincial Government of British Columbia appropriated two hundred thousand dollars for preliminary improvements, in the construction of roads and pavements, of sewers and water mains, before the town site was opened. While the Provincial Government makes Prince Rupert its headquarters for the northern part of the Province, with a court-house and buildings for offices, the Dominion Government is erecting a permanent and handsome post-office and customs house. Surrounded by a country whose richness and variety of resources are beyond comparison, its rapid growth is inevitable.

The easy proximity of Prince Rupert to Alaska is one of the most important things in connection with this unique and brilliant young seaport of the Pacific. Seattle and Skagway are 1000 miles apart, and thus the round trip between Seattle and Skagway is 2000 miles; but from Prince Rupert to Skagway is of course a sail of far less distance. The trip is one of entrancing scenery, fiords, bays all mountain-locked in supreme majesty and beauty, arms of the sea extending into coast indentations with an unexcelled panorama of glancing lights, play of colours, and moving-picture panoramas of grandeur and picturesqueness. Between Seattle, Prince Rupert, and Skagway the entire round trip occupies some eleven days. It is a voyage unmatched on the entire globe. In the distance the towering peaks clothed in snow of dazzling whiteness rise beyond the mountain ranges in their royal purple with evanescent flitting gleams of gold and rose from the brilliant sun; the green water of the bays is alive with thousands of leaping salmon; and the shores are defined by the dark pine forests, standing in an impenetrable tangle of ferns and trailing undergrowth. Through this "Inside Passage," as it is called, a fleet of steamers has been employed by the Grand Trunk Pacific in a splendid coast service between Seattle and Skagway. "I am in the writing-room on the upper deck of the *Prince George* sailing amid such ineffable glory that I only write about one word to every ten minutes," said an enthusiastic voyager in a personal letter to a friend in the early September days of 1915; "only one word in ten minutes will be allotted to you, for I must LOOK! It is the time of my life, and I can write letters (at all events to you, to whom they write themselves) anywhere. But this voyage—it is the dream of a lifetime! I have sailed the enchanted Mediterranean with our rapturous callings at Algiers, rising on terraced hills in her unspeakable beauty; at Naples, with all the Neapolitan coast a very vision of the ethereal realms; I have sailed on to Genoa, with Ischia, dream-haunted by Victoria Colonna, Italy's immortal woman-poet, and made my pilgrimage to the island and over the ancient Castel d'Ischia by local boats from Naples; I once sailed through the Ionian Isles in the late afternoon of a May day that was all azure and gold; I have sailed the Italian lakes and cruised about on the Alpine lakes of Switzerland: but it still remained for this one enchanted voyaging to give me that thrill of untranslatable ecstasy. This combination of the sea and mountains in what they call the 'Inside Passage' is simply superb. And the *Prince George* is perfectly ideal in all conditions.

"I have a large, beautiful state-room alone—every state-room on these steamers is an outside one; the entire steamer is richly carpeted in soft moss-green; finished in the native woods, polished till you could use the woodwork for a mirror (and if it reflected you how decorative it would be!); beside that, there are mirrors galore, of the regulation order, and a news-stand with all the world's literature, so to speak; the most delightful bathrooms, but I don't spend the entire time at sea in salt baths, as you unkindly assert; the table is excellent, being rather noted, I am told, for its fine cuisine, and there is to me a very direct connection between delicious coffee and various accompaniments, and feeling 'up' to things for the day; anyway, everything is delicious, and the splendid, spacious decks to enjoy a paradise of walking on; writing-desks well stocked with stationery at every turn, on every deck; and these steamers are 'twin-screw' if you know what that means! I confess I don't! but apparently people who do know consider a 'twin' screw as of far more importance in the universe than one lone, lorn screw; and they are equipped with wireless telegraph (I do know what that means) and with oil engines, and every modern device of safety, and with fairly luxurious comfort; and, indeed, the whole voyage is ideal and has only one fault—alas! alas! that it will come to an end. If only it would never end! I count off the flying hours as a miser counts his gold, I can hardly bear to sleep to miss one hour of its glory and loveliness, yet sleep, too, is a joy in this magical air, and, at all events, this voyage will not be ended when it is over. I shall have it all the rest of my life ... to live over again and again 'in the ethereal,' where all outer experiences find their record. I am quite sure the Recording Angel sets this down in illuminated pages."

From Puget Sound 500 miles of the voyage is through Canadian waters, so vast is the Dominion. For one hundred and twenty miles the steamer is sailing through the Straits of Georgia, which separates the main land of British Columbia from Vancouver Island, with the range of the Olympic Mountains astern, from whence the gods look down on mortals. Do they not, indeed, dwell on Olympian heights? Passing into the Seymour Narrows from the Georgian Strait, the Channel is hardly more than one third of a mile wide, and the rocky walls with the lofty mountains just behind are so overgrown with trees as to present an almost solid wall of emerald green, tempting the passenger to reach out his hand and grasp the cedar needles that seem so near. On sunny days the reflections in the water are bewilderingly clear, and here and there pour down rushing cataracts of foam-crested water from the melting snow of the mountains.

Indians spearing Salmon in Bulkley Cañon

"Queen Charlotte Sound," writes Ella Higginson,[1] "is a splendid sweep of purple water.... The warm breath of the Kuro Siwo, penetrating all these inland seas and passages, is converted by the great white peaks of the horizon into pearl-like mist that drifts in clouds and fragments upon the blue waters. Nowhere are these mists more frequent, nor more elusive, than in Queen Charlotte Sound. At sunrise they take on the delicate tones of the primrose or the pinkish star-flower; at sunset, all the royal rose and purple blendings; all the warm flushes of amber, orange, and gold. Through a maze of pale yellow, whose fine, cool needles sting one's face and set one's hair with seed pearls, one passes into a little open water-world where a blue sky sparkles above a bluer sea, and the air is like clear, washed gold. But a mile ahead a solid wall of amethyst closes in this brilliant sea; shattering it into particles that set the hair with amethysts instead of pearls.... It is this daily mist-shower that bequeaths to British Columbia and Alaska their marvellous and luxuriant growth of vegetation, their spiced sweetness of atmosphere, their fairness and freshness."

[1] *Alaska; the Great Country*, by Ella Higginson. New York: The Macmillan Company.

Forty miles north of Prince Rupert is Dixon's Entrance, that marks the international boundary between the Canadian and Alaskan waters. Some haunting impress left upon the air by the great navigators who made their pioneer voyages in these intricate waterways—Perez and Valdez, Duncan, Vancouver, Meares, Caudra—their dauntless courage and their perils fling spectra on the passing winds and waves. The scenic effects grow more and more sublime as the steamer advances. At a distance of about seventy-five miles north of Prince Rupert the traveller comes in sight of a remarkable series of mountain terraces, rising more than six thousand feet into the air, with sheer walls and castellated summits.

The first call at port after Prince Rupert is at Ketchikan, seven hundred miles from Seattle, with a population of some two thousand people, the distributing point for the mines and fisheries of Southern Alaska. On its crescent-shaped harbour and with its eternal guard of mountains, with its lake and its falls and its wonderful gorge, three miles distant into the woodlands, it is a picturesque town, and with its electric lighting and steam heating it leaves little to be desired for comfortable residence. Between Ketchikan and Wrangell are the Wrangell Narrows, a channel where ethereal vapours, many-hued, like tropical flowers, are breeze-blown in the air; and the long, green moss, on the trees on either side, sways like drapery. Miss Scidmore, writing of Wrangell Narrows, thus pictured it with her fascinating pen:

"It was an enchanting trip up that narrow channel of deep water, rippling between bold island shores and parallel mountain walls. Beside clear emerald tide, reflecting tree and rock, there was the beauty of foaming cataracts leaping down the sides of snow-capped mountains and the grandeur of great glaciers pushing down through sharp ravines and dropping miniature icebergs into the sea. Touched by the last light of the sun, Patterson Glacier was a frozen lake of a wonderland, shining with silvery lights, and showing a pale ethereal green and deep, pure blue in all the rifts and crevices of its icy front."

From Wrangell on to Juneau the entrance to Taku Inlet is passed. The far-famed Taku Glacier is differentiated by the extreme brilliancy of its colouring from all other glaciers of the Alaskan regions. Taku Inlet, with its forty-five ice streams, is a fitting approach to this marvel of Nature. Every blast of the steamer's whistle is as the call of a giant monster which is answered by masses of ice that, detached by the vibration, plunge headlong into the sea with a noise like thunder. "That day on the Taku Glacier will live forever as one of the rarest and most perfect enjoyment," again writes Alaska's vivid interpreter, Miss Scidmore: "The grandest objects in Nature were before us, the primeval forces that mould the face of the earth were at work, and it was all so out of the every-day world that we might have been walking a new planet, fresh fallen from the Creator's hand." The Taku Glacier has a sheer, precipitous front three hundred feet high, the colour making it seem one gigantic sapphire, so intense is the blue. Yet again there are glints of green and rose and gold that flash out as if a casket of jewels had been flung over it, or an avalanche of star-dust, windswept, from the far spaces of the universe. John Muir, the great naturalist, whose vision was that of the artist and whose spirit was always open to the message of the eternal world, was deeply impressed by Taku and by Sundum fiords, and in one allusion he says of Taku:

"A hundred or more glaciers of the second and third class may be seen along these walls, and as many snowy cataracts, which, with the plunging bergs, keep all the fiord in a roar. The scenery is of the wildest description, especially in their upper reaches, where the granite walls, streaked with waterfalls, rise in sheer massive precipices, like those of Yosemite Valley, to a height of three and four thousand feet."

The poetic eye of John Burroughs keenly recognised the grandeur of all this voyage and the especial splendour that lies between Prince Rupert and Skagway; and of the gleaming brilliancy of the glacier regions he said that it was as if "the solid earth became spiritual and translucent."

This new route to Alaska, which is under the auspices of the Grand Trunk Pacific, has greatly increased the tourist travel, as the safety of the "Inside Route," combined with the luxurious conditions and the ineffable panorama of beauty, render the journey as easy and feasible as it is delightful. There is a saving of three days by journeying over the Grand Trunk Pacific to Prince Rupert and there embarking for Alaska. In January of 1916, the well-known traveller and writer, Mr. Frank G. Carpenter, made this trip of which he wrote:

"... I despair of giving you any idea of the beauties of this voyage, they are so many and so varied. Now you have the wonders of the Swiss Lakes, now those of the Inland Sea of Japan, and now beauties like those on the coasts of New Zealand. There are all sorts of combinations of sea and sky, of evergreen slopes and snow-capped mountains. The colour effects are beyond description and the sunsets indescribable in their changes and beauties. The islands are of all shapes and sizes and they float upon sapphire seas. Many of the islands have snow-capped mountains that rise in green walls almost straight up from the water, and their heads are often crested with silver."

Juneau, the capital and principal metropolis of Alaska, is on Gastineau Channel, which is eight miles in length and more than a mile wide at the entrance, gradually growing less as it nears the mainland, till it becomes like a narrow avenue of blue water through which the sunset pours in the late afternoon with an almost unearthly beauty. Mount Juneau, in the centre of the town, rises to a height of 3000 feet, with sloping sides of a pale green down which rush numberless cascades of silvery, sparkling water. Juneau is already an important business centre, with incalculably rich mining properties tributary to the city, and with almost every branch of business and the industries represented. It is the commercial supply centre of all the camps; it is on the direct line of travel from Seattle to the Upper Yukon, and has its banks, assay laboratories, transportation facilities, and good schools, while it is the residence of the Governor of Alaska and the seat of all the Federal offices. There is a Chamber of Commerce, and there are women's clubs and imported gowns. The hospitalities of Juneau are already famous, and social life rises to a gaiety and whirl that leaves the Parisian life, as it existed in its social tide before the war, quite in the shade. The Parisienne is seldom reckless in her extravagance; a certain well-adjusted economy is a part of French life, even among the most fashionable and wealthy. But economy can hardly be said to have achieved much for itself in Juneau. Is not Alaska stuffed with gold? Not a few of its residents live as if that conviction were their financial basis. The entertaining is on a lavish scale; the women are dressed so smartly as to put a modest traveller quite to rout; and money is apparently regarded as something to be put into immediate circulation.

Life is at high tide. Juneau has a creditable library, it has several cleverly edited newspapers, and the general vitality of the social and commercial life is not unworthy of the sparkling splendours of the scenic setting. As Juneau was founded in 1880, its initial mining camp developing towards a town, the period of its existence that antedates the dawn of the twentieth century is regarded by its up-to-date residents as ancient history. The Rome of the fifth century is not more remote from the Rome of 1916 than is the decade of the 'eighties from Juneau. The people are the true "futurists" in every sense. No grass grows under their glancing feet. They drive, and dress, and dine, and dance. They begin where the older cities leave off, so to speak. If they are remote from the great world centres, so much the worse for the same centres! Life is perpetually *en fête* in Juneau. The vital exhilaration, the sparkling energy, the eye on the future, and the disregard of the past, are characteristics of the general march of progress.

It is interesting to recall that the first book ever written on Alaska was by Eliza Ruhamah Scidmore of Washington, the capital of the United States, a book published by the Lothrop house in Boston (U.S.A.) early in the decade of 1880-90. Miss Scidmore was the first American woman to visit Alaska, sailing from San Francisco by a freight steamer some time before any passenger service was inaugurated for that wonderful voyage. An adventurous spirit, her eager imagination always flitting before to penetrate some unknown region, Miss Scidmore thus began, in her early girlhood, the extensive and somewhat remarkable travels which have been continued in her picturesque life. Since those days of her first youthful achievement her name has flown widely on the wings of fame as that of one of the most brilliant and able women writers of her country. Taking the Orient for her happy hunting-ground, Miss Scidmore has made numerous voyages over the Pacific, with many prolonged sojourns in China, Japan, and India; making a pilgrimage to Java and writing of its old temples and mysterious customs in a richly illustrated paper that appeared in the *Century Magazine* and which attracted wide attention. Among her books *A Winter in China* and *Jinrikisha Days* have come to be regarded as almost indispensable handbooks for travellers as well as the enchanters of the fireside or the summer piazza; and by means of many years' residence in Tokio and Yokohama, Miss Scidmore has become an acknowledged authority on Oriental art, a connoisseur whose judgment has been sought by more than one of the great art collectors in the States. With her keen intellectual grasp she has also entered into the politics of the Far East; and to *The Outlook*, and other leading reviews in both London and New York, Miss Scidmore has contributed articles so able in their discernment as to be widely quoted and discussed.

Miss Scidmore's initial trip to Alaska, interpreted in a book offering a series of singularly vivid impressions, combined, too, with a study of facts and prevailing conditions, and fascinating pictorial descriptions of this "water-colour land" as she termed it, from the faint evanescent hues of sunshine on the glaciers, perhaps contributed more than any other single cause to stimulate the demand for passenger excursions to this country.

Miss Scidmore's description of Muir Glacier, an exquisite piece of word-painting, has often been reproduced; and of her last, lingering view of this spectacle she wrote:

"The whole brow was transfigured with the fires of sunset; the blue and silvery pinnacles, the white and shining front dreamlike on a roseate and amber sea, and the range and circle of dull violet mountains lifting their glowing summits into a sky flecked with crimson and gold."

Somewhere about 1889 another gifted American woman, Kate Field, author, lecturer, and a charming figure in society, visited Alaska; and to Miss Field belongs the honour of having delivered the first lecture ever given in that country. It was in Juneau, in a primitive and unfinished room, that Miss Field gave this lecture, utilising a rough table as a platform. Her audience included miners in their working garb, prospectors, many of the usual camp-followers, a few Indians, and several of her fellow-passengers from the steamer. Her theme was that of good citizenship, and one of her hearers afterwards reported that she gave them wholesome truths with characteristic vehemence and earnestness. Miss Field was rewarded by being presented with the "freedom" of the town (then hardly more than a mining-camp), with a pair of silver bracelets made by the Indians, a bottle of virgin gold, and a totem pole. These picturesque tributes were highly valued by their witty and graceful recipient, and she often displayed them with pride and pleasure to her friends in Washington, New York, Paris, or London. Visiting the Muir Glacier at this early period when its unequalled grandeur was at its perfection (for of late years earthquakes and devastations have changed its contour) Miss Field thus described it:

"Imagine a glacier three miles wide and three hundred feet high, and you have a slight idea of Muir Glacier. Picture a background of mountains fifteen thousand feet high, all snow-clad, and then imagine a gorgeous sun lighting up crystals with rainbow colouring. The face of the crystal takes on the hue of aquamarine—the hue of every bit of floating ice that surrounds the steamer. This dazzling serpent moves sixty-four feet a day, tumbling headlong into the sea, startling the air with submarine thunder."

PRINCE RUPERT, BRITISH COLUMBIA

Prince Rupert, British Columbia

Miss Field's experience in Juneau must have been, indeed, a contrast to the scenic setting of her girlhood, when, in Florence, Italy, she studied music and art; where Walter Savage Landor taught her Latin and wrote classic verse to her; where Robert and Elizabeth Barrett Browning welcomed her to their poets' home in Casa Guidi; and where she met George Eliot, whose genius kindled her own. With her literary talent stimulated and all aglow in this radiant atmosphere, Miss Field wrote that exquisite series of monographs on Landor, Mrs. Browning, Madame la Marchesa Ristori, and several of the Italian poets, which were published in the *Atlantic Monthly* (then the magazine which was the very arbiter of American literary destiny), a series that has been often erroneously attributed to the eminent sculptor and poet, William Wetmore Story, as in those days the *Atlantic Monthly* preserved the silence of the gods regarding the identity of its contributors.

It is something to have passed one's early youth in Arcady; and between those Florentine days, and her appearance as the first lecturer in Alaska, there lay a series of richly varied years and achievements. Kate Field seemed to be always winging her shining way, and it was during an interlude in Hawaii, whose beauty steeped her in gladness, that she fared forth, on a golden day in the Maytime of 1896, on still another journey; a mystic journey into those realms of the Life More Abundant, and entered on a new phase of experiences, even those of the Adventure Beautiful.

From Juneau the Grand Trunk Pacific Line of steamers proceeds to Skagway, through the Lynn Canal, considered, all in all, the most beautiful of the fiords of Alaska. Skagway rejoices in the poetic designation of "the flower City of Alaska" from the amazing luxuriance and loveliness of the riotous floral growth in the gardens of the town and also in the outlying country. Skagway is the gateway to the Yukon, and the tourist who wishes to visit Canada's portion of this great Northland embarks on the White Pass and Yukon Railway, which affords easy access to Lake Atlin and down the Yukon to Dawson, the capital of Yukon Territory.

The future importance of Skagway depends largely on the success of the White Pass and Yukon Railway. Of this, however, there is practically no question. Skagway has a population of more than two thousand; and it is splendidly equipped with cable, telephone and telegraph services; with electric lighting; with good schools and churches; and with shops and stores furnishing an adequate assortment for all needs of utility and of taste and beauty; it has a very attractive resident region, and its gardens are already famous. During the Klondike excitement of 1897-98, Skagway was the base of operations for many thousands of prospectors who thronged this region. It is especially attractive to the devotees of ethnological science, as it is near some of the more interesting Indian villages, and it has supreme attractions for the artist. The glaciers of Davidson and Mendenhall are near, and nowhere are the enchantments of a summer in the far northlands more alluring and spellbinding to the lover of flowers and fragrances, of stars and sunsets, of the beauty that flashes from solid mountain walls of opal pinnacles and glittering palisades, in an atmosphere prismatic in colour—nowhere are there more lovely "lands of summer beyond the sea" than in and around Skagway.

It has been more or less generally supposed that the climate of Alaska was inevitably severe and fairly arctic in its character. On the contrary, the mean temperature of Juneau for July is fifty-seven degrees and the thermometer often ranges from seventy to even ninety. Thus the mean temperature of Juneau for July is only one degree less than that of San Francisco for August. The equability of the temperature in Southern Alaska is a feature of importance. The entire land, in summer, is covered with a dense vegetation.

One of the great marvels of nature in the Alaskan and Yukon regions is that of the matchless spectacle of the Northern Lights. Not even the glacier can rival Aurora Borealis. It is Robert Service who is the bard of the mystic illuminations that are fairly before the eye of the reader of that scintillating poem, the "Ballad of the Northern Lights."

"And soft they danced from the Polar sky and swept in the
    primrose haze;
And swift they pranced with their silver feet, and pierced with

a blinding blaze.
They danced a cotillion in the sky; they were rose and silver shod;
It was not good for the eyes of man, 'twas a sight for the eyes of God.

"And the skies of night were alive with light, with a throbbing, thrilling flame
Amber, and rose, and violet, opal and gold it came.
Pennants of silver waved and streamed, lazy banners unfurled;
Sudden splendours of sabres gleamed, lightning javelins were hurled;
There in our awe we crouched and saw with our wild, uplifted eyes,
Charge and retire the hosts of fire in the battleground of the skies."

Prince Rupert and Alaska! They offer the traveller the very glory of the world and of all the heavenly spaces.

CHAPTER X

PRINCE RUPERT TO VANCOUVER, VICTORIA, SEATTLE, AND THE GOLDEN GATE

The voyage from Prince Rupert to Alaska is unparalleled in its glory of scenic enthralment; it is a trip unique and, indeed, quite unrivalled by any that this terrestrial sphere has disclosed to the wanderer over her spaces; yet hardly less interesting in a different way is that lovely sail of two days and two nights from Prince Rupert to Seattle, with calls at the ports of Vancouver and Victoria. The one enchants the imagination; the other relates itself to the great social order of human life. The latter reveals the vast resources of British Columbia; the almost infinite possibilities for the transcendent future of a new and still higher civilisation; the regions of the homes, the development, the nobler and still nobler culture of life in its evolutionary progress.

The comfort and beauty of these Grand Trunk Pacific steamers are, as noted in the preceding chapter, responsible for much of the enjoyment of the voyage. To be comfortable—even to have the senses gratified with beauty in one's immediate environment—is by no means the chief end or aim of life, but it is assuredly a means to an end; after that other things. He who is

"Alive to gentle influence
Of landscape and of sky,
And tender to the spirit-touch,"

can hardly escape the immediate sense of a reinforcement of energy by the subtle charm of a pleasing environment. It is like the influence of music, harmonising and co-ordinating all one's powers of achievement.

The coast of British Columbia, stretching away to the southland, has its own order of beauty, as has already been described in the description of the voyage which begins at Seattle extending to Skagway. The two days of return from Prince Rupert are only too brief for the traveller with an eye for the singular beauty of precipitous cliffs, forest-crowned, that rise, from the shores, brilliantly diversified with the waterfalls, islands, and glimpses of hanging glaciers, now and then seen under radiant skies.

For tourists who, arriving at Prince Rupert, are not able to make the Alaskan voyage, this sail to Seattle will yet hold so much of majesty and beauty that, while not fully compensating for the northern cruise, is yet singularly satisfying in itself. Leaving Prince Rupert at nine in the morning the steamer calls at Vancouver at four in the afternoon of the next day; and hardly is she at her dock before the enterprising municipal motor car company sends a representative on board to announce a "one-dollar-an-hour-and-a-half" trip about the city in a number of spacious motor cars in waiting, which offers to all who embrace the opportunity the interest of seeing the famous Stanley Park, covering a thousand acres, together with the Shaughnessy Heights, the marine drive, and all points of interest, with the sightseers assured that they should be delivered at their steamer in good time for its departure.

Vancouver's growth has been truly remarkable. It began thirty years ago with a few log-cabins in a clearing overlooking Burrard Inlet. In 1901 the population of the city was about 27,000; to-day, 200,000 people are citizens of Vancouver and suburbs. Its wharfs are crowded with shipping, more than 18,000 vessels using the port in a single year, while its customs revenue amounts to five millions of dollars annually.

The business and residential sections of Vancouver are extremely interesting and no tourist would willingly miss seeing something of the largest Canadian city on the Pacific Coast. On the evening of February 14, 1916, the first long-distance telephone conversation was held between Vancouver and Montreal. Previous to this, telephonic communication had been opened between New York and San Francisco, a distance of 3400 miles; but on the occasion of the opening between Montreal and Vancouver the human voice was heard at a distance of 4227 miles!

The marvellous progress made in telephone service is illustrated by some records dating back more than forty years. It was in Boston in the spring of 1875 (March 10, 1875, to be exact), that Professor Bell was first able to send an intelligible sentence from one room to another in a building at No. 5, Exeter Place, in that city. This message to the next room was to Thomas Augustus Watson, and consisted of the words, "Mr. Watson, Mr. Watson, I want you; come here." In the summer of 1915, Professor Bell sent the same message from New York to Mr. Watson who was in San Francisco.

Pure Bred Jerseys, Western Canada

Miss Kate Field, the brilliant American critic and lecturer, was among those fascinated by Dr. Bell's initial experiments of 1875 demonstrating his new invention. Miss Field, while residing in England, took an important part in bringing the telephone to public notice. In the biography of Miss Field there appears a number of extracts from her diary of this period, of which one, under the date of January 14, 1878, runs as follows:

"Drove early to Osborne Cottage (Isle of Wight) where Sir Thomas Biddulph invited me to come in the evening. Arrived there all fine in my new gown at 8.30 P.M. Met Lady Biddulph, Sir Thomas, General Ponsonby, Mrs. Ponsonby, and others. Very polite and very courteous about telephone. I sang Kathleen Mavourneen to the Queen who was delighted and thanked me telephonically. Sang Cuckoo Song, Comin' Thro' the Rye, and recited Rosalind's epilogue. All delighted. Then I went to Osborne House and met the Duke of Connaught. Experiments a great success."

So comprehensive were Miss Field's convictions of the wide scope and resistless nature of scientific advance that she once remarked to a friend, "I look to see science prove immortality." Her faith in immortality was not wanting, but she believed it to be within that order of truth which might actually be demonstrated by science.

Victoria is only some six hours' sail from Vancouver—beautiful Victoria, worthy of the greatest queen of the ages whose name the city so proudly bears. Not only for its signal attractions, but as the capital of British Columbia, Victoria has especial interest, and the tourist who is wise will disembark and remain in this delightful city until the next steamer arrives continuing the voyage to Seattle. An English city dropped into the American continent is Victoria. It is neither Canadian nor yet of the United States, but it is practically an English city located on Vancouver Island. It is already an important port, and the equable climate attracts residents and visitors from the entire continent.

It is called, indeed, "the city of sunshine," and it has both wealth and health in measure to impress the visitor, if it does not transform him into at least a temporary resident. The aristocratic residential district has entrancing views of the sea, islands, bays, and mountains, and more than three miles of coast line. The beauty of the architectural effects, the equable climate, the delightful drives afforded by the wide asphalt-paved boulevards, and the variety of amusements and entertainments—yachting, golf, fishing, country clubs with all manner of sports and games, together with its good schools, numerous churches, and library, attract a population of refinement and of a notable order of intellectuality.

To arrive at Seattle in the early dawn is to arrive at the psychological moment.

"If them would'st view fair Melrose aright
Go visit it by pale moonlight,"

counsels Sir Walter; and to view Seattle at her most typical and representative moment one should see her first in the golden glow of a morning, that illuminates all her crescent harbour and reveals her streets alive in the new energy of the day. Seattle is known as "the Seaport of Success." She takes the opposite pole from the motto Dante saw over the red city of Dis. Far from any abandonment of hope by "those who enter here," the very spectacle of her eager, intense life reinvigorates the newcomer. Has he not entered the Seaport of Success? "If you want success—Succeed!" counsels Emerson. Of course one will succeed in Seattle. That is what he is there for. He is "born for the job." Seattle is the marvel of the day. One quite sympathises with the citizen who met a press correspondent from New York on a train and begged him to include Seattle in his glowing interpretations. "But I was in Seattle last week," rejoined the writer. "Oh, but you should see Seattle *now!*" replied the up-to-date resident.

Seattle has a population of nearly three hundred and fifty thousand; she has four transcontinental railways; and fifty-seven steamship lines. Lake

Washington, lying just outside the city, a sheet of water twenty-five miles in length and averaging three miles in width, offers one of the most ideal and poetic regions for suburban homes, and one whose privileges are apparently appreciated. The beautiful residences that adorn its shores render it a locality well worth seeing. The lake extends to the foothills of the Cascade range, whose peaks, perpetually covered with ice and snow, are from five thousand to more than fourteen thousand feet in height. With this majestic mountain range on one hand, and Puget Sound on the other, Seattle has an environment that rivals, in natural beauty, any other city of the world. The boulevards of Seattle are famous, and of these ex-President Taft declared that they formed one of the most magnificent combinations of modern city and mediæval forest. From these boulevards of thirty miles in extent, connecting a chain of thirty-eight parks, there are continual vistas of lake, and sea, and snow-capped mountains, and the drive is often among arbours and flowers and shrubs revealing rare skill and taste in gardening.

The State of Washington has wisely inaugurated a system of splendid roadways, whose skilful engineering has rendered the broad boulevards, the country highways, a veritable paradise of comfort to motorists. More than fifty thousand miles of such road thoroughfares stretch in all directions from Seattle. Four of these great highways, those of the Pacific, Sunset, Olympic, and National Parks, were built and are maintained at the expense of the state. One important feature of these is the Pacific Highway, a thoroughfare of 2000 miles in length, connecting British Columbia with the southern limit of California. It is the longest drive of the world and has a picturesque beauty unsurpassed by that of any known region.

Nor are the ardent residents of Seattle in any way inclined to reticence regarding her allurements. To one voyager on board, who was a native of the States, but who had been so spellbound by her first wonderful trip through Canada that she longed to "assume a virtue, though she had it not" and pass herself off as a native of the Dominion—to this tourist a Seattle lady rather importunately insisted that she ought to remain at least a week in the "Seaport of Success" and revel in its amazements. "You would see parks of hundreds of acres," exclaimed the loyal resident of the capital city of the State of Washington, among other enumerations of the glories to be revealed. "Oh, is that all?" unkindly responded the voyager. "Why, in Canada we are accustomed to parks of over four thousand square miles." The devotee of Canadian landscapes endeavoured to say this with the air of one born and bred in the Dominion, and she was quite charmed with her evident success when the Seattle lady replied, "Oh, you are a Canadian? I thought you were one of our own people." "Did you, indeed?" returned the masquerading Canadian, non-committantly, with the most innocent and unconscious air that it was possible to assume.

MOUNT ROBSON, BRITISH COLUMBIA

Mount Robson, British Columbia

It is an interesting and picturesque trip by rail from Seattle to Portland (some seven hours) and from Portland out to its port, Flavell-Astoria, is another picturesque little journey, some two hours by rail. Here awaits one of the Pacific steamers of the Great Northern Company, with its top deck glass-enclosed, making the vast sweep of ocean view possible in all weather; with four other promenade decks, with its ballroom, its conveniences for games of all sorts, and its enormous crowds of gay passengers. The sail from Flavell-Astoria to San Francisco is only thirty-six hours; too brief for a lover of beauty, yet a great deal of enjoyment can be crowded into that time by those who surprise the secret.

It was not only the ideal way by which to approach the Panama-Pacific Exposition of 1915, but it remains the ideal way in which to approach San Francisco. The first instinctive thought of the tourist is that he can only enjoy this approach if he arrives from Hawaii, or Japan, or some port in the Orient. On the contrary, he can enjoy one of the great and one of the most picturesque trips that the resources of this world afford, by journeying to California, via Prince Rupert, and on, by sea, by land, by sea again, through Vancouver and Seattle; thence by way of Portland, and Flavell-Astoria, to the triumphant entrance by the Golden Gate. It was a marvellous tour for the vanished Exposition summer of 1915, and it will remain marvellous for all the summers to come, growing as the years pass more beautiful, more feasible, and more familiar to the travelling public.

CHAPTER XI

CANADA IN THE PANAMA-PACIFIC EXPOSITION

The year of 1915 will forever remain illuminated in the history of Canada and of the United States as that of the celebration of two momentous events: the completion of the Panama-Pacific Canal, uniting the Atlantic and the Pacific Oceans; and the bridging the entire continent, from Montreal to Vancouver, from New York to San Francisco, by human speech. The achievement of the Panama Canal was at a cost of three hundred and ten millions of dollars; the achievement of "the voyage of the voice" across the continent, by the Bell telephone system, cost that company twice the amount of the expenditure demanded by the canal. During the next decade, the Bell Company propose to expend an even greater sum in the perfecting of all the future possibilities that may arise.

The completion of the Panama Canal is one of the signal events in the world's history. It changes the great currents of commerce; it has reduced the distance between the central points of the Atlantic and the Pacific coasts from 13,000 to 5000 miles, and it will greatly reduce the cost of coaling on voyages from coast to coast. From Colon, on the Atlantic side of the Isthmus, to Balboa, on the Pacific side, was formerly, by the water route around Cape Horn, a distance of 10,500 nautical miles; through the canal the distance is 44 miles. The time required between these two points formerly approximated to 126 days; now the distance between is but one day. These elementary statistics reveal to some degree the inestimable value of the achievement to all the nations of the world.

It was fitting that such an achievement should be celebrated with an exposition of the arts, the resources, the productions, and the inventions of the civilised world. It was the vivid drama of international achievement. There were more than eighty thousand single exhibits, and groups of related exhibits, representing every phase of the highest efforts of man in contemporary progress. Industries and economics, inventions and discoveries, arts and sciences, education and ethics, met under the striking architectural beauty and in a scenic setting never before equalled in any land. Against a background of the blue Pacific lying under a glowing western sky, with a splendour of decoration hardly paralleled, the scene was one worthy to be forever perpetuated in the world's history. It struck the note of a new life. The contrast between this illustration of the development of the arts of peace—the vision of the spirit that united East and West in the common cause of all that ennobles and exalts—and those awful scenes of carnage that were raging in central Europe on the other side of the globe, was a contrast that might well employ the genius of Thucydides to depict, with a pen lighted from the living coal on the altar. Yet, such is the leading of divinely-guided destiny, each was doing its work in the regeneration of the world. The seemingly irreparable calamity of the war was sweeping away old conditions that the new life of spiritualisation should enter in; it was the preparing the way of the Lord and making His paths straight. Faith constantly discerned the triumphant exhortation:

"Lift up your heads, O ye gates; and be ye lift up, ye everlasting doors; and the King of Glory shall come in!"

More than three hundred congresses met in these palaces under the shadow of the Tower of Jewels; in the halls of music, of art, or in the terraced pavilion of the Court of the Universe. All were welcomed with that royal hospitality that has ever characterised the generous heart of San Francisco. These congresses dealt for the most part with the vital topics of the day. They concerned themselves less with the life of literature and more with the life of nature; less with the life that takes note of abstract and profound intellectual problems and more with the practical applications of ethical truth. The congresses thus discussed open-air life, foods, clothing, motoring, the political enfranchisement of women, new theories in education, hygiene, economics, charities. In the building of Liberal Arts there was one exhibit from the Observatory on Mount Lowe, labelled by the director of that institution, as the stuff of which the universe and man were made: that of electrons and mentoids. The distinctively new note of the twentieth century was everywhere in evidence. The Exposition planted its standard in an approaching Future, not in a receding Past. By this standard alone could it be truly judged. The salons of fine art did not measurably offer, in any extent, the quality of art displayed at Chicago in 1893, nor was it comparable with that transcendently superb collection of paintings and sculpture that concentrated the inspiration of the centuries in the Paris Exposition of 1900. Naturally, there were physical barriers of space and the barriers of war conditions that effectually determined this. It was easy for Europe and the Orient to send to Paris their most adequate representation. And France, alone, is so rich in her national treasures of art, both of the past and of contemporary work, that her own display alone would have made a profound impression. For San Francisco, in 1915, conditions effectually debarred her from securing much of the great art of the world. Very wisely, she did not dash herself blindly and unavailingly against destiny, but wisely struck the key of desire from a new centre. The result was in that the Exposition suggested its own ideals with but slight reference to traditions.

Singularly fortunate was it, indeed, in its administration. President Charles C. Moore seemed the man best fitted for the high and responsible place that he so ably filled. Never was a great world-exposition conducted with a more remarkable combination of wisdom, courtesy, admirable judgment, and comprehensive treatment. Not less fortunate was the great undertaking in its vice-presidents: William H. Crocker, R. B. Hale, I. W. Hellman, jun., M. H. De Young, Leon Sloss, and James Bolph, jun., while Dr. Frederick J. V. Skiff, as Director-in-Chief; George Hough Perry, at the head of the Publicity Department; and Mr. A. M. Mortesen, as Traffic Manager, were all felicitously equipped for their special service.

"The Future is our kingdom,"

said George Sterling, the poet of the day, whose poem entitled *The Builders* was read by George Arlett, a member of the California State Commission, at the closing ceremonies.

Mr. Sterling struck the keynote of the splendid enterprise in these stanzas:

"We do but cross a threshold into day.
  Beauty we leave behind
  A deeper beauty on our path to find
And higher glories to illume the way.
  The door we close behind us is the Past;
  Our sons shall find a fairer door at last.

"A world reborn awaits us! Years to come
  Shall know its grace and good,
  When wars shall end in endless brotherhood
And birds shall build in cannon long since dumb.
  Men shall have peace, though then no man may know
  Who built this sunset city long ago."

Only nine years had passed since San Francisco had been practically destroyed by a sudden and terrible calamity. But the spirit of the Golden Gate laughs at calamity and with a magician's wand transmutes it into success. Only two years after this devastation San Francisco raised millions for the exposition she had planned. No earthquake could entomb her spirit, nor could it be drowned by any tidal wave that the Pacific is capable of providing. With that lofty poet, William Vaughan Moody, who, alas, "died too soon" for the nation which his lyre entranced, San Francisco might well declare:

"From wounds and sore defeat
  I made my battle-stay;
Winged sandals for my feet
  I wove of my delay."

The Panama-Pacific Exposition opened on February 15, 1915, and closed on December 4 of the same year. It was participated in by the Argentine Republic, Bolivia, Brazil, Canada, Chile, China, Costa Rica, Cuba, Denmark, Dominican Republic, Equador, France, Guatemala, Haiti, Holland, Honduras, Italy, Japan, Liberia, Mexico, Nicaragua, New Zealand, Panama, Persia, Peru, Portugal, Salvador, Spain, Sweden, Uruguay, and Venezuela.

This enumeration of the countries participating will of itself suggest the somewhat new class of exhibits, as differing from those of older countries in former world-displays. The Panama-Pacific was thus its own precedent. Its claims to the novel and the unique were extremely well sustained. It was the second exposition held on the Pacific coast, and it had the longest duration by four months of any ever held before.

The grounds comprised over 600 acres, with a water-front of two and a half miles, on San Francisco Bay, just east of the Golden Gate. On the other three sides they were partly enclosed by hills, thus forming a natural amphitheatre. There were eleven colossal palaces with many lesser buildings. These palaces were grouped in a series of rectangles connected by courts and arcades with an Andalusian charm. The courts fascinated the eye by their colonnades, arches, domes, and glittering minarets. They were adorned by mural paintings of symbolic significance, by fountains, sunken gardens, and sculptured art, with niches and restful seats. Festival Hall, with its superb organ, where a concert was held every day, contained an auditorium seating three thousand people, and there were also ten smaller halls. The National Government staged its own special exhibit on a ten-acre space, appropriating two million dollars for this purpose, and this exhibit included a representation of the building of the Panama Canal.

In all this imposing world-panorama of twentieth-century exhibits, Canada led the procession. Whatever the enthralling nature of spectacles offered by other nations, it was the Dominion that set the pace. Canada, an entrancing, garlanded figure, aglow with her abounding enthusiasms; her resistless energy; her dreams of a future that crystallise themselves in her all-conquering empire building—Canada the Spellbinder assumed her place as if by divine right, and certainly by common consent, as the very Winged Victory flying on into a golden future. The Canadian Building, whose classic beauty would have done no discredit to the Parthenon had it also occupied a place on the "Holy Hill" that overlooks all Attica; this structure, so simple yet so rich in architectural effect, her main portal guarded by great lions sculptured on either side, was one of the most impressive creations of the entire Exposition. With a singular comprehensiveness of grouping, the exhibits in this building represented the Dominion in her completeness. It was no one province that engaged the attention to the exclusion of another; it was the Dominion herself, in the unity of her vast empire, rather than any merely tributary feature of the country. In the inscrutable magic that wrought this effect lay the secret of its spellbinding quality. It was a power that enthralled every visitor who crossed the threshold, and brought him back to study it again.

How was this result achieved? The question was in the air. Every one asked it. No one could exactly answer it, but every one shared the wonder. The statistical data of the Dominion was impressive enough for almost any commensurate influence; yet mere facts and figures could give little clue to the mysterious effect on the throngs of visitors. One might read that the population of Canada had increased from five millions to seven millions in ten years; and that fifty-five per cent. of this population was engaged in conquering Nature, and transmuting her plains into golden harvests as a granary of the world; that her Government is expending ten millions a year in agricultural instruction alone; that her root and fodder crop each year is valued at almost two hundred millions of dollars, representing an area of nine million acres, and that the value of her field crops annually is five hundred and fifty millions of dollars. One might read that her live stock, valued at a given time at seven hundred millions, increased a hundred and fifty per cent. within one decade only. This visitor might recall the shrewd assertion of James J. Hill that "there is land enough in Canada, if thoroughly tilled, to feed every person in Europe"; and that, while at present only thirty-six million acres are under cultivation, there are four hundred and forty millions, thirty per cent. of her entire area, that are available for agricultural use. Yet not all these impressive statistics can alone account for the innate magic, the indescribable witchery, that Canada flings about all who come to look upon these marvellous panoramas in her building. Statistical data have their uses and inspire respect, while one cons them by heart and feels sure he is thereby equipped to give a reason for the faith that is in him; but in his heart he knows that all the figures in the realm of mathematics could not really account for his consciousness of the fascinations of the Dominion. A leading journal of San Francisco, advocating the desire that the Californian exhibit should be made a permanent one, proceeded to point the moral and adorn the tale by pointing to the Canadian exhibition. The editorial argument thus ran:

"Canada, with her complete exhibit, has won much praise from Exposition sightseers and has set the precedent for a permanent exhibit. One reason why our northern neighbour was able to make such a splendid impression at the Jewel City from the first was because, as its display was permanent, much of it had been installed in a European exhibition and had come directly here from across the Atlantic. The packing cases were ready to be opened and the best arrangement for the resources of Canada had been determined by experience.

"California needs to be an active participant in future expositions, as active as the Dominion of Canada.

* * * * * * * *

"With a permanent exhibit California will be ready at the first sound of an exposition reveille to rush to the front, full panoplied in luscious armour of golden butter, armed with 42-cm. cases of preserved fruits and with glittering shields of virgin gold.

"Then bring on your Canada!"

The skill with which the Canadian exhibit was grouped impressed itself first as a work of art, and only secondarily as a thing of commercial value. This skill in presentation was not the least element in its attractiveness. Here was Dawson, shooting out rays of violet, vermilion, and orange, myriads of lights in all the colours of the spectrum. A panoramic view of a wheat belt that would feed the world; Vancouver, with the great elevator at the water's edge; and with that, was Vancouver's prophetic dream of 1923, when three hundred millions of bushels of grain will be sent from Canada to Europe by the way of the Panama Canal; again there were the homes of farmers, attractive and realistic; an orchard scene introducing real fruit, and where realism ended and art began it was difficult to discover; the trees were laden with fruit; apples lay in heaps under the shade of the trees; young men and maidens were gathering the rosy and the golden fruit, tripping over the green turf so naturally that one half wondered if they as well as the apples were not actual? Here was a section out of British Columbia showing a sportsman's happy hunting-ground; there were snow-capped mountains, but with real water trickling down; an eagle, fierce, tempestuous, with widespread, flapping wings, is hovering in the air in a manner that would do credit to Heller, the wizard of necromancy on the stage. From yawning crevices bears emerge, until the visitor instinctively shrinks away, and the beaver is seen constructing his dam. Was it Governor Frontenac who recommended to the King of France that the beaver should be adopted as Canada's trade mark?

There are mounted duck, grouse, elk, buffalo, and sullen, scowling carabou gazing at the surging throng. There are buffalo from the Peace River region, a thousand miles north of the border between Canada and the States, where these hordes formerly ranged in countless droves, and which to-day is one of the finest of wheat-growing regions.

Nothing is more interesting to the curious visitor than are the views of typical Canadian homes. Some that are shown are but the growth of twelve years; from the time of the first turning of the plough in the prairie soil to completion of the two-storied, balconied house, with its broad piazza, set in the pretty grounds whose shady trees were planted as seedlings, with gay parterres of flowers in and around the curving walks and paths. The facilities for thus acquiring a home, by taking up the usual allotment of a hundred and sixty acres of land, which can be done on such favourable terms, turned the attention of many visitors toward the Dominion.

Another exhibit of great interest was that of power plant models, for every industrial centre in Canada has this abundance of power at very low rates, owing to the enormous supply of water power in the country. The canneries, too, form one of the most important industries, and their extent is well illustrated in the display made in the Canadian building.

There are cases upon cases of specimens of Canada's precious minerals: gold from British Columbia, silver ore from Cobalt, gold from the Yukon, and copper and various other minerals, with representative specimens of coal deposits. Other glass cases again display much of the flora of Canada, in a profusion of flowers whose rich and brilliant colouring attracts attention; and there are curious grasses and rare plants and foliage.

In one corridor are a group of life-like portraits in oil of King George and Queen Mary, of several of the Governors-General of the Dominion, and of many of the Government officials, Sir John A. Macdonald, Sir Wilfrid Laurier, and Premier Borden. In this connection it is rather interesting to recall that the appellation of the term Dominion to the country was due to a member of Parliament who, after Sir John Macdonald had arranged for the confederation of the nine provinces, and a name was being discussed, said that he had that morning read in his Bible the words: "His Dominion shall be from sea to sea," and the happy augury was seized and the term applied to the vast and splendid country.

Colonel William Hutchinson's hospitable offices were a favourite rendezvous for appreciative visitors. Here gathered Canadians and Canada-lovers to discuss the latest news from the Dominion. So largely, however, had Colonel Hutchinson's life been passed in the noted national and international expositions of the world that for fifteen years he has hardly been more than three months at a time in his home in Ottawa.

The Grand Trunk building offered, daily, a moving picture exhibition that attracted many onlookers, and so real were the effects that when in one a torrent of water came rushing over a cataract, the visitor near involuntarily turned for a seat farther back. In this building, as in the national one, the

Dominion was laid under tribute in representation that interpreted the essential life of Canada.

The superb collection of photographs of the scenic mountain route of the Grand Trunk Pacific was a perennial attraction to visitors in the exhibit made by this transcontinental railway. It revealed anew how the completion of the Grand Trunk System is an achievement which in its daring, its magnitude of interests, and the enterprise involved was one of the great twentieth-century events, and one only to be compared with the opening of the Panama-Pacific Canal itself.

LOOKING TOWARDS MOUNT MUNN FROM THE VALLEY OF FLOWERS

Looking towards Mount Munn from the Valley of Flowers

The Reverend Arthur Barry O'Neill, C.S.G., after visiting the Exposition, wrote that he considered the Canadian and the Grand Trunk buildings as instances of "artistic genius beyond all praise," and as a "lasting honour and credit to the Canadian Government." In a sonnet in which Mr. O'Neill celebrates the youth of Canada, the brave lads who have gone to the front, and who

"... have writ a score
Of valour true, surpassing old romance.
And lent new pride to each Canadian's glance,"

the poet adds:

"And here, as well, where contests fair of Peace,
The nations wage along the Golden Gate,

Huge throngs acclaim the Maple Leaf, nor cease
The chorused praise that makes our hearts elate."

It is not the aim in this chapter to describe the whole of this interesting and beautiful Exposition, but only the contribution made by Canada; yet one can hardly refrain from noting the charm of the Alaskan exhibit with its panoramic presentation of the Muir glacier; nor that of the Santa Fe Railway in the "Zone," where the very realistic and wonderful portrayal of the Grand Canyon in Arizona was one of the great attractions of the entire grounds.

The Palace of Transportation was one of the extremely interesting features of the Exposition. Here could be studied the latest scientific methods of the day in many details not familiar to the general public, as, for instance, the method of handling mails on fast trains and the delivery at stations while the full speed of the train is maintained; many types of marine transportation; and still more of aircraft, the navigation of the air being one of the things constantly demonstrated to throngs of people who were absorbingly interested in the possibilities of aerial flight.

The experimental panorama of the Panama Canal itself was an appropriate feature. At the Exposition in Paris in 1900 the journey on the Trans-Siberian Railway was produced with extraordinary realism. The traveller entered a luxurious train, a very real train comprising drawing-room and dining cars, as well as a library car, and the passing of the long panorama of the entire scenery of that noted route gave a very vivid idea of what one would see in the actual journey. The California Exposition arranged a similar exhibit of a journey through the Panama Canal. The voyager was invited to the deck of a steamer, and ingenious illusions illustrated the sailing from ocean to ocean.

San Francisco was a gala city through the entire summer. Not the least of the enjoyments were the sails in the splendid local boats, with glass-enclosed decks, across the Bay to Oakland and to Berkeley, the latter city the seat of the University of California. There were excursions for every day in the week for those who wished to vary the scene, and the Exposition itself constantly presented new attractions and new features with the great number of congresses, the numerous lectures, and perpetual fêtes.

The close of the Panama-Pacific Exposition was a scene worthy to live in historic pageantry. The day was one of June dropped into the heart of December. The sun was burning against a cloudless sapphire sky. Within the very radiance of the Tower of Jewels, on one of the terraces of the Court of the Universe, was erected a stand on which were assembled the Directors, the Commissioners of Foreign Governments, the representatives of the Army and Navy of California, and the representatives of the City of San

Francisco. From the arches of the Rising and the Setting Sun the sculptured figures looked down. There was orchestral music, and the reading of Mr. Sterling's poem from which lines have been quoted in preceding pages. The message of Woodrow Wilson, President of the United States, was flashed around the world at the moment it was given to the Exposition. President Wilson well expressed the significance of the undertaking as one "eloquent of the new spirit which is to unite East and West and make all the world partners in the common enterprises of progress and humanity."

The guards marched away; the sailors fired a salute; the Exposition banner descended. President Moore's pictorial words have immortalised the scene:

"Night came on, and the world's wonder of lights; the Exposition lights that would never shine again—a red glow on Kelham's towers, rose flame in the porches of the Machinery Palace, dim reflections in the Lagoon of the Palace of Fine Arts and the broad basin in the Court of the Four Seasons, the splendour of the giant monstrances in the Court of Abundance, the silver phosphorescence of the Adventurous Bowman on his column and the Lord of the Isthmian Way on his rack-o'-bones horse, the tremulous frosty shimmer of the hundred thousand jewels of the great spire; and over all, the long bands, like lambent metal, of bronze and crimson and green and blue, from the forty-eight searchlights on the Yacht Harbour Mole, bands that barred the heavens so far that they deceived the eye and in the south-east appeared to converge beyond the hills of the city.

"Not abruptly, but slowly and gently, the lamps grew dark, the beams of the searchlights faded, and arches and courts and colonnades and towers and sculptured forms of men and women and angels and great beasts receded into the friendly night, lighted now by the glimmer of the winter stars, Orion and Sirius, Aldebaran and the Hyades. And through the starlight 'Taps' dropped in liquid notes from bugles high on the Tower of Jewels."

Bulkley Gate (150 feet high), Bulkley River

CHAPTER XII

CANADIAN POETS AND POETRY

"My guide is but the stir to song."

"But Love must kiss that mortal's eyes
　Who hopes to see fair Arcady;
No gold can buy you entrance there,—
No wisdom won with weariness."

"'Tis strange you cannot sing,' quoth he,
'The folk all sing in Arcady.'"

Arcady, or Canada, are they one and the same? The pipes of Pan echo throughout the entire Dominion. The Poet—

"Born and nourished in miracles,"

writes his scroll by every shining lake, in the deep, dim interior of the forest, on every majestic mountain height. He renders constant service to the inward law, and it is the poet who is the real historian of his country. It is he who immortalises her heroic deeds; who paints her landscapes in unfading colours; who crystallises her greatness into song. One line of the poet's may outweigh a volume of descriptive prose.

"His instant thought a Poet spoke
　And filled the age his fame."

It would be a marvel if the Canadian colour and atmosphere did not produce a choir of singers, if not, indeed, a nation of poets. Nor can national poetic feeling be measurably restricted to the comparatively few greater poets in any land or literature; to the supreme masters in the lyric art. The greatness of Wordsworth, Landor, Shelley, Keats, Coleridge, of the Brownings, Tennyson, and of Swinburne, does not detract from, even though it overshadows, the charm of a score of the lesser poets, each of whom has his individual place. Had the lives of Browning and Tennyson been of the comparatively brief duration of Stephen Phillips, how much of their noblest work would have been unwritten? Had not Wilfrid and Alice Meynell, with angelic goodness, rescued Francis Thompson from destitution, what might not the world of poetic literature have missed? It is not alone by the standard of Dante, Shakespeare, Goethe, or Petrarca that the art of poetry should be estimated. To no inconsiderable degree the number as well as the quality of the poets of a nation are typical of the national inspiration.

The fact that Canada, as a country that looks back to hardly more than a century and a half of organised life and whose literary expression has been almost entirely within the past half century, should have produced a body of poetry that has just claims to being considered national literature is as impressive as it is interesting.

"Has Canada a voice of her own in literature distinct from that of England?" questions Thomas Guthrie Marquis. "In Poetry, at least," he adds, "the Canadian note is clear and distinct, and of permanent value." There was little Canadian verse produced until well within the nineteenth century; and the first poem of real claim to distinction was the "Saul" of Charles Heavysege, published in 1857, a poem written "in the grand manner," the author presenting his ideas "with a dignity, austerity, and epic grandeur that are found in few poetic compositions." It was, however, with the decade of 1880-90 that the era of the modern and artistic poetic literature of Canada really opened, its keynote sounded by a poet, then hardly twenty years of age—Charles George Douglas Roberts—whose name has come to be widely known as that of one whose lips have been touched with the divine fire. His initial volume, *Orion and Other Poems*, revealed something in the quality that established his right to poetic rank. His very crudities, faults of construction inevitable to youthful ardour and inexperience, were still more suggestive of promise than higher technical excellence that might be recognised among contemporary verse. The classical tendency and temperamental assimilation were very obvious; the young man was evidently a devotee of Shelley and Tennyson; but he might easily have had worse masters. Six years later came his second volume of verse, *In Divers Tones*, that at once laid special claim on lovers of poetry; and when, in 1893, his *Songs of the Common Day* appeared, with its exquisite *Ave*, commemorating the centenary of Shelley, many people felt that a new star had arisen to shine with permanent splendour in the poetic firmament. There are lines and stanzas in the *Ave* that are worthy to hold their immortality so long as the art of poetry lives to bless and ennoble and inspire life. Shelley—

"the breathless child of change,
Urged ever by the soul's divine unrest."

And again:

"But all about the tumult of his heart
Stretched the great calm of his celestial art."

And this stanza:

"Thyself the lark melodious in mid-heaven;
    Thyself the Protean shape of chainless cloud.
Pregnant with elemental fire, and driven

>   Through deeps of quivering light, and darkness loud
> With tempest, yet beneficent as prayer. "

And the breathing line:

"And speechless ecstasy of growing June,"

condensing in itself all the rapture of summer hours; or the beautiful stanza:

> "O heart of fire, that fire might not consume!
>   Forever glad the world because of thee;
> Because of thee forever eyes illume
>   A more enchanted earth, a lovelier sea!
> O poignant voice of the desire of life,
>   Piercing our lethargy, because thy call
> Aroused our spirits to a nobler strife
>   Where base and sordid fall,
> Forever past the conflict and the pain
> More clearly beams the goal we shall attain!"

Perhaps the most perfect lyric of Charles G. D. Roberts, and one that, while in no sense an imitation, yet suggests the *Break, Break, Break* of Tennyson, is that entitled *Grey Rocks and Greyer Sea*:

> "Grey rocks, and greyer sea,
>   And surf along the shore—
> And in my heart a name
>   My lips shall speak no more.
>
> "The high and lonely hills
>   Endure the darkening year—
> And in my heart endure
>   A memory and a tear.
>
> "Across the tide a sail
>   That tosses, and is gone—
> And in my heart the kiss
>   That longing dreams upon.
>
> "Grey rocks, and greyer sea,
>   And surf along the shore—
> And in my heart the face
>   That I shall see no more."

One of the stirring poems is that of *An Ode for the Canadian Confederacy*, in which occur the lines:

"Awake, my country, the hour of dreams is done!
   Doubt not, nor dread the greatness of thy fate."

The lyre of Charles G. D. Roberts is one of many strings, and the temptation is rather irresistible to quote from him at still greater length.

Within the opening years of the decade of 1860-70 were born Charles G. D. Roberts, William Wilfred Campbell, Archibald Lampman, Bliss Carman, George Frederick Scott (now Canon Scott), and another who, though bearing the same name, is only related to the Reverend Canon by the ties of poetic brotherhood, Duncan Campbell Scott. William Henry Drummond (known especially as "The Poet of the Habitant") and Isabella Valancy Crawford belonged to the preceding decade, and although ranked as Canadian poets, were born in Ireland, coming to the Dominion at an early age.

William Wilfred Campbell is the poet both of Nature and of human interests. No adequate view of an art so many-veined and so fine as his can be presented within the limited space of these pages, but from his noble poem on *England* this stanza is taken:

"And if ever the smoke of an alien gun
   Should threaten her iron repose,
Shoulder to shoulder against the world.
   Face to face with her foes,
Scot and Celt and Saxon are one
   Where the Glory of England goes."

And this from *The Hills and the Sea*:

"Give me the uplands of purple,
   The sweep of the vast world's rim,
Where the sun dips down, or the dawnings
   Over the earth's edge swim,
With the days that are dead and the old earth-tales,
   Human, and haunting, and grim."

A discerning critic says of Mr. Campbell that his poems are "something akin to the whisper of silence, the magic of moonlight, the sadness of art." Yet perhaps more than all one finds the tender human strain, as in *The Last Prayer*, of which these stanzas are representative:

"Master of life, the day is done;
   My sun of life is sinking low;
I watch the hours slip one by one
   And hark the night-wind and the snow.

* * * * * *

"And must thou banish all the hope,
   The large horizon's eagle-swim,
The splendour of the far-off slope
   That ran about the world's great rim,

"That rose with morning's crimson rays
   And grew to noonday's gloried dome,
Melting to even's purple haze
   When all the hopes of earth went home?

* * * * * *

"Yea, thou mayst quench the latest spark
   Of life's weird day's expectancy,
Roll down the thunders of the dark
   And close the light of life for me.

"Melt all the splendid blue above
   And let these magic wonders die,
If thou wilt only leave me, Love,
   And Love's heart-brother, Memory."

His *Canadian Folk Song* has become a popular favourite. The last stanza runs:

"The firelight dances upon the wall,
Footsteps are heard in the outer hall,
And a kiss and a welcome that fill the room,
And the kettle sings in the glimmer and gloom—
Margery, Margery, make the tea,
Singeth the kettle merrily."

It is in the setting of Canada's wonderland to music that much of the best work of Mr. Campbell lies; in his *Manitou, The Legend of Restless River, Dawn in the Island Camp*, and the musical *Vapour and Blue*. He has made himself the interpreter of Nature in all her moods, as has also Archibald Lampman, of whom William Dean Howells said that his pure spirit was electrical in every line; and that "the stir of wing, of leaf, of foot; the drifting odours of wood and field," thrilled his readers in his verse.

Canoeing on the Fraser River

In his *Passing of Autumn* Mr. Lampman gives this delicate picture:

"The wizard has woven his ancient scheme—
   A day and a star-lit night;
And the world is a shadowy-pencilled dream
   Of colour, and haze, and light."

And who would not turn to his *April in the Hills* to greet the springtime?

"I break the spirit's cloudy bands,
A wanderer in enchanted lands,
I feel the sun upon my hands;
   And far from care and strife
The broad earth bids me forth. I rise
With lifted brow and upward eyes.
I bathe my spirit in blue skies,
   And taste the springs of life.

"I feel the tumult of new birth;
I waken with the wakening earth;
I match the bluebird in her mirth;
   And wild with wind and sun,
A treasurer of immortal days,
I roam the glorious world with praise,

The hillsides and the woodland ways,
    Till earth and I are one."

Mr. Lampman was a master of the sonnet and one of these entitled *Outlook* touches a high note, while another, *The Railway Station*, so interprets the poetic side of common experiences as to be rather distinctive among all his work and so claims reproduction here:

"The darkness brings no quiet here, the light
    No waking; ever on my blinded brain
    The flare of lights, the rush, the cry, and strain,
The engines' scream, the hiss and thunder smite:
I see the hurrying crowds, the clasp, the flight.
    Faces that touch, eyes that are dim with pain:
    I see the hoarse wheels turn, and the great train
Move labouring out into the bourneless night.
So many souls within its deep recesses,
    So many bright, so many mournful eyes:
Mine eyes that watch grow fixed with dreams and guesses;
    What threads of life, what hidden histories,
What sweet or passionate dreams and dark distresses,
    What unknown thoughts, what various agonies!"

Bliss Carman has long been recognised by the critical lover of poetic art as a poet of unusual distinction and grace. When, in the days of his early youth, his poem *Low Tide on Grand-Pré* appeared in the *Atlantic Monthly*, all connoisseurs in poet-lore felt the magical touch. Over all the barren reaches on which the sun had gone down the poet saw the "unelusive glories":

"Was it a year or lives ago
    We took the grasses in our hands.
And caught the summer flying low
    Over the waving meadow lands,
    And held it there between our hands?

* * * * * *

"And that we took into our hands—
    Spirit of life, or subtler thing—
Breathed on us there, and loosed the bands
    Of death, and taught us, whispering,
    The secret of some wonder thing."

That the poem is faintly, vaguely reminiscent of Swinburne's *Félise* is only an added charm. Like a refrain of music lingers the last stanza:

"The night has fallen, and the tide ...
   Now and again comes drifting home,
Across these aching barrens wide,
   A sigh like driven wind or foam:
   In grief the flood is bursting home!"

Mr. Carman has kept faith with the poetic dreams of his youth. Could there be found in the songs of any land a lyric more subtle, more delicately exquisite in expression, than this which he calls *The Unreturning*?

"The old, eternal spring once more
   Comes back the sad, eternal way;
With tender, rosy light, before
   The going out of day.

"The great white moon across my door
   A shadow in the twilight stirs;
But now, forever, comes no more
   That wondrous look of Hers!"

Master of many and varied orders of song, Mr. Carman has the rare art of the ballad; and his blank verse, as his lyrical, is enticing. A series of the daintiest lyrics, *Songs of the Sea Children*, call up a very fairyland in which to wander. One of these (the lyrics form a sequence) thus portrays the mysteries of spring:

"In the blue mystery of the April woods,
      Thy spirit now
Makes musical the rainbow's interludes,
      And pink the peach-tree bough.

"In the new birth of all things bright and fair,
      'Tis only thou
Art very April, glory, light, and air,
      And joy and ardour now."

Bliss Carman is a word-painter as well as a poet in his lyrical work. With what fairy-like magic he pictures the landscape, the colouring, the very breath of the summer wind, the rustle of leaves, and the swaying of the flower on its stem.

From a multitude of examples, here is one poem, entitled *The Dance of the Sunbeam*:

"When morning is high o'er the hilltops.
   On river and stream and lake.
Whenever a young breeze whispers,
   The sun-clad dancers wake.

"One after one upspringing,
   They flash from their dim retreat,
Merry as running laughter
   Is the news of their twinkling feet.

"Over the floors of azure
   Whenever the wind flaws run,
Sparkling, leaping, and racing,
   Their antics scatter the sun.

"As long as water ripples
   And weather is clear and glad,
Day after day they are dancing,
   Never a moment sad.

"But when through the field of heaven,
   The wings of storm take flight,
At a touch of the flying shadows
   They falter and slip from sight.

"Until, at the grey day's ending,
   As the squadrons of cloud retire,
They pass in the triumph of sunset
   With banners of crimson fire."

Mr. Carman is pre-eminently the poet of nature, as how else could he be when, in *The Breath of the Reed*, he makes this appeal?

"Make me thy priest, O mother.
   And prophet of thy mood,
With all the forest wonder
   Enraptured and imbued";

or when he thus expresses himself in *The Great Return*?

"When I have lifted up my heart to thee,
   Then hast thou ever hearkened and drawn near,
And bowed thy shining face close over me,
   Till I could hear thee as the hill-flowers hear.

"When I have cried to thee in lonely need,
   Being but a child of thine bereft and wrung,
Then all the rivers in the hills gave heed
   And the great hill winds in thy holy tongue—

"That ancient incommunicable speech
   The April stars and Autumn sunsets know—
Soothed me and calmed me with solace beyond reach
   Of human ken, mysterious and low."

Mr. Carman is, however, more than a writer of exquisite lyrics, more even than a painter and hymner of nature in its various aspects and moods. He is more deeply concerned with the mystery which we call life than with anything else, and again and again seeks to understand and express his sense of that mystery. His *Behind the Arras*—described by a recent writer as the most distinctive book of poems issued in English in the past quarter of a century—is a record of such attempts. We quote here the opening verse of *The Players*:

"We are the players of a play
   As old as earth,
Between the wings of night and day,
   With tears and mirth."

And here the first verse of *In the Wings*:

"The play is life; and this round earth
   The narrow stage whereon
We act before an audience
   Of actors dead and gone."

And here are some lines from *Beyond the Gamut*, which for philosophic insight are surely hard to equal in modern poetry:

"As all sight is but a finer hearing,
   And all colour but a finer sound,
Beauty, but the reach of lyric freedom,
   Caught and quivering past all music's bound;

"Life, that faint sigh whispered from oblivion,
   Harks and wonders if we may not be

Five small wits to carry one great rhythmus,
    The vast theme of God's new symphony.

"As fine sand spread on a disc of silver,
    At some chord which bids the notes combine,
Heeding the hidden and reverberant impulse,
    Shifts and dances into curve and line,

"The round earth, too, haply, like a dust-mote,
    Was set whirling her assigned sure way,
Round this little orb of her ecliptic
    To some harmony she must obey."

The temptation to go on quoting from Mr. Carman's work (which is more varied and touches more chords than most persons—even among those who endeavour to keep in touch with the poetry produced in our day—are aware) has to be resisted, but space must be found for a portion of a recent poem, *A Mountain Gateway*, in which, in beauty and clarity of thought and expression, the poet reaches perhaps his highest point:

"I know a vale where I would go one day,
When June comes back and all the world once more
Is glad with summer. Deep with shade it lies,
A mighty cleft in the green bosoming hills,
A cool dim gateway to the mountains' heart.

"On either side the wooded slopes come down,
Hemlock and beech and chestnut. Here and there
Through the deep forest laurel spreads and gleams,
Pink-white as Daphne in her loveliness—
That still perfection from the world withdrawn,
As if the wood gods had arrested there
Immortal beauty in her breathless flight.

* * * * * *

"And where the road runs in the valley's foot,
Through the dark woods a mountain stream comes down,
Singing and dancing all its youth away
Among the boulders and the shallow runs,
Where sunbeams pierce and mossy tree trunks hang
Drenched all day long with murmuring sound and spray.

"There, light of heart and foot-free, I would go
Up to my home among the lasting hills,

* * * * * *

And in my cabin doorway sit me down.
Companioned in that leafy solitude
By the wood ghosts of twilight and of peace,
While evening passes to absolve the day
And leave the tranquil mountains to the stars.

"And in that sweet seclusion I should hear,
Among the cool-leafed beeches in the dusk,
The calm-voiced thrushes at their evening hymn,
So undistraught, so rapturous, so pure,
It well might be, in wisdom and in joy,
The seraphs singing at the birth of time
The unworn ritual of eternal things."

In the Reverend George Frederic Scott, D.C.L., F.R.S.C., Canon of the Cathedral in Quebec since 1894, Canada has a poet of high poetic seriousness of especial distinction, and with just claims to more than a national recognition. A long poem entitled *Evolution*, written by Canon Scott in 1887, stands as something unique in English-speaking poetry, in its presenting a great scientific truth with poetic expression. Of this some stanzas follow:

"Life out of death, death out of life,
   In endless cycles rolling on,
And fire-gleams flashing from the strife
   Of what will come and what has gone.

* * * * *

"But what art thou and what am I?
   What place is ours in all this scheme?
What is it to be born and die?
   Are we but phases in a dream?

* * * * *

"And we are present, future, past—
   Shall live again, have lived before.
Like billows on the beaches cast
   Of tides that flow for evermore.

* * * * *

"That may be so; but to mine eyes
   A being of wondrous make thou art—

The point at which infinities
    Converge, touch, and forever part.

"Thou canst not unmake what has been,
    Nor hold back that which is to come;
We dwell upon the waste between
    In the small 'now' which is our home.

* * * * *

"But in the ages thou shalt be
    A link from unknown to unknown,
A bridge across a darkling sea,
    A light on the world's pathway thrown.

* * * * *

"And we must pass—we shall not die;
    Changed and transformed, but still the same.
To grander heights of mystery,
    To fairer realms than whence we came.

"God will not let His work be lost;
    Too wondrous is the mind of man,
Too many ages has it cost
    The huge fulfilment of His plan.

"But on we pass, for ever on,
    Through death to other deaths and life;
To brighter lights when these are gone,
    To broader thought, more glorious strife,

"To vistas opening out of these;
    To wonders shining from afar.
Above the surging of the seas,
    Above the course of moon and star;

"To higher powers of will and deed,
    All bounds, all limits left behind;
To truths undreamt in any creed;
    To deeper love, more God-like mind.

* * * * *

"Great God! we move into the vast;
    All questions vain—the shadows come!

We hear no answer from the past;
    The years before us all are dumb.

"We trust Thy purpose and Thy will;
    We see afar the shining goal;
Forgive us, if there linger still
    Some human fear within the soul!

* * * * *

"But lo! the dawn of fuller days;
    Horizon-glories fringe the sky!
Our feet would climb the shining ways
    To meet man's widest destiny.

"Come, then, all sorrow's recompense!
    The kindling sky is flaked with gold;
Above the shattered screen of sense,
    A voice like thunder cries, 'Behold!'"

In Canon Scott's *Requiescat*, in memory of General Gordon, is one of the thrilling lyrics of memorial verse:

"O thou twice hero,—hero in thy life
    And in thy death!—we have no power to crown
Thy nobleness; we weep thine arm in strife;
    We weep, but glory in thy life laid down.

* * * * * *

"Saint! hero! through the clouds of doubt that loom
O'er darkling skies, thy life hath power to bless;
We thank thee thou hast shown us in the gloom
Once more Christ's power and childlike manliness."

A quatrain on Darwin's tomb in Westminster Abbey is worthy to be held in memory:

"The Muse, when asked what words alone
    Were worthy tribute to his fame,
Took up her pen, and on the stone
    Inscribed his name."

Full of tender and beautiful feeling is this little lyric of Canon Scott's that he entitles *Beyond*:

"My heart it lies beyond, dear,
   In the land of the setting day,
Where the whispers are soft and fond, dear,
   Of the voices that pass away;
And oft, when the night is falling,
   And a calm is on the sea,
I fancy I hear them calling
   From that far-off land for me.

"It is only idle dreaming
   But the dream is full of rest.
And up where that glory is streaming
   From the gates of the golden west,
I wander away in spirit,
   With a mingled joy and pain,
Till I almost seem to inherit
   The sweet dead past again.

* * * * *

"Yes, my heart it lies beyond, dear,
   Where that sun is burning low,
And were you not so fond, dear,
   I might perhaps—but no!
Are you weary already with walking?
   And tears! What tears, dear, too!
How selfish of me to be talking,
   My darling, in this way to you!"

One of the most widely known and frequently quoted of the poems of Canon Scott is the *Van Elsen*:

"God spake three times and saved Van Elsen's soul:
He spake by illness first, and made him whole;
      Van Elsen heard Him not,
        Or soon forgot.

"God spake to him by wealth; the world outpoured
Its treasures at his feet, and called him lord;
      Van Elsen's heart grew fat
        And proud thereat.

"God spake the third time when the great world smiled,
And in the sunshine slew his little child;
  Van Elsen like a tree
  Fell hopelessly.

"Then in the darkness came a Voice which said:
'As thy heart bleedeth, so My heart hath bled;
  As I have need of thee
  Thou needest Me.'

"That night Van Elsen kissed the baby feet,
And kneeling by the narrow winding-sheet,
  Praised Him with fervent breath
  Who conquered death."

Canon Scott, who may well be recognised as the most spiritual of Canadian poets, has published five volumes of poems, *The Soul's Quest*, *My Lattice and Other Poems*, *The Unnamed Lake*, *Poems Old and New*, and *In the Battle Silences, Poems Written at the Front*. There is a depth of thought, an appealing grace and tenderness of feeling in his work that insures his poems a treasured place in Canadian life.

Duncan Campbell Scott has the fascination of the spontaneous singer, and how all the entrancement of the Dominion is caught into these lines:

"Oh, Land of the dusky balsam,
 And the darling maple-tree,
Where the cedar buds and berries,
 And the pine grows strong and free!
My heart is weary and weary
 For my own country."

Something in this song recalls, like remembered music, Katherine Tynan's (Mrs. Hinkson) haunting poem, *Homesick*, of which two lines run:

"But my heart flies back to an Abbey gray
Where the dead sleep sweet, and the living pray."

The professional critic could find many poems of Mr. Scott's with intrinsically greater claim than this lovely little chanson, *To B. W. B.* (now Mrs. Duncan Campbell Scott), but something in the lilting cadence enchains the reader:

"The world is spinning for change
    And life has rapid wings;
Oh, one needs a steady heart
    Not to falter while he sings.

"But this is made for my Dear One
    When we are far apart,
That she may have, wherever she goes
    A song of mine in her heart.

"A song that will serve as an anchor,
    Compass, and pilot, and chart,
A song that will bid her remember
    That Love is the crown of Art.

* * * * *

"With a star from her open window
    When the cuckoo wakes with a start:
Oh, can she ever forget me
    With a song of mine in her heart?"

In *The Voice and the Dusk* what a play of colour:

"The slender moon and one pale star,
    A rose leaf and a silver bee
From some god's garden blown afar,
    Go down the gold deep tranquilly.

"Within the south there rolls and grows
    A mighty town with tower and spire,
From a cloud bastion masked with rose
    The lightning flashes diamond fire."

A poet's *nom de plume* is that of "Katherine Hale," so well known in private life as Mrs. John W. Garvin, who to her own charm as a poet must add still another as the wife of a poet and a critic of distinction as well. The gods endowed "Katherine Hale" with a resplendent lyre, and her poems have flown to many lands. Perhaps no poem of the war has more closely touched the universal heart than has "Katherine Hale's" poem, so intense in its restrained power, entitled *Grey Knitting*, so widely known that from it only these three stanzas will be given:

"All through the country, in the autumn stillness,
   A web of grey spreads strangely, rim to rim;
And you may hear the sound of knitting needles.
   Incessant, gentle—dim.

"A tiny click of little wooden needles,
   Elfin amid the gianthood of war;
Whispers of women, tireless and patient,
Who weave the web afar.

* * * * * *

"I like to think that soldiers, gayly dying
   For the white Christ on fields with shame sown deep,
May hear the fairy click of women's needles
   As they fall fast asleep."

What a spell of potent witchery she weaves in her song *I used to Wear a Gown of Green*:

"I used to wear a gown of green
   And sing a song to May,
When apple blossoms starred the stream
   And Spring came up the way.

"I used to run along with Love
   By lanes the world forgets,
To find in an enchanted wood
   The first frail violets.

"And ever 'mid the fairy blooms
   And murmur of the stream,
We used to hear the pipes of Pan
   Call softly through our dream.

"But now, in outcry vast, that tune
   Fades like some little star
Lost in an anguished judgment day
   And scarlet flames of war.

"What can it mean that Spring returns
   And purple violets bloom,
Save that some gypsy flower may stray
   Beside his nameless tomb!

"To pagan Earth her gown of green,
   Her elfin song to May—
*With all my soul I must go on
   Into the scarlet day.*"

The poets have been the celebrants of many of the historic epochs of Canada and the recorders of her great names; and in this especial line John Daniel Logan has rendered an interesting service in his *Songs of the Makers of Canada*. In these Dr. Logan has celebrated Cartier as the "dauntless discoverer," Champlain as the "first Canadian," Laval as "the high-priest of knowledge," Wolfe as the "illustrious victor," Brock the "valiant leader," Drummond the "indomitable soldier," Ryerson the "renowned educator," Howe the "champion of self-government," Macdonald the "great confederationist," Laurier the "prophetic imperialist." Such a collection, in its vigour and vividness of personal characterisation, is the very intellectual panorama of Canada. Of Macdonald, the "great confederationist," the First Premier of the Dominion (1867), we find Dr. Logan saying:

"Macdonald, though thy soul hath passed away
From wonted wolds in our Canadian land,
Where thou wast chiefest of the fervid band
   That sought to give the people fullest sway
      O'er their own destiny, thy spirit goes
         Triumphant in this Canada of ours
         Resplendent now before the elder Pow'rs
      Who mark how virile our young nation grows!

"Thy wisdom was the vision of a seer
Who knew the meaning of the pregnant days
Which gen'rous Time should father into ways
   For unity...."

In the memorial lyric to William Henry Drummond, whom Dr. Logan enshrines as "Sovereign of Joy and Prince of Tears," the poet touches perhaps his most musical note in the lines:

"O Lost Canadian Singer of the winsome lays,
How farest thou along the Elysium ways,—
   Art thou companionless as we
         And sorrowing?

* * * * * *

"O gentle heart, we wonder if thou farest happily
   With Homer and the Attic strain,
   With Milton and the Tragic train."

Among the younger Canadian poets are two sisters, Annie Campbell Huestis and Ethel Huestis Butler, who have each won distinction. One little lyric of Mrs. Butler's, *On Life's Highway*, is singularly poetic in its motive, contrasting the experiences of walking as companioned with Grief, or with Joy, and is expressed with much tenderness of feeling. The work of Miss Huestis suggests that she makes her pilgrimages to the "holy hill," and brings away with her all the fragrance of the thyme. A poem of hers entitled *Aldaran, the Singer*, has somewhat of that sustained sweetness and music that so signally characterised Mrs. Browning's *Catarina to Camoens*. From Miss Huestis's *Aldaran* are these extracts:

"Aldaran, who loved to sing,
     Here lieth dead.
All the glory of the spring,
All its birds and blossoming,
     Near his still bed
Cannot waken him again.
Cannot lure to hill and plain,
     Aldaran, the Singer,
       Who is dead.

"Aldaran, who loved to sing,
     Here lieth low;
Not again his heart shall spring
At the time of blossoming,
     Ah, who can know?
Still at dusk or break of day,
 Some can hear him on his way,
     Aldaran, the vanished one,
     Walking, hidden, in the sun;
Moving, mist-like, by the streams
When the early twilight dreams;
     Speeding on his quiet way,
     Never seen by night or day,

"But in pity drawing near
To the help of those who fear.
     To the beds of those who die,
     Singing low their lullaby,
Singing still, when they are far

Where the mist and silence are,
    Singing softly still that they
    May not fear the hidden way.
So, to those whose day is sped,
In the hour lone and dread,
    Cometh Aldaran, the Singer,
        Who is dead!"

For her *Magdalen*, whose beauty of phrasing attracted attention when published in a leading critical review of New York, and in which there is a haunting reminiscence of Christina Rossetti, room must here be made, as it represents Miss Huestis in what is perhaps her most artistic mood:

"'Where are you going, weary feet.
    Feet that have failed in storm and flood?'
'I go to find a flower sweet
    I left, fresh growing, near a wood.
The winds blow pure from many a hill,
    And hush to tender stillness there.
Shall not this restless heart be still,
    And grow more innocent and fair?'
'Not so; for sin and bitter pain
Can never find Youth's flower again!'

"'Where are you going, wistful face,
    Face with the mark of shame and tears?'
 'I go to find a quiet place
    Where no one sees and no one hears.
The beauty and the silence there
    Shall thrill me through and still my pain.
Shall touch my hardness into prayer,
    And give me back my dreams again.'
'Not so; for Sin has closed the door
On Youth's fair dreams forevermore.'"

"'Where are you going, heart of woe.
    Pitiful heart of fear and shame?'
'A strange and lonely way I go,
    Where none shall pity, none shall blame.
Far with my sin and misery
    I creep on doubtful feet, alone;
No human heart can follow me
    To mark my tears or hear my moan.'

'*Nay; but the never-ceasing sting,*
The clearness of remembering!'

"'What do you see, O changing face,
   Alight with strange and tender gleams?'
'I near the hushed and holy place
   Of One who gives me back my dreams.'
'Where are you daring, eager feet,
   Feet that so wild a way have trod?'
'O bitter world, no scorn I meet.
   Sinful and hurt, I go to God!
On my dark sin, forevermore,
A sinless Hand has closed the door.'"

Miss Huestis dons her singing-robes too infrequently; but who may venture on any prediction regarding the poetic production of one who is still on the threshold of achievement? For the poet, himself, least of all, may foresee his own future, nor is it given to those who love his songs to discern his future in the magic glass. The poet is ever a subject in a kingdom of untraced laws and unmapped territory.

"For voices pursue him by day
   And haunt him by night;
And he listens, and needs must obey
   When the Angel says 'Write!'"

Forever does he await the Voice and the Vision.

Louis Frechette is the French-Canadian Laureate, who was crowned by the French Academy, in 1881, for the striking merit of his tragedy, *Papineau*. Doctor Frechette (born in 1841) has contributed greatly to the fame of his country. In his *La Decouverte du Mississippi*, and in *Le Drapeau Anglais, Saint-Malo*, and others, is his real distinction felt. His poems are so long and so closely woven as hardly to lend themselves to extracts.

Thomas O'Hagan is one of the favourite poets of the Dominion, and aside from his own notable contribution to poetry, he has done and is doing a wonderful work in his scholarly and critical lectures on poets. His published lectures interpretative of Shakespeare, of Dante, and of Browning, Tennyson, Longfellow, and others, are in constant demand. In *A Gate of Flowers, An Idyll of the Farm, The Bugle Call*, and the timely production *I Take Off my Hat to Albert*, are poems that inspire the popular favour; and in a lyric entitled *Ripened Fruit* these stanzas are especially calculated to awaken response:

"I know not what my heart hath lost;
   I cannot strike the chords of old:
The breath that charmed my morning life
    Hath chilled each leaf within the wold.

"The swallows twitter in the sky,
   But bare the nest within the eaves;
The fledglings of my care are gone,
    And left me but the rustling leaves.

"And yet, I know my life hath strength,
   And firmer hope and sweeter prayer,
For leaves that murmur on the ground
    Have now for me a double care.

"The glory of the summer sky
   May change to tints of autumn hue;
But faith that sheds its amber light
    Will lend our heaven a tender blue.

"O altar of eternal youth!
   O faith that beckons from afar.
Give to our lives a blossomed fruit—
    Give to our morns an evening star!"

Very distinctive is the work of Doctor William Henry Drummond, the poet of the "habitant" life. *De Nice Leetle Canadienne* and *Leetle Bateese* have become household songs. In the former one stanza runs:

"O she's quick, an' she's smart, an' got plaintee heart,
   If you know correc' way go about;
An' if you don' know, she soon tole you so.
   Den tak' de firs' chance an' get out;
But if she love you, I spik it for true,
   She will mak' it more beautiful den,
An' sun on de sky can't shine lak' de eye
   Of dat nice leetle Canadienne."

Leetle Bateese is a favourite with reciters who master the dialect, and who frequently delight their audiences by the mingled humour and tenderness of the picture:

"Too sleepy for sayin' de prayer to-night?
Never min', I s'pose it'll be all right;
Say dem to-morrow—ah! dere he go!
Fas' asleep in a minute or so—
An' he'll stay lak dat till de rooster crow,
    Leetle Bateese!

* * * * * *

"But, leetle Bateese! please don' forget
We rader you're stayin' de small boy yet,
So chase de chicken an' mak' dem scare,
An' do w'at you lak wit' your old gran'pere
For we'n you're beeg feller he won't be dere—
    Leetle Bateese!"

John W. Garvin, who has manifested his devotion to the muses by compiling a notable anthology of Canadian poets (recently published), is also a poet of recognition, and one of his productions, entitled *Majesty*, is especially original in conception. Mr. Garvin's devotion to the poetic literature of his country has rendered great service in the way of making the poets known to the general reading public and bringing together, within convenient limits, much that is best in poetic art.

The names come to mind of Alfred Gordon, a young and gifted English poet now a resident of Montreal; of Ethelyn Wetherald, Robert Norwood, E. Pauline Johnson, the daughter of Chief Johnson of the Mohawks; of Virna Sheard, Alma Frances McCollum, Albert D. Watson, William McLennan, and William Douw Lighthall (whose recognition extends far beyond his native country); of Charles Mair, whose *Tecumseh* contains much that is excellent in poetic lore. Marjorie L. C. Pickthall has already established a claim to the wide recognition that opens before her, and her poem *The Lamp of Poor Souls* must be especially remembered. Jean Blewett is one of the most thoughtful and beautiful of the present choir of singers. Mrs. Blewett is Canadian born, and something of the high seriousness of life that characterises the Reverend Canon Scott seems reflected in the poems of Mrs. Blewett; as in the following, entitled *Discontent*:

"My soul spoke low to Discontent:
    Long hast thou lodged with me,
Now, ere the strength of me is spent,
    I would be quit of thee.

"Thy presence means revolt, unrest,
    Means labour, longing, pain;
Go, leave me, thou unwelcome guest,
    Nor trouble me again.

"Then something strong and sweet and fair
    Rose up and made reply:
Who gave you the desire to dare
    And do the right? 'Twas I.

"The coward soul craves pleasant things,
    Soft joys and dear delights—
I scourged you till you spread your wings
    And soared to nobler heights.

"You know me but imperfectly—
    My surname is Divine;
God's own right hand did prison me
    Within this soul of thine,

"Lest thou, forgetting work and strife,
    By human longings prest,
Shouldst miss the grandest things of life,
    Its battles and unrest."

Breaking Camp

Breaking Camp

Helena Coleman has much of that spiritualisation of vision which was so evident in Adelaide Proctor, and which was exalted to the supremest poetic art by Mrs. Browning. From Miss Coleman's *Love's Higher Way* these stanzas are taken:

"Constrain me not! Dost thou not know
That if I turn from thee my face
'Tis but to hide the overflow

"Of love? We need a little space
And solitude in which to kneel
And thank our God for this high grace

"That He hath set His holy seal
Upon our lives. My heart doth burn
With consciousness of all I feel

"And own to thee, and if I turn
For one brief moment from thy gaze,
'Tis but that I may better learn

"To bear the unaccustomed blaze
Of that white light that like a flame
Thy love has set amidst my days."

Of Isabella Valancy Crawford, who flashed like a glancing star across Canadian skies, and whose death in 1887 (at the age of thirty-six) was a signal loss to her adopted country, Mr. Garvin, at once her biographer and the editor of the complete edition of her poems, well says: "A great poet dwelt among us and we scarce knew her." William Douw Lighthall pronounces Isabella Valancy Crawford the most impressive Canadian poet next to Roberts. "This wonderful girl, living in the 'Empire' Province of Ontario, early saw the possibilities of the new field around her, and had she lived longer might have made a really matchless name. It was only in 1884 that her modest volume came out. The sad story of unrecognised genius and death was re-enacted."

This volume of Miss Crawford's was handicapped by an infelicitous title. *Old Spookses' Pass; Malcolm's Katie, and other Poems*, was hardly a description to invite further investigation. The book passed almost unnoticed, and within three years its author died. "She was a high-spirited, passionate girl," says Mr. Lighthall, "and there is little doubt that the neglect of her book was the cause of her death. Afterward her verse was seen to be phenomenal.... It was packed with fine stuff."

Malcolm's Katie is the story of a man and a maid, the man going forth in the woodlands to hew a home with his axe, and the maid remaining in faith and devotion in her home. It is a long poem in blank verse, strewn with occasional lyrics, of which one runs:

"O Love builds on the azure sea,
   And Love builds on the golden sand,
And Love builds on the rose-winged cloud,
   And sometimes Love builds on the land!

"O if Love build on sparkling sea,
   And if Love build on golden strand,
And if Love build on rosy cloud,
   To Love these are the solid land!

"O Love will build his lily walls,
   And Love his pearly roof will rear
On cloud, or land, or mist, or sea—
   Love's solid land is everywhere!"

Mr. Lighthall is himself a poet of distinction and one of the best translators of French poetry. Among his finest work is a poem on Homer, breathing the very spirit of classic ages. Another is entitled *Canada Not Last*, a sonnet series to Venice, Florence, and Rome, the concluding sonnet, which follows, relating to Canada:

"Rome, Florence, Venice—noble, fair, and quaint,
   They reign in robes of magic round me here;
But fading blotted, dim, a picture faint,
   With spell more silent only pleads a tear.
Plead not! Thou hast my heart, O picture dim!
   I see the fields, I see the autumn hand
Of God upon the maples! Answer Him
   With weird, translucent glories, ye that stand
Like spirits in scarlet and in amethyst!
I see the sun break over you; the mist
On hills that lift from iron bases grand
Their heads superb!—the dream, it is my native land!"

Another genuine poet is Peter McArthur, one time editor of New York *Truth* and now farming at his old home in Ontario. Mr. McArthur has published but one volume of verse, but that volume is enough to place him securely well up among the truly authentic voices in the Canadian choir. Everything he writes has a markedly individual quality. There is nothing in him, as one writer has said, of the mere æsthetic or dilettante; he is alive to his finger tips. Mr. McArthur has a keen eye and ear for the common things of the life about him, as witness *A Thaw*.

"The farmhouse fire is dull and black,
   The trailing smoke rolls white and low
Along the fields till by the wood
It banks and floats unshaken, slow;
   The scattering sounds seem near and loud,
   The rising sun is clear and white.
And in the air a mystery stirs
   Of wintry hosts in coward flight.

"Anon the south wind breathes across
   The frozen earth its bonds to break,
Till at the call of life returned
   It softly stirs but half awake.
The cattle clamour in their stalls,
   The house-dog barks, he knows not why.
The cock crows by the stable door,
   The snow-birds, sombre-hued, go by.

"The busy housewife on the snow
   To bleach lays out her linen store,
And scolds because with careless feet
   The children track the spotless floor.

With nightfall comes the slow warm rain,
    The purl of waters fills the air,
And save where roll the gleaming drifts
    The fields lie sullen, black, and bare."

But Mr. McArthur does not write simply of the life around him; the life within is of greater import to him. Here, as evidence of this, is a fine sonnet of his, entitled *Summum Bonum*. Mr. McArthur, it might be noted in passing, is a real master of the sonnet for all his few accomplishments in that form of verse:

"How blest is he that can but love and do,
    And has no skill of speech nor trick of art
Wherewith to tell what faith approveth true
    And show for fame the treasures of his heart.
When wisely weak upon the path of duty
    Divine accord has made his footing sure
With humble deeds he builds his life to beauty,
    Strong to achieve and patient to endure.
But they that in the market-place we meet,
    Each with his trumpet and his noisy faction,
Are leaky vessels, pouring on the street
    The truth they know ere it hath known its action:
Yet which, think ye, in His benign regard,
Or words or deeds shall merit the reward?"

Agnes Maule Machar is another of the group of patriotic poets whose theme is often that of the Empire. She discerns the imperial conditions, and she is intensely in sympathy with the richness and beauty of the land. In Miss Machar's *A Prayer for Dominion Day* these fine lines occur:

"O God of nations, who hast set her place
    Between the rising and the setting day,
    Her part in this world's changeful course to play,
Soothe the conflicting passions that we trace
In her unrestful eyes—grant her the grace
    To know the one true, perfect love, that may
    Give noble impulse to her onward way—
God's love, that doth all other love embrace!"

Lloyd Roberts, one of the young poets of the Dominion, the eldest living son of Charles G. D. Roberts, is true to his poetic birthright, and is the author of an impressive war poem, *Come Quietly, England*, which opens as follows:

"Come quietly, England, all together, come!
   It is time!
We have waited, weighed, and blundered, wondered
Who had blundered;
     Stared askance at one another
     As our brother slew our brother,
And went about our business,
Saying, 'It will be all right—some day.
   Let the soldiers do the killing—
   If they're willing—
     Let the sailors do the manning,
     Let the cabinets do the planning.

Let the bankers do the paying
And the clergy do the praying.
   The Empire is a fixture,
     Walled and welded by five oceans,
   And a little blood won't move it,
     Nor a flood-tide of emotions.'
Well, now we know the truth
   And the facts of all this fighting;
How 'tis not for England's glory
   But for all a wide world's righting.

* * * * *

   "What Washington starved and strove for
In the long winter night;
     Lincoln wept for, died for,—
Do we doubt if he were right?

* * * * *

   "And who would fear to follow
When Nelson sets the course?
   And who would turn his eyes away
From Wellington's white horse?
   Not one, I warrant, now—
Not one at home to-day;
   In England? In Scotland?
In the Green Isle cross the way?

No, nor far away to Westward
   Beyond the leagues of foam—
They are coming, they are coming,
   Their feet are turning home.
In Canada they're singing,
   And love lies like a flame
About their throats this morning
   Their sea-winds cannot tame.
Africa? Australia?
   Aye a million throats proclaim
That their Motherland is Mother still
   In something more than name!

"It is time! Come, all together, come!
Not to the fife's call, not to the drum;
     Right needs you; Truth claims you—
   That's a call indeed
   One must heed!

Not for the weeping
   (God knows there is weeping!)
Not for the horrors
   That are blotting out the page;
Not for our comrades
   (How many now are sleeping!)
     Nor for the pity nor the rage,
But for the sake of simple goodness
   And His laws
We shall sacrifice our all
   For the Cause!"

One of the most brilliant of Canadian poets is Arthur Stringer, though he is more widely known as a novelist, his *Silver Poppy* and *Wire Tappers* having been the successes of their day. Mr. Stringer's poetic work is striking for its variety and range. He has written lyrics and sonnets of almost Keats-like quality, and with as ready facility has written poems in the most modern form of *vers libre*. Then he has turned to the literature of ancient Greece and given us such things of pure beauty in blank verse as *Hephæstus* and *Sappho in Leucadia*, which do not shrink in comparison with any other modern work of their kind; and again has presented us with such pitilessly realistic and convincing pictures as *The Woman in the Rain*. He has also written verse of the Celtic order, his volume of *Irish Poems* being a well of true Irish humour and feeling. And yet, withal, Stringer is Canadian in every nerve and fibre of him. Listen to his *Going Home*:

"I tread each mountain waste austere,
   I pass dark pinelands, hill by hill;
Each tardy sunrise brings me near,
   Each lonely sunset nearer still.

"Sing low, my heart, of other lands
   And suns we may have loved, or known:
This silent North, it understands,
   And asks but little of its own!

"So where the homeland twilight broods
   Above the slopes of dusky pine,
Teach me your silence, solitudes;
   Your reticence, grey hills, be mine!

"Whether all loveliness it lies,
   Or but a lone waste scarred and torn,
How shall I know? For 'neath these skies
   And in this valley I was born."

Here is a characteristic poem of Stringer's entitled *War*, written years ago, and yet reading as if the ink in which it was written were still wet:

"From hill to hill he harried me;
   He stalked me day and night.
He neither knew nor hated me;
   Not his nor mine the fight.

"He killed the man who stood by me,
   For such they made his law.
Then foot by foot I fought to him,
   Who neither knew nor saw.

"I aimed my rifle at his heart;
   He leapt up in the air.
My screaming ball tore through his breast,
   And lay embedded there.

"Lay but embedded there, and yet
   Hissed home o'er hill and sea,
Straight to the aching heart of one
   Who'd wronged not mine nor me."

As a specimen of Stringer's skill in handling of blank verse, here is a portion of the farewell between Sappho and Phaon in *Sappho in Leucadia*:

Sappho. But you,—
You will forget me, Phaon; there the sting.
The sorrow of the grave is not its green
And the salt tear upon its violet;
But the long years that bring the grey neglect,
When the glad grasses smooth the little mound,—
When leaf by leaf the tree of sorrow wanes
And on the urn unseen the tarnish comes,
And tears are not so bitter as they were,
Time sings so low to our bereavèd ears,—
So softly breathes, that, bud by falling bud,
The garden of fond Grief all empty lies
And unregretted dip the languid oars
Of Charon thro' the gloom, and then are gone.

Phaon. Red-lipped and breathing woman, made for love,
How can this clamouring heart of mine forget?

Sappho. You will forget, e'en though you would or no,
And the long years shall leave you free again;
And in some other Spring when other lips
Let fall my name, you will remember not.

Phaon. Enough,—but let me kiss the heavy rose
Of your red mouth.

Sappho. Not until Death has kissed
It white as these white garments, and has robed
This body for its groom.

Another characteristic poem of Stringer's, entitled *A Prayer in Defeat*, will bear comparison with William Ernest Henley's famous *Unafraid*:

"Still hurl me back, God, if Thou must!
   Thy wrath, see, I shall bear—
I have been taught to know the dust
   Of battle and despair.

"Bend not to me this hour, O God,
   Where I defeated stand;

I have been schooled to bear thy rod,
   And still wait, not unmanned!

"But should some white hour of success
   Sweep me where, vine-like, lead
The widening roads, the clamouring press—
   Then I thy lash shall need!

"Then, in that hour of triumph keen,
   For then I ask thine aid;
God of the weak, on whom I lean,
   Keep me then unafraid!"

Space cannot be found for it here, but following are a few verses from another beautiful poem, *St. Ives' Poor*. The idea of this poem is found in the old saying that in the giving of alms the Christ is revealed:

"For O, my Lord, the house-dove knows her nest
   Above my window builded from the rain;
In the brown mere the heron finds her rest,
   But these shall seek in vain.

"And O, my Lord, the thrush may fold his wing,
   The curlew seek the long lift of the seas,
The wild swan sleep amid his journeying;
   There is no place for these.

"Thy dead are sheltered; housed and warmed they wait
   Under the golden fern, the falling foam;
But these Thy living wander desolate,
   And have not any home."

And here is an exquisite poem, *The Immortal*, which is full of Miss Pickthall's own music:

"Beauty is still immortal in our eyes,
When sways no more the spirit-haunted reed,
When the wild grape shall build
No more her canopies,
When blows no more the moon-grey thistle seed,
When the last bell has lulled the white flocks home,
When the last eve has stilled
The wandering wing, and touched the dying foam,

When the last moon burns low, and, spark by spark,
The little worlds die out along the dark—

"Beauty that rosed the moth-wing, touched the land
With clover-horns and delicate faint flowers;
 Beauty that bade the showers
Beat on the violet's face,
Shall hold the eternal heavens within their place,
And hear new stars come singing from God's hand."

We cannot resist, before leaving Miss Pickthall, quoting a lovely little lyric of hers called simply *Serenade*:

"Dark is the Iris meadow,
   Dark is the ivory tower,
And lightly the young moth's shadow
   Sleeps on the passion flower.

"Gone are our day's red roses,
   Lovely and lost and few,
But the first star uncloses
   A silver bud in the blue.

"Night, and a flame in the embers
   When the seal of the years was set;
When the almond bough remembers
   How shall my heart forget?"

Passing mention has been made of the names of Ethelwyn Wetherald and Pauline Johnson, but the work of these poets is too distinctive to avoid some reference to it. Miss Wetherald has published some half-dozen books of verse, all made up chiefly of short lyrics, and all possessing an individual quality which may well be called unique. Here is one of her strongest poems, entitled *Prodigal Yet*:

"Muck of the sty, reek of the trough,
   Blackened my brow where all might see,
Yet while I was a great way off
   My Father ran with compassion for me.

"He put on my hand a ring of gold
   (There's no escape from a ring, they say);
He put on my neck a chain to hold
   My passionate spirit from breaking away.

"He put on my feet the shoes that miss
   No chance to tread in the narrow path;
He pressed on my lips the burning kiss
   That scorches deeper than fires of wrath.

"He filled my body with meat and wine,
   He flooded my heart with love's white light!
Yet deep in the mire, with sensuous swine,
   I long—God help me!—to wallow to-night.

"Muck of the sty, reek of the trough,
   Blacken my soul where none may see.
Father, I yet am a long way off—
   Come quickly. Lord! Have compassion on me!"

It has been indicated that Pauline Johnson, whose death a few years ago is still fresh in the memory of those who knew her and her work, was Indian by birth and her poetry is marked by the vigour and virility which such a fact would imply. *How Red Men Can Die* and *The Cry of an Indian Wife* are perhaps her best-known poems, but they are too long to quote here. Following, however, is a little poem, *The Honey Bee*, which shows Miss Johnson's keen feeling for colour, as well as her fine lyric quality:

"You are belted with gold, little brother of mine,
   Yellow gold, like the sun
That spills in the west, as a chalice of wine
   When feasting is done.

"You are gossamer-winged, little brother of mine,
   Tissue winged, like the mist
That broods where the marshes melt into a line
   Of vapour sun-kissed.

"You are laden with sweets, little brother of mine,
   Flower sweets, like the touch
Of hands we have longed for, of arms that entwine,
   Of lips that love much.

"You are better than I, little brother of mine,
   Than I, human-souled,
For you bring from the blossoms and red summer shine,
   For others, your gold."

The poet has no country save that of the kingdom of song, or rather, all countries are his own, and while Canada cannot claim Robert W. Service by birth, it is he who has so made himself the poet of her scenic grandeur and her primitive human experiences in the deepest emotions of life, love, death, sacrifice, revenge, that no sketch of Canadian poetry could omit the name of one who has made the Dominion known, in its grandeur and its mountain solitudes, the world over. Mr. Service has inevitably been much quoted in these pages; no one can travel in Canada, no one can write of Canada, without this perpetual consciousness of the vivid way in which he has translated her landscapes and her life. What a ring of the vitality that conquers the wilderness is in his *Call of the Wild*!

"Have you suffered, starved, and triumphed, grovelled down,
    yet grasped at glory,
  Grown bigger in the bigness of the whole?
'Done things' just for the doing, letting babblers tell the story,
  Seeing through the nice veneer the naked soul?
Have you seen God in His splendours, heard the text that
    nature renders
  (You'll never hear it in the family pew),
The simple things, the true things, the silent men who do
    things?—
  Then listen to the wild—it's calling you.

"They have cradled you in custom, they have primed you with
    their preaching,
They have soaked you in convention through and through;
 They have put you in a showcase; you're a credit to their
    teaching—
  But can't you hear the wild?—it's calling you.
Let us probe the silent places, let us seek what luck betide us;
  Let us journey to a lonely land I know.
There's a whisper on the night-wind, there's a star agleam to
    guide us,
  And the wild is calling, calling ... let us go."

In *The Law of the Yukon* we find:

"This is the law of the Yukon, and ever she makes it plain;
'Send not your foolish and feeble; send me your strong and
    your sane;
Strong for the red rage of battle; sane, for I harry them sore;

Send me men girt for the combat,—men who are grit to the core;
Send me the best of your breeding, lend me your chosen ones;
Them will I take to my bosom, them will I call my sons;
Them will I gild with my treasure, them will I glut with my meat;
But the others, the misfits, the failures,—I trample under my feet.

* * * * * * *

"'I am the land that listens, I am the land that broods;
Steeped in eternal beauty, crystalline waters and woods.
Monstrous, moody, pathetic, the last of the lands and the first,
Visioning campfires at twilight, sad with a longing forlorn.'

* * * * * * *

"This is the law of the Yukon, that only the Strong shall thrive;
That surely the Weak shall perish, and only the Fit survive;
Dissolute, damned, and despairful, crippled and palsied and slain,
This is the law of Will of the Yukon,—Lo, how she makes it plain!"

Robert Service has many moods, and in the tender little lyric *Unforgotten* he dramatises the way in which one's real life lies in his consciousness rather than enchained with the bodily presence:

"I know a garden where the lilies gleam,
   And one who lingers in the sunshine there;
   She is than white-stoled lily far more fair.
And oh, her eyes are heaven-lit with dream.

"I know a garret, cold and dark and drear,
   And one who toils and toils with tireless pen,
   Until his brave, sad eyes grow weary—then
He seeks the stars, pale, silent as a seer.

"And ah, it's strange, for desolate and dim
   Between these two there rolls an ocean wide;
   Yet he is in the garden by her side
And she is in the garret there with him."

One of the wonderful poems of Mr. Service is that of *My Madonna*. The artist "haled" him "a woman from the street" for his model; he painted her:

"I painted her as she might have been
   If the Worst had been the Best,"

and she "laughed at the picture and went away," but a connoisseur came and exclaimed:

"'Tis Mary, the Mother of God."

"So I painted a halo round her hair,
   And I sold her, and took my fee,
And she hangs in the church of Saint Hilaire,
   Where you and all may see."

Mount Robson, at a Distance of Ten Miles

No attempt to transcribe any impressions of Canada could attain to success that did not include some reference, even one so slight and imperfect as this, to her poets. Any adequate comment on her poetic literature would fill more than one volume of itself. They who make the songs of a people are traditionally held to be not less in influence than are they who make her laws; and that the future will be still more enriched with the enthusiasms and the strange and thrilling elements of the life of the Dominion is a foregone conclusion.

CHAPTER XIII

THE CALL OF THE CANADIAN WEST

The call of the Canadian West is far less the call of the adventurer, of the speculator, of the seeker of vast and sudden wealth than it is the call to carry an enlightened civilisation into the vast new region that beckons to humanity invested with all the alluring glory of the Promised Land. It is nearly three hundred years ago that the Pilgrim Fathers landed in New England to conquer the wilderness. But the Pilgrims did not find that the railways had gone before and prepared the way with luxurious trains of Pullman cars, or that telegraph and telephone service, in all varieties, to say nothing of Marconigrams, daily mails, motor cars, and various other amenities of life, were awaiting them. The New England of to-day is more indebted to the past half century for its advance than it is to the preceding two and a half centuries. So it may be fairly claimed that the Canadian West begins with the degree of progress, so far as mechanical conveniences and resources go, to which older countries have but just advanced. It is the heir of all the ages.

In normal times, before the War, there was an annual immigration into Canada that approximated to the number of four hundred thousand people, of whom more than fifty thousand were from the United States. There was said to be in round numbers from fifty to seventy thousand who were neither from the States nor from the British Isles, while the remainder were chiefly from England, Scotland, or Wales. The Irish immigration is more attracted to the States, as more than twelve millions of their race are already incorporated into the population of that country.

Two leading factors produce this large immigration into the Dominion. One is that Canada is a country whose richness of resources, climatic conditions, and scenic beauty are incomparable; the other is that there are wise and liberal provisions made by the government to offer desirable and attractive conditions and judicious inducements to the right sort of men to establish their homes in Canada. Thousands of prosperous farmers already scattered over Western Canada began, not many years ago, with inconsiderable capital, but their intelligence, industry, and integrity have carried the way and developed conditions of living that are eminently satisfactory.

The excellent character of the land in Western Canada is well displayed in the great region opened up by the Grand Trunk Pacific. Following for fifty miles the valley of the Assiniboine River, the line of railway goes through the drainage basin of Qu'Appelle River, and on into the great basin of the south Saskatchewan River, crossing it at Saskatoon, the width of this basin being some 200 miles. Then on through the western part of Saskatchewan and the eastern part of Alberta, the railway makes a gradual ascent through sandhills and ridges until crossing the third steppe it proceeds for the remaining 130 miles, to Edmonton, over a level country. With the exception, and that an inconsiderable one, of these sandhills and ridges, there is no waste land between Winnipeg and Edmonton.

In the whole region now opened to civilisation by the Grand Trunk Pacific, there extends a belt of rich farming land from 300 to 500 miles in width from north to south and some 1000 miles in length from east to west. From Winnipeg to the west, the physical properties of the land are found by trained experts to be exceptionally advantageous for the growing of wheat, oats, barley, and flax; "in fact," says Professor Clifford Willis (a recognised authority on soil physics), "the yields of small grain of this type were the best that I have seen anywhere in the best tilled fields of the United States." Professor James H. Pettit, of Cornell University, who won his doctor's degree from the University of Göttingen for work in soil fertility and bacteriology, finds that this recently opened up region possesses some of the richest soils, and that this is due to the alluvial deposits of the large area once covered by the old glacial Lake Agassiz. These deposits have left a soil of silt and clay that is capable of producing thirty-five or forty bushels of wheat, and eighty or ninety bushels of oats to the acre.

To "mixed farming" as well as to the production of grain alone, or of live stock, all this enormous region lends itself. Before the country was opened and rendered accessible by the Grand Trunk Pacific, the region was practically a wilderness. The land was fertile, the numerous rivers and the lakes provided a sufficiency of water and generally promising conditions, but until transit was provided all these were unavailing. Prosperous towns have now sprung up all along the line of the railway, and the settlement of the country progresses with incredible swiftness. The settler arrives with his twentieth-century equipment. The contrast between the manner in which Canada is being gracefully and luxuriously settled, and that of the mid-nineteenth-century settlement of the western part of the United States, is something with which to reckon. The Canadian pioneer arrives in his Pullman car instead of the "prairie schooner" that slowly and wearily traversed the plains west of the Mississippi. He starts a steam engine to plough the land, and if trees or stumps come in his way he exterminates them with celerity by machinery. When the harvesting time comes, wonderful mechanisms cut the grain and bind it, while his trucks are perhaps equipped with motor power and swiftly carry the grain direct from the threshing-machines to the elevators, from which it is shipped to market. Wherefore, indeed, should he taste drudgery? Is he not the heir to all the ages?

The marked liberality of the Canadian Government in its universal provision for higher education is one of the features of the Dominion that can never be too deeply emphasised. Winnipeg, Saskatoon, and Edmonton are all seats of universities, whose privileges are open to women on equal terms. At both Winnipeg and Saskatoon are also agricultural colleges, offering practical instruction in scientific farming, and the ways of wealth are at once made plain for the youth of the region.

Mount Robson Glacier

The telephone service is practically universal, welding into unity all the labour on a great farm of hundreds of acres, and enabling the farmhouse to be in touch with city and town. Appreciating the importance of this, the government of each province lends substantial aid in the instalment of telephone service, and the main telephone lines in these three western provinces are owned and operated by the government. Thus all agricultural communities are linked together in close contact and communication.

Social conditions thereby establish themselves on a satisfactory basis. The comfort of the rural home is assured. There is no isolation to be encountered. Good roads, railway facilities of the best order that the world can afford, telephones, and telegraphs make possible a social life impossible under former pioneer conditions.

Churches spring up wherever there are people, for religion and education go hand in hand in Canada.

The garden facilities are not the least of the attractions to settlers. The abundance with which garden stuff of all kinds—potatoes, peas, beans, onions, turnips, pumpkins, and squash, as well as lettuce, radishes, rhubarb, and small fruits—grow in all this region is something to see.

This agricultural empire is so great in its promise for the future, so interesting and enchaining in its present development, that there is hardly a limit to the imagination regarding its importance in a not distant period.

The "great North-West" is a term which has been commonly employed to designate the provinces of Manitoba, Saskatchewan, Alberta, and the northern part of British Columbia. It is rather a vague term; yet it indicates, if it does not exactly define, a region of unrivalled scenic grandeur, and of such potential resources and favourable conditions of climate as to virtually add a new continent to the world. Such is the march of progress, however, that at the time of writing the "North-West," strictly speaking, is that portion of the land north of these provinces stretching eastward to Hudson Bay and northward to the Arctic Ocean and including that part of the Yukon on the Canadian side of the Alaskan border. This definition is according to Watson Griffin's map of the Dominion of Canada in his accurate and authoritative work, *Canada of the Twentieth Century*, which appeared in May, 1916, bringing all matter pertaining to the country up to date with statistical accuracy. It is pointed out by Mr. Griffin that in the older provinces, such as Quebec and Ontario, the climate has been virtually transformed by the culture of the soil. In southern Manitoba it is also on record that while the early settlers lost their crops by summer frosts, no such disasters are now experienced. The experiments in agriculture have proved that the soil under cultivation stores up the heat received during the long, bright days, and that the radiation of this heat at night prevents the fatal frosts. Climatic conditions are not, therefore, arbitrary and fixed beyond control, but are largely amenable to civilisation. It is this fact that lends probability to the expectation of creating prosperous conditions for living in the region north of the sixtieth parallel. "In fact," says Mr. Watson Griffin, "at some of the Hudson's Bay Company posts in these territories the clearing, draining, and cultivation of the land has already had a remarkable effect, and if this is true where very small areas have been brought under cultivation, it is conceivable that the cultivation of wide areas might have a very great influence in preventing summer frosts." If well-cultivated soil does receive and store the sun's heat it seems reasonable to suppose that in these northern districts, where the summer days are so long, the general opening of the soil to the sun and air should have a marked effect.

The most reliable experts unite in the conviction that the Mackenzie Basin is capable of supporting an agricultural population. The soil is rich; and in that part of the Basin alone, lying between Athabasca Lake and the Arctic Ocean, there is a belt of land 940 miles long and over 60 miles wide. Ninety miles south of latitude sixty-three ripe strawberries are found. A little farther to the south currants and other small fruits grow luxuriantly. There are already scanty settlements, remote and apart, in this country, and an increasing population of huntsmen, fur-traders, and tourists to whom sport is the attraction; and the first consideration that would occur to the traveller, or to any student of this almost unmapped region of infinite space, would be as to the ways and means for safeguarding human life and for the maintenance of law and order. For untold centuries this region has been the home and haunt of the Indians and of wild and ferocious animals. The Indian tribes possessed all this district in which to roam at will. Their means of subsistence were hunting and fishing, and their resources for clothing consisted in the skins and furs of captured animals. Any adequate conception of the wildness of this unbroken wilderness is almost impossible to grasp. The primæval forests impenetrable with their dense growth of underbrush, fallen trees, colossal rocks washed bare by the beating storms of centuries, with uncounted and fairly innumerable leagues of lakes, rivers, swamps—how unconquerable this primitive world of Nature! Yet the call of the North-West, even this remote and unknown North-West, has sounded, and the ear of poet, prophet, and priest is that which registers the cry unheard and unheeded by others.

It is a significant commentary on human life, in its assertion of that divinity which man feels within him, that the first white men to fare forth to penetrate this wilderness were the French missionary priests, and that the intense motive that drew them into hardships and dangers incredible was that of the love of God and the longing to make known to the untamed Red Man the help and comfort of the Divine Power—to bring to these children of nature something of the message of a diviner destiny. "To Pierre Radisson and his comrade, the Sieur Groseillers, belong the credit of having first penetrated this vast tract of undiscovered country," writes Mr. A. L. Haydon in his remarkable book, *The Riders of the Plains*. No romance was ever more enthralling than this volume, nor would it be possible to offer any adequate interpretation of the great North-West that did not take account of Mr. Haydon's work. With the thrilling adventures of these French missionaries all students of history are acquainted; and it is such a chapter in life and in literature that any transcription of the experiences would of itself make a volume. In its fulness it can only perhaps be found in the pages of the Recording Angel. "They plunged into the unknown," says Mr. Haydon; "took the daring leap that all such pioneers are called upon to take; and along the paths they blazed followed a host of others hardly less intrepid. He who would read of the further discovery and exploitation of the North-West of Canada must study the glowing life-stories of Marquette, Joliet, La Salle, De la Verendrye, and others."

There were also temporal as well as spiritual leadings. The adventurous fur-traders pushed further and further into the primæval wilderness and established forts as centres of supplies and as definite places for their barter with the Indians. Two separate and important companies entered on this quest, the famous Hudson's Bay Company and the North-West Fur Company. The outposts that each of these energetic associations established were like lighted torches into the darkness; even this untrodden wilderness began to respond to the first conquest of humanity. Myths and traditions also led on. There were rumours in the air, whisperings of voices on the wind, that some vast and unknown sea lay between the western coast and Japan. The Pacific Ocean was known, but these nebulous intimations pointed to a body of water never yet discovered. In 1731 the Sieur De la Verendrye, as gallant a gentleman as ever sought his fortune in the new world, started gaily from Montreal upon the quest for this great sea. With his company he took the route up the Red River to its junction with the Assiniboine, making camp at Fort Rouge, the site of the present city of Winnipeg. Rumours still haunted the air of "mighty waters beyond the mountains," and over the infinite and trackless expanse of prairie they still further extended the march, but the formidable foothills of the Rocky Mountains proved too great a barrier, and it was due to the persistence, and probably, too, also to the greater physical vigour of a young fur-trader, Alexander Mackenzie, of the North-West Company, that the mysteries of the mountain ranges were penetrated, the foothills crossed, and the river traced that now bears his name.

These two fur-trading companies became important factors in the development of the North-West. There was an intense rivalry between them, yet the very intensity of the discord and ill feeling became an added impetus in the rivalry of exploration. Many and diverse qualities are brought into play in the conquering of a wilderness. Evil and good are always sown together like the wheat and the tares, and even the evil has its part to play and its work to do. Of this fierce rivalry between the two was born that activity which created so large a number of trading-posts, and the energy that founded numerous settlements, many of which are now recognised as prosperous centres.

In 1670, under the patronage of Prince Rupert, there was incorporated the "Honourable Company of Merchant-Adventurers Trading into Hudson's Bay," which developed later into the Hudson's Bay Company.

Pierre Radisson and the Sieur Groseillers, both among the most daring and heroic explorers the world has known, excited a wave of enthusiasm in England by the reports of the wilderness they carried back with them. For more than a century the Company under the patronage of Prince Rupert continued to carry on a prosperous business, and after this was merged into the Hudson's Bay Company, and again after the two rival associations united, a splendid business was developed. But while the rivalry had conduced to enterprise and exploration, the monopoly was as naturally concerned in not making too widely known the rich resources that might thus serve to attract other competitors.

Farming in Shellbrook District, Saskatchewan

Early in the nineteenth century a large Scotch settlement, under the auspices of the Earl of Selkirk, was established in the Red River region. They encountered almost every phase of hardship and trial. Great floods devastated their land and ruined their attempts at agriculture. The severe winters, with their enshrouding snow-drifts, their icy blasts, the imprisoning character of the elements, the remoteness from any vestige of human habitations or contact with civilisation, went far towards annihilating even the most persistent efforts to found a settlement that should withstand these conditions.

By the mid-nineteenth century, however, the settlements of the great North-West had become so numerous that there began to be requirements for larger means of protection. The Hudson's Bay Company, at this time, held territory to the extent of over two million square miles. All this expanse was admitted into the confederation, to the reassurance and great satisfaction of the settlers scattered over this wide region; but to the alarm and prevailing dissatisfaction of another order of the inhabitants, the French half-breeds, who were themselves a force with which a reckoning had to be made. Their alarm culminated in the Rebellion of 1869, an outbreak suppressed by Colonel (later Lord) Wolseley. Soon after this outbreak was quelled there came the formation of the Province of Manitoba, and from this event there dated a new epoch in the history of this part of the country. The conditions grew worse rather than better. The United States were also a contributing factor to greater discord. The treatment of the Indians by the government of the States had apparently left much to be desired (to put it mildly) and the turbulent warfare that went on almost continually in the western part of that country drove many of the Indian tribes into frenzy. Many of these tribes now crossed the border line into Canada to seek British protection. There were at this time in Canada some seventy thousand Indians to whom the Imperial government had promised protection, and the coming of these fresh tribes from the States, largely, too, in conditions of revolt and resentment at what they felt to be unjust and cruel treatment, could not but be regarded with grave apprehensions by the white settlers. They were alarmed at the close proximity of these unknown savage tribes as well as apprehensive of the effect they might produce on the Canadian Indians.

In the summer of 1872 the Canadian Adjutant-General, Colonel Robertson-Ross, was dispatched by the Government of the Dominion to make a tour of inspection through the North-West. He found that a party of lawless traders and smugglers from the States had established a trading-post which they had named Fort Hamilton, about sixty miles north of the border-line between the Dominion and the United States; and that they were conducting a species of barter with the Blackfeet Indians, supplying them with firearms and with ardent spirits, in direct opposition to the laws of both countries. They were paying no customs duty for the merchandise they were thus introducing into Canada. Colonel Robertson-Ross found the demoralisation that they were working to be very great and of great injury, not only to the Indians, but to the entire country. "At Fort Edmonton," said the Adjutant-General in his Report, "whisky was openly sold to the Blackfeet and other Indians trading at the Fort by smugglers from the United States, who derived large profits therefrom, and whom, on being remonstrated with by the official in charge of Hudson's Bay Post, coolly replied that they very well knew they were defying the laws, but as there was no force to prevent them they would do as they pleased."

All this inciting to intemperance and brawling led to other offences against law and order. The Indians took to horse-stealing, and the entire population of the North-West was at their mercy. Neither property nor life was safe. On dishonesty and robbery followed murder as a not uncommon occurrence and other crimes of a serious nature were not infrequent. Sir John Macdonald was at this time the Premier of Canada. It was on his initiative that Colonel Robertson-Ross had been sent on this reconnaissance to find out to what extent the lawless marauders were demoralising the entire country and the nature of the protection and safeguards that should be instituted for the population. The Adjutant-General earnestly recommended the establishment of a trained and disciplined military body, to be subject to its own rules, and to be distinct from any civil force, though acting as an addition to whatever civil force might also be formed. "Whatever feeling may be entertained toward policemen, animosity is rarely, if ever, felt toward disciplined soldiers wearing her Majesty's uniform in any portion of the British Empire," stated Colonel Robertson-Ross, and he added: "In the event of serious disturbance a police force, acting alone and unsupported by a disciplined military body, would probably be overpowered in a province of mixed races, where every man is armed, while to maintain a military without any civil force is not desirable."

Colonel Robertson-Ross also urgently recommended that a chain of military posts should be established from Manitoba to the Rocky Mountains; that a stipendiary magistrate for the Saskatchewan should be appointed, who should also act as an Indian Commissioner and who should fix his residence in Edmonton. "The individual to fill this post," he said, "should be one, if possible, already known to the Indians, and one in whom they have confidence." He also pointed out that this Indian Commissioner should always be accompanied by a military force. "A large force is not necessary," he said; "but the presence of a certain force will, I believe, be found indispensable for the security of the country, to prevent bloodshed and preserve peace."

This is the story of the way in which the Royal North-West Mounted Police of Canada came into being. These "Riders of the Plains" stand alone and unparalleled in the world in their organisation, their peculiar field of work, and the nature of their control over the vast region entrusted to their care. This Mounted Police Force comprises about six hundred officers and men, whose territory is an area as extensive as all Central Europe, or a region five times as large as Great Britain; extending for two thousand miles from east to west, and a thousand miles from north to south. In this great area are twelve divisional posts and one hundred and fifty detachments. The organisation of this body was carried out in the autumn of 1873. The first one hundred and fifty of the Mounted Police were stationed at Lower Fort Garry in Manitoba. They were under the command of Lieutenant-Colonel George A. French, an officer of the Royal Artillery who had been the Inspector of Artillery at the School of Gunnery in Kingston, Ontario. Colonel French at once, on arriving in Manitoba, urged upon the Government the need of strengthening the force by at least doubling the number of men. Two hundred more were enlisted in Toronto, and the expedition to the Far West was fixed for an early date in the spring.

The picturesque aspect of the Royal North-West Mounted Police is notable. It was Sir John Macdonald's idea that the dominant note in their uniform should be scarlet as "this colour conveys the strongest impression to the mind of the Indian, through his respect for 'the Queen's soldiers.'" To accentuate the military character of the force and to distinguish them from the blue-coated soldiers of the States was a point of real importance.

This first detachment of the Royal Mounted Police made an expedition in the summer of 1874 into the very heart of the Blackfeet country, and returned to Dufferin in November, having made an effective campaign in the interests of law and order, from which very important and momentous results have ensued since that time. That the small body of less than seven hundred men should exercise such control, not only over so vast an area of almost unknown wilderness, inhabited by such a diversity of human beings scattered widely apart, is practically an isolated fact in all history. To this magnificent Force is largely due, to-day, the conditions that invest the North-West with such promise and prosperity.

"The Force may be said to have largely completed the work it originally set out to do," writes Frank Yeigh[1]; "so far as the frontier provinces are concerned, a work that is worth many times its cost, as an object-lesson of the power and authority of government existing behind all real civilisation."

[1] *Through the Heart of Canada*. T. Fisher Unwin, London, 1910.

Still, the task of the mounted patroller is by no means yet completed. The present force costs the country nearly three-quarters of a million dollars a year. Their outposts are being set farther and farther afield. Thus, from the promontory of Cape Chidley, at almost the most northerly point of Labrador, the barracks overlook Hudson Straits; another guards Hudson Bay, while a third protects the Arctic seaboard, and the most western post serves to protect the gold land of the Yukon. It is a fact, and a striking one, that on the three-hundred-mile road from White Horse to Dawson the traveller is as safe as in any part of Canada. Of the life of this Royal Force Mr. Haydon says:

"The stories of the daily life of these rough-riders of the plains are the very essence of romance, of high courage, of Herculean tasks performed and great difficulties overcome. The Mounted Police kept down lawlessness when the Canadian Pacific Railway was being built, they fought bravely during the Riel Rebellion of 1885, they kept well in hand the gold rush to the Klondyke in 1889-90, and not a few served in South Africa during the Boer War. But the deeds of the individual men call for high praise. Their qualities of fidelity, devotion to duty, and their fearlessness are constantly being exemplified. A thousand miles on the ice, 'mushing' by dog-team and komatik, through unexplored haunts of bear and wolf, is a common marching order for these splendid pioneers."

One individual instance among the many that might well be related to add to the annals of human heroism is the remarkable journey made in 1906 by Constable Sellers, who, with an interpreter and an Eskimo, drawn by a dog-team, left the west coast of Hudson Bay in February of that year to discover the locality of a Scottish ship in the Arctic waters, to collect the customs due, and to inspect the conditions of this region. The trip lasted two months, and before his return in April Constable Sellers had experienced all the hardships of an Arctic winter. Many pages might be filled with the thrilling accounts of the adventures and the noble and self-effacing sacrifices of these brave defenders of the law, these magnificent protectors of human life and property, the very guardians of all that makes for civilisation and lends value and significance to life. Mr. Yeigh's description of the conditions of life of the force on Herschell Island is extremely graphic. He says:

"The life of the Mounted Policeman on Herschell Island presents many features of interest. Stranded in this far-off corner of the Dominion in the Canadian 'Land of the Midnight Sun,' he lives as near the North Pole as possible. It is a circumscribed island home, moreover, with a shoreline of only twenty-three miles, and with cliffs rising five hundred feet from the Arctic Sea. Though so far north, in latitude 69°, Herschell Island is covered with a luxuriant growth of grass and carpeted with innumerable wild flowers. The island possesses the one safe harbour in all these northern waters—a harbour in which fifty ships could safely winter."

This island is distinguished as the centre of the whaling grounds of the Arctic regions.

No adequate interpretation of the conditions that prevail in the Dominion could be possible that did not include some account of the "Riders of the Plains." The service of these faithful guardians is by no means exclusively limited to their official responsibility; they add to this that of being the friends, the helpers, of the settlers, under all the new unforeseen conditions that confront them in the new country. All over the Canadian land the watchword "Safety first" meets the eye. The watchword "Humanity first" seems to be that of the Royal Mounted Police. Their careful and tender ministrations are given to the invalid and the helpless; they risk their lives to warn and save settlers when a raging fire is sweeping over woodlands or prairie; they aid the new arrival to set up his camp the first night; they help him to repair vehicles or mechanism that has given out; they assist him to build his first primitive shelter, and even to cook his meals and to care for his live stock. The safety of the incoming inhabitants, the essential conditions that render possible their establishment of a home, have depended so essentially on the protection and the safe-guarding afforded by the "Riders of the Plains" that their splendid service is not only a fundamental factor in Canadian life and history, but is a shining page in the records not made with hands.

A touching incident has been narrated in the chronicles of the Mounted Police Force. It was required some years ago to send dispatches to a distant post during the severest rigour of winter weather. A young constable, a University graduate, gently born and bred, set out with these dispatches, but days passed into weeks, and weeks into months, and no trace of him could be discovered. At last, in the following spring, a storm-worn uniform and the bones of a human body were discovered by a patrol in a secluded spot, and on the order he was carrying was scrawled: "Lost—horse dead. Am trying to push ahead. Have done my best." Who could read with eyes undimmed by tears such a testimony as this to the young constable's high sense of honour and utter sacrifice of anxiety for his own personal safety? No soldier at the front ever more gallantly faced death in the discharge of his duty. Indeed, the stranger who comes to Canada and enters with any degree of sympathy and understanding into the national life is more impressed with the unwritten watchword of "Duty first" than with the legend of "safety" that meets his eye. Is it too much to say that the Dominion is the nation of heroes? It is certainly no exaggeration to say that heroes abound in this country where the unmeasured richness of the resources of Nature is yet far exceeded by the nobility of man's mind.

The growth and expansion of Canada has proceeded very rapidly within the first part of the twentieth century. The problems involved in this swift expansion have increased in number and importance. They assume a varied character, because the vast extent of the empire inevitably raises such diverse questions of political, educational, and social requirements, that of the bi-lingual problem being not least in importance. Then there are the problems of immigration, of transportation and communication, including matters of railway highways, inland navigation, foreign commerce, and postal facilities. Sir James Grant, speaking before the Empire Club of Toronto in the December of 1915, reviewed the remarkable development of Canada since about 1850, and said that, marvellous as was this record, it would be exceeded by the tremendous developments of the immediate future. Of the new territory in northern Ontario, opened on the clay belt, Sir James predicted that it would be settled by thousands of people, and that it would become one of the most attractive parts of the country. In this region the supply of wood and water is practically inexhaustible, and the splendid transit facilities bring it into easy communication with the markets. Apart from the agricultural, there is the mining outlook.

Even the great and disastrous war that began in August, 1914, will not be wholly disastrous, or even antagonistic, to the future of Canada. Great trade facilities will be opened between Russia and Canada. Vast numbers of British soldiers who have left their industrial occupations for the front will have so accustomed and acclimatised themselves to open air and exposure that they will look for life in the open rather than to any return to shops or manufactories. Canada confidently anticipates at least a million settlers from among these ranks. They would be particularly qualified for the order of life required for the hardy pioneer of that North-West defined by Mr. Watson Griffin as lying north of Manitoba, Saskatchewan, Alberta, and British Columbia, and stretching eastward to Hudson Bay and northward to the Arctic Ocean. They would be prepared to bring to this rigorous and exacting part of the country a hardy vigour and invincible courage in the conquering of nature in a degree quite in excess of that now demanded in the more settled regions. The young and eminently enterprising western Provinces have already made the establishment of Winnipeg as one of the greatest wheat markets in the world an accomplished fact. "In 1904," asserts a New York financial journal, "they raised fifty-eight million bushels of wheat in Manitoba, Saskatchewan, and Alberta; five years later the yield was one hundred and fifty million bushels, and in 1913 the crop approximated to two hundred millions of bushels of wheat. At this rate of progress," continued this journal, "Canada must soon pass France and India, and stand third in the line of wheat producers. Ultimately she will dispute with Russia and the United States for the first position. Wheat has been the pioneer of our development, and undoubtedly it will prove the same with Canada.... No vivid imagination is needed to see what the future development of Canada means to the people of the United States."

That the great problem of food for the people of Europe will largely devolve on Canada and the States for many years after the end of the war is quite evident.

The Minister of Public Works, the Honourable Robert Rogers, in an interview with a press representative, said not long ago:

"The prairie country will do its share in saving Canada when the war is over.... There will be a vast tide of immigration. Where will the European emigrants go? Will they go to foreign lands, lands where they will be lost forever to the

Allies, or will they come to Canada, where they will be under the British flag? That is the vital question for Canada, for the Empire, for the Allies, for civilisation.

"We want to be able to go practically to the door of every European who is thinking of a home elsewhere, and show him the Canadian West—tall wheat, ample railway connections, growing cities and all.

"It will be the finest thing in the world for him and the satisfaction of Canada. Moreover, it will be the solution of most of the problems which now confront him, as, for instance, how to make our transcontinental railways paying propositions; how to enable our industries to find new tasks when the war orders stop; how to adjust our mercantile system to the changed conditions; how to till our farm lands and start again the late lamented boom....

"The West is empty. Its natural resources are inexhaustible. We could take care of the entire British white population there. And think what it would mean for the West, and so for all Canada, if we got five million new people out there after the war? Winnipeg, Brandon, Regina; Prince Albert, Calgary, Edmonton; Medicine Hat, Portage la Prairie, Dauphin, Saskatoon, Lethbridge, Swift Current, and many other centres would become great cities. The salubrious British Columbia coast would seethe with new activity and new populations; our railways would become great earners; industries would spring up all over the West. The industries of the East would find a new market within their own tariff fence. Banking would boom, wholesale trade would flourish, young clerks in the East would become prosperous proprietors in the West."

In the eager and many-sided activities that are springing up and fairly treading upon each other's heels in Canada, Technical Schools hold a distinctive place. The late Lord Strathcona was a zealous and influential advocate of trade and technical schools as one of the most effective means of bettering the condition and elevating the life of the working-man. The great West is not behind in the establishment of these.

THRESHING WHEAT, MANITOBA

Threshing Wheat, Manitoba

Now as to the conditions that await the settlers in western Canada. The land is fertile; the climate, the water supply, and the transit and traffic facilities are of the best. But favourable conditions do not of themselves work miracles, and pioneer life has its difficulties. Prosperity is not magically invoked by any entreaty of the gods, nor does it fall down out of the blue sky upon its votaries. But with health, integrity, and a reasonable amount of capital, the achievement of prosperous and happy living is possible within a comparatively short time. It is related that after the annual harvest there are people who go on pleasure trips to New York and San Francisco, and "think nothing of expending thousands of dollars before their return." There are farms where the owner has his motor car; his house, commodious and handsome, is steam-heated and electric-lighted, as he generates electricity from his own plant. There is a music room with a grand piano, and perchance a violin for the music-gifted young son or daughter as well; there is a library with a good and always growing collection of books, for it is realised that reading is not a mere passive entertainment but a creative activity as well. A good book sets the entire mental mechanism in motion. It is as a motor force, a power, applied to the mind. To give one's self to intervals of reading is not merely to be borne through the realms of thought in a golden chariot, but is, rather, the conquering of a region of new capabilities and powers, applicable to the entire range of the problems of life. "The key to every man is his thought," says Emerson. Books are food for the mental and spiritual life, and from all good reading there results a certain transubstantiation into energy that refines and exalts the quality of life. The broad piazzas, the shaded lawns, of these prosperous farmhouses are a revelation to the traveller and their own commentary on Canadian conditions.

Not longer ago than 1900 agriculturalists contended that wheat could not be grown north of the fiftieth degree of latitude. The best quality of the grain is now raised in the regions north of the fifty-fifth degree. All the vast expanse of the Peace River country, for some 700 miles or more north of the Grand Trunk Pacific Railway, offers rich and attractive soil that well repays cultivation. As has been noted in preceding pages, regions that were formerly supposed to be adapted only to the most primitive conditions of life—to hunting, fishing, canoeing, or dog-sledging—are now found to be entirely amenable to ordinary life and pursuits, with a climate even less rigorous than is sometimes experienced in the winters of northern Dakota or Minnesota. The Japanese chinook wind that blows in tempers the air, and many of these northern lakes are now free from ice, for the most part, during the winter. This change of the climate has largely been brought about by the opening up of forests and dense undergrowth, which so intercepted the sun's rays that ice would be found at midsummer in the dense shades.

The valley of the Athabasca, stretching away from the portals of Jasper and of Jasper Park, is an Alpine wonderland; it is enshrined in legendary history; it is unrivalled in splendour of scenery and richness of colour; and traversed as it is by the most modern of our transcontinental lines, it becomes as easily accessible to tourists as are the romantic mountain haunts of Colorado. No more beautiful summer resort could be dreamed than that afforded by this valley. It is destined to become one of the famous mountain haunts of the world. Fine carriage roads are being constructed in Athabasca Valley that will add to the famous drives of the world, and rank with that never-to-be-forgotten drive from Sorrento to Amalfi, or that of the Corniche road on the Riviera. The Athabasca Valley and Jasper Park and Mount Robson Park will be developed into places of great international resort, as are the Yellowstone Park, the Grand Canyon in Arizona, and the Yosemite in the United States.

After the Bear Hunt—Moose River Forks

In the *de luxe* conditions of travel through all these regions to-day, it is as difficult to realise the conditions that prevailed there before the arrival of the railway line as it was for the little lad at school to transport himself into the pre-historic days before the telephone had established its universal sway. Reproved by his instructor for not knowing the date on which Columbus discovered America, he replied that he could not find it. "Not find it!" replied the irate master, "there it is, right before your eyes, 1492!" The lad looked at it. "Why, I thought that was his telephone number," he rejoined. It is quite as difficult for the traveller to-day to project himself backward, even into the environment of only a past century. The world into which we are born seems to have existed forever. It is a curious fact, but one that seems borne out by experience, that any event which just preceded one's own consciousness and memory is practically as remote as if it were many centuries away. This truth regarding the phenomena of consciousness might well enlist the scrutiny of that analyst of Time and Memory, the brilliant Henri Bergson.

Is it amid all the transcendent beauty, all the scenic glory of the great North-West that one shall listen for the call and watch for the beckoning to the Promised Land? Its prairies and valleys provide every resource for the support of life, its forests offer the most incalculable yield in lumber, its lakes and rivers teem with fish, its mountains are rich in mineral wealth, it has water power to be utilised in manufactures, lighting, and traction to an extent that defies prediction; there is every contributing cause for great cities to arise, with universities, with their laboratories and observatories for science, while, with such a port as that of Prince Rupert, the commerce of the world will be brought to these shores; nor does it require any undue effort of imagination to see, as in a vision, the libraries, the conservatories of music, the museums of art that will arise, the splendour of cities "with room in their streets for the soul." The Call of the North-West is to art, to science, to poetry, to religion. It is the call to the great spiritual realities of the spiritualised life, "the power of conduct, the power of intellect and knowledge, the power of beauty, and the power of social life and manners." The real task of man is that of the discerner of spiritual truth. "The universe is the externalisation of the soul." And in this eternal quest man shall press forward "without haste, without rest," consoled by his divination of spiritual ideals; a dweller in the atmosphere of spiritual splendour expressed in those immortal lines:

"I will wait heaven's perfect hour
Through the innumerable years!"

www.ingramcontent.com/pod-product-compliance
Ingram Content Group UK Ltd.
Pitfield, Milton Keynes, MK11 3LW, UK
UKHW041019120225
455007UK00004B/227